Greg Perry
Dean Miller

WITHDRAWN

Sams **Teach Yourself**

Beginning
Programming

in **24**
Hours

Fourth Edition

SAMS

Sams Teach Yourself Beginning Programming in 24 Hours, Fourth Edition

For information about buying this title in bulk quantities, or for special sales opportunities (which may include electronic versions; custom cover designs; and content particular to your business, training goals, marketing focus, or branding interests), please contact our corporate sales department at corpsales@pearson.com or (800) 382-3419.

For government sales inquiries, please contact governmentsales@pearsoned.com.

For questions about sales outside the U.S., please contact intlcs@pearson.com.

Library of Congress Catalog Card Number: 2019951973

ISBN-13: 978-0-13-583670-5

ISBN-10: 0-13-583670-0

1 2019

Editor-in-Chief
Mark L. Taub

Acquisitions Editor
Kim Spenceley

Managing Editor
Sandra Schroeder

Development Editor
Chris Zahn

Senior Project Editor
Lori Lyons

Technical Editors
John Fonte
Michael Garcia

Production Manager
Aswini Kumar/
codeMantra

Indexer
Ken Johnson

Proofreader
Abigail Manheim

Cover Designer
Chuti Prasertsith

Compositor
codeMantra

Contents at a Glance

To access the online appendixes, go to informit.com/register to register your book. After your book is registered, enter the product ISBN 9780135836705 and go to the Downloads tab below the book description. Click the link to download the appendixes.

Table of Contents

Part V: Other Programming Languages

To access the online appendixes, go to informit.com/register to register your book. After your book is registered, enter the product ISBN 9780135836705 and go to the Downloads tab below the book description. Click the link to download the appendixes.

About the Author

Greg Perry is a speaker and writer in both the programming and applications sides of computing. He is known for bringing programming topics down to the beginner's level. Perry has been a programmer and trainer for two decades. He received his first degree in computer science and then earned a Master's degree in corporate finance. Besides writing, he consults and lectures across the country, including at the acclaimed Software Development programming conferences. Perry is the author of more than 75 other computer books. In his spare time, he gives lectures on traveling in Italy, his second-favorite place to be.

Dean Miller is a writer and editor with more than 20 years of experience in both the publishing and licensed consumer products businesses. Over the years, he has created or helped shape a number of bestselling books and series, including *Sams Teach Yourself in 21 Days*, *Sams Teach Yourself in 24 Hours*, and the *Unleashed* series, all from Sams Publishing. He has written or cowritten 15 books on computer programming and professional wrestling and is still looking for a way to combine the two into one strange amalgam.

Dedication

Dean: *To Fran, Margaret, John, and Alice—Thanks for being the absolute best family someone could ask for.*

Acknowledgments

Greg: My thanks go to all my friends at Pearson. Most writers would refer to them as editors; to me, they are friends. I want all my readers to understand this: The people at Pearson care about you most of all. The things they do result from their concern for your knowledge and enjoyment. On a more personal note, my beautiful bride, Jayne; my mother Bettye Perry; and my friends, who wonder how I find the time to write, all deserve credit for supporting my need to write.

Dean: I'd like to thank Greg Perry for creating outstanding book that continues to educate generations of new computer programmers. It's been a highlight of my career to work with him as both his editor and co-author over the years. Thanks to Kim Spenceley for working with me to create this new edition. I appreciate the amazing work Lori Lyons, Kitty Wilson, and the production team at Pearson put into this book. Special thanks to my technical reviewers, John Fonte and Michael Garcia, for improving the quality of the book with their thorough reads. On a personal level, I have to thank my three children, John, Alice, and Maggie, and my wife Fran for their unending patience and support.

We Want to Hear from You

As the reader of this book, *you* are our most important critic and commentator. We value your opinion and want to know what we're doing right, what we could do better, what areas you'd like to see us publish in, and any other words of wisdom you're willing to pass our way.

You can email to let us know what you did or didn't like about this book—as well as what we can do to make our books stronger.

Please note that we cannot help you with technical problems related to the topic of this book, and that due to the high volume of mail we receive, we might not be able to reply to every message.

When you write, please be sure to include this book's title, edition number, and author, as well as your name and email address. We will carefully review your comments and share them with the author and editors who worked on the book.

Email: community@informit.com

Register Your Book

Register your copy of **Sams Teach Yourself Beginning Programming in 24 Hours, Fourth Edition** at informit.com for convenient access to downloads, updates, and corrections as they become available. To start the registration process, go to informit.com/register and log in or create an account. Enter the product ISBN **9780135836705** and click Submit. Once the process is complete, you will find any available bonus content under "Registered Products."

Introduction

Learning how to program computers is easier than you might think. If you approach computers with hesitation, if you cannot even spell *PC*, if you have tried your best to avoid the subject altogether but can do so no longer, the book you now hold contains support that you can depend on in troubled computing times.

This 24-hour tutorial does more than explain programming. This tutorial does more than describe the difference between JavaScript, C++, and Java. This tutorial does more than teach you what programming is all about. This tutorial is a *training tool* that you can use to develop proper programming skills. The aim of this text is to introduce you to programming using professionally recognized principles, while keeping things simple at the same time. It is not this text's singular goal to teach you a programming language (although you will be writing programs before you finish it). This text's goal is to give you the foundation to become the best programmer you can be.

These 24 one-hour lessons delve into proper program design principles. You'll not only learn how to program, but also how to *prepare* for programming. This tutorial also teaches you how companies program and explains what you have to do to become a needed resource in a programming position. You'll learn about various programming job titles and what to expect if you want to write programs for others. You'll explore many issues related to online computing and learn how to address the needs of the online programming community.

Who Should Use This Book?

The title of this book says it all. If you have never programmed a computer, if you don't even like them at all, or if updating the operating system of your phone throws you into fits, take three sighs of relief! This text was written for *you* so that, within 24 hours, you will understand the nature of computer programs and you will have written programs.

This book is aimed at three different groups of people:

▶ Individuals who know nothing about programming but who want to know what programming is all about.

- Companies that want to train nonprogramming computer users for programming careers.

- Schools—both for introductory language classes and for systems analysis and design classes—that want to promote good coding design and style and that want to offer an overview of the life of a programmer.

Readers who seem tired of the plethora of quick-fix computer titles cluttering today's shelves will find a welcome reprieve here. The book you now hold talks to newcomers about programming without talking down to them.

What This Book Will Do for You

In the next 24 hours, you will learn something about almost every aspect of programming. The following topics are discussed in depth throughout this 24-hour tutorial:

- The hardware and software related to programming

- The history of programming

- Programming languages

- The business of programming

- Programming jobs

- Program design

- Internet programming

- The future of programming

Can This Book Really Teach Programming in 24 Hours?

In a word, yes. You can master each chapter in one hour or less. (By the way, chapters are referred to as "hours" or "lessons" in the rest of this book.) The material is balanced with mountains of shortcuts and methods that will make your hours productive and hone your programming skills more and more with each hour. Although some chapters are longer than others, many of the shorter chapters cover more detailed or more difficult issues than the shorter ones. A true attempt was made to make each hour learnable in an hour. Exercises at the end of each hour will provide feedback about the skills you learned.

Conventions Used in This Book

This book uses several common conventions to help teach programming topics. Here is a summary of those typographical conventions:

▶ Commands and computer output appear in a special `monospaced` computer font. Sometimes a line of code will be too long to fit on one line in this book. The code continuation symbol (➥) indicates that the line continues.

▶ Words you type also appear in the monospaced computer font.

▶ If a task requires you to select from a menu, the book separates menu commands with a comma. Therefore, this book uses File, Save As to select the Save As option from the File menu.

In addition to typographical conventions, the following special elements are included to set off different types of information to make it easily recognizable.

TRY IT YOURSELF ▼

The best way to learn how to program is to jump right in and start programming. These Try it Yourself sections will teach you a simple concept or method to accomplish a goal programmatically. The listing will be easy to follow and then the programs' output will be displayed along with coverage of key points in the program. To really get some practice, try altering bits of the code in each of these sections in order to see what your tweaks accomplish.

NOTE

Special notes augment the material you read in each hour. These notes clarify concepts and procedures.

TIP

You'll find numerous tips that offer shortcuts and solutions to common problems.

CAUTION

The cautions warn you about pitfalls. Reading them will save you time and trouble.

HOUR 1
Hands-On Programming

You have this book because you want to go further than the typical computer user. You don't just want to use computers; you want to write programs for them. You want the skills necessary to make computers do exactly what you want.

This 24-hour tutorial shows that you don't have to be a wizard to become a proficient (or even an expert) programmer. By the time you finish this one-hour lesson, you will have reviewed your first computer program and its results. This chapter springboards you into programming so you can get a feel for programming right away. Once you've had this hands-on experience, subsequent hours will explain more of the background you need to understand how to design and write programs.

The highlights of this hour include the following:

- ▶ Learning what a program does
- ▶ Understanding the truth behind common programming myths
- ▶ Mastering source code concepts
- ▶ Reviewing your first program

Get Ready to Program

You'll find this hour divided into these two areas:

- ▶ An introduction to the nature of programming
- ▶ Hands-on practice with your first programming language

Most new programmers want to start programming right away. However, some background is necessary. This hour attempts to take care of both demands by offering an introductory background look at programming and then quickly jumping head-first into hands-on programming. If you went straight into a new programming language with absolutely no background first, you might miss the entire point of programming. So, the next few pages bring all readers up to a level playing field so that everyone who takes this 24-hour course can begin to write programs right away.

What a Computer Program Does

Most people today are surrounded by computers, and those computers are getting incredibly powerful. For example, the CPU that powers your smartphone is actually more powerful than the computer that was used to put the first man on the Moon. Not only do we have desktop and laptop computers, as well as tablets and smartphones, but appliances like televisions and your car have computers embedded in them. All those computers perform specific tasks, depending on where they are located. Your laptop can help you balance your checkbook or track your inventory if you run a business. Your phone is filled with apps to enhance productivity or have fun. The computer in your car helps maintain the vehicle's temperature. These jobs happen thanks to computer programs that an individual or team created.

If you want to begin programming, chances are you have probably been using a computer for some time. Nevertheless, as a future programmer, you should review some fundamental computing concepts before you can master the ins and outs of a new computer language.

At its simplest level, a computer *processes data*. Figure 1.1 shows this as the primary goal of all computer programs. Many businesses call their computer programming departments *data processing departments* because computers process data into meaningful information. You may not have considered the difference between the words *data* and *information* before, but there is a tremendous difference to a computer professional. Raw data consists of facts and figures, such as hundreds of days of stock prices. A program might process that data into meaningful information, such as a line chart that shows the overall trend of the stock prices over time. It is the computer *program* that tells the computer what to do. Sometimes, a program might simply process data from another program without showing any output for the user. The processed data is still information because the program's output, stored on the disk, is changed in some way. For example, a program that closes monthly account balances may collect data from various accounting systems in a company and combine, balance, and close that data, resetting the data for the following month.

FIGURE 1.1
Programs convert raw data into meaningful information.

A *program* is a list of detailed instructions that the computer carries out. The program is the driving force behind any job that a computer does. The computer cannot do anything without a program. It is the job of the programmer to design and write programs that direct the computer to transform raw data into meaningful information for the end user. The *end user* (usually just called the *user*) of the computer is generally the nontechnical, nonprogramming person who needs the results (the information) that the program provides.

You, as the programmer, are responsible for guiding the computer with the programs you write. Learning to program computers takes a while, but it is certainly rewarding. Computer programming offers the advantage of instant feedback, unlike a lot of other jobs you can train for.

Common Programming Misconceptions

This book aims directly at the heart of the matter: Computers are easy to use and easy to program. A computer is nothing more than a dumb machine that "knows" absolutely nothing. Without programs, the computer doesn't know what to do. A computer is like a robot that waits on your every command and acts out your instructions exactly as you give them. Sometimes your program instructions are incorrect. If they are, the computer goes right ahead and attempts them anyway.

NOTE
_____

Don't fear computer programming. Computers are tools to help you get your job done. You can learn to program.

_____

Many misconceptions about computers exist and stem from a lack of understanding about how computers work and what computers are physically capable of doing. This book wants to shoot down the myths and improve your understanding of these machines. You'll be programming computers in no time. The computer is nothing more than a tool that helps you do certain types of work. The computer itself is not bad or good. A hammer is a tool you can use for good (to build houses) or for bad (to break things). A computer in the wrong hands can be used for bad purposes, but that isn't the computer's fault, any more than it is the hammer's fault if someone misuses it.

The next three sections attack the three most popular computer myths. Have you heard any of them? Did you think some were true?

Myth 1: Only Math Experts Can Program Computers

Thank goodness this is a myth and not reality, or thousands of people would be out of work (including most computer book authors!). Computers would be elitist machines used by only the best engineers and scientists; the casual user could not master them. Computers would still be beneficial in some areas, but they would not provide the benefits that so many people can enjoy.

Not only can you be poor at math, you don't even have to like math or have the desire to learn math to be a good computer programmer. The computer does all the math for you; that's one of its jobs. There are countless expert computer programmers in the world who cannot tell you the area of a circle or the square root of 64. If you thought this myth was reality, you can relax.

Programming can provide beneficial side effects. It turns out that, as you become a better programmer, you may find your math skills improving. Developing programming skills tends to improve your overall capability for logical thinking, which underlies many skills in math as well. Therefore, being better in math might be a result of programming, but it's not a prerequisite.

TIP

People who favor logic puzzles, crosswords, anagrams, and word-search games seem to adapt well to programming, but again, liking these gaming activities is not a programming prerequisite. You will find that you can learn to program computers—and actually become extremely good at it—without liking math, being good at math, or having any flair at all for puzzles or word games.

Myth 2: Computers Make Mistakes

You might have heard the adage "To err is human, but to *really* foul things up takes a computer!" This might be accurate—but only in that a computer is so very fast that it duplicates a person's mistakes rapidly.

Computers do not make mistakes; people make mistakes. If you have heard a bank teller tell you that $24 was incorrectly deleted from your savings account because "the computer program made an error," the teller probably has no idea what really happened. People program computers, people run them, and people enter the data that the computers process.

The odds of a computer randomly fouling up a customer's bank balance are minute. Computers simply do not make random mistakes unless they are programmed incorrectly. Computers are finite machines; when given the same input, they always produce the same output. That is, computers always do the same things under the same conditions. Your job, as you learn to program, will be to reduce the chance of computer mistakes.

When a computer malfunctions, it does not make a simple mistake; rather, it *really* messes things up. When a computer fails, it typically breaks down completely, or a storage device breaks down, or the power goes out. Whatever happens, computers go all out when they have a problem, and it is usually very obvious when they have a problem. The good news is that computers rarely have problems.

Before people invented computers, banks kept all their records on ledger cards. When a teller found a mistake (possibly one that the teller had made), do you think the teller said, "The ledger card made a mistake"? Absolutely not. Computers can have mechanical problems, but the likelihood of small mistakes, such as an incorrect balance once in a while, is just too small to consider. Such mistakes are made by the people entering the data or by (gulp) the programmers.

Myth 3: Computers Are Difficult to Program

Computers are getting easier to use—and to program—every day. If you used a microwave, drove a car, or watched a television recently, then chances are good that you used a computer when you did. Did you know you were using a computer? Probably not. The makers of computers have found ways to integrate computers into your everyday life to monitor and correct problems that might otherwise occur without them.

Of course, if you are reading this book, you want to learn enough about computers to write your own programs. Writing computer programs does take more work than using a microwave oven's computerized timer functions. The work, however, primarily involves getting down to the computer's level and learning what it expects.

Not only are computers getting easier to program every day, but you have more opportunities to learn about them than ever before. Cable television channels are loaded with educational shows about using and programming computers. Books and videos on the subject are all around you. The Internet itself contains scores of classes on all aspects of computers and other topics. YouTube hosts hundreds of videos on programming. There is probably a computer programming class happening within 15 minutes of your house as you read this.

Many Programs Already Exist

Although there are many programs already written for you to use, sometimes you need a program that fills a specific need and you cannot find one that does exactly what you want. When you are done with this book, you will know exactly what you need to design and write your own programs.

Programmers Are in Demand

Look at help-wanted websites. You'll find that there is a shortage of computer programmers. Amid the requests for Java programmers, C++ programmers, C# programmers, mobile app developers, systems analysts, senior systems analysts, object-oriented programmers, systems programmers, HTML coders, and application programmers, you may find yourself lost in a sea of uncertainty and *TLAs* (three-letter acronyms) that might, at first, seem hopeless. Do not fret; this book will help direct you toward areas of programming that might be right for you.

Hour 22, "How Companies Program," explores the chain of computer jobs and describes what each type of programming job is all about. If you are just starting out, you probably won't be able to go to work as the most senior-level programmer, but you will be surprised at the salary your programming skills can bring you.

The Real Value of Programs

Although the prices of individual computer programs are decreasing, companies and individual computer owners invest more and more in programs every year. Not only do people purchase new programs as they come out, they update the older versions of programs they already have.

Businesses and individuals must factor in the cost of programs when making computer decisions. Whereas an individual usually buys a computer—called *hardware* because the machine isn't changed often or easily—and is done with the hardware purchasing for a while, the purchasing of programs—the *software*—never seems to end because software changes rapidly. For a future programmer, this is welcome news because it means a secure career. For the uninformed computer purchaser, the cost of software can be staggering.

A business must also factor in the on-staff and contract programmers and the time needed to write the programs it uses. More information on the programming and support staff appears in the next section.

Users Generally Don't Own Programs

When a company purchases software, it most often purchases a *software license*. If a company wants to buy a word-processing program for 100 employees, legally it must purchase 100 copies of the program, or at least buy a *site license* that allows the company to use the software on more than one machine. When a company buys a program, it does not own the program. When you buy a record, you do not own the music; you have only purchased the rights to listen to the music. You cannot legally alter the music, record it, or give away recordings of it, and, most importantly, you cannot sell recordings that you make of it. The same is true for software that you buy. The license for individual software grants you permission to use the software on one computer at any one time.

Giving Computers Programs

Figure 1.2 shows the code for a simple program by a computer programmer. As a matter of fact, that computer programmer is about to be you after you create the code using Python.

Remember: A computer is only a machine. To give a machine instructions, your instructions might be fairly readable, as those in Figure 1.2 are, but the *code* (another name for a program's instructions) must be fairly rigid and conform to a predefined set of rules and regulations according to the programming language you use. Therefore, to write a program in the Python programming language, you must conform to Python's rules of proper command spelling and placement. This programming language grammar is called *syntax*. (And you thought syntax was just a levy placed on cigarettes and liquor!)

```
# Set the ages for a and b
a = 13
b = 16

print("Anna is", a, "years old!")
print("Trey is", b, "years old!\n")
print("Trey is", b-a,"years older than Anna")
print("In two years, Anna will be", a+2, "years old!\n")

# Create a list of sports
sports = ["basketball", "football", "soccer", "skateboarding"]

# Loop through all the sports
for sport in sports:
    print("One of Anna's favorite sports is", sport)

# Create a list of colors
colors = ["blue", "red", "yellow"]

#Now list all the sneakers Trey has
for color in colors:
    print("Trey has a",color,"pair of sneakers")
```

FIGURE 1.2
A program's instructions are somewhat cryptic but human readable.

NOTE

It is important to understand that the first section of this book is teaching you the basics of computer programming using the Python language, but it is not a complete Python tutorial. This may seem like the same thing, but it is not. The aim of the book is to teach you basic computer programming techniques (with examples in Python code) in the first half of the book and introduce you to a variety of programming languages and jobs in the second half. There are scores of excellent books, including *Teach Yourself Python in 24 Hours*, also by Sams Publishing, that can take you through every in and out of the Python language. That book will take you far more in-depth into the language than this book. Now that we've properly calibrated your expectations, let's get back to beginning programming!

Source Code

Even after you make the effort to learn a computer language such as Python, and after you go to the trouble of typing a well-formed and syntactically accurate program such as the one in Figure 1.2, your computer still will not be able to understand the program! The program you write is called *source code*. It is the source code that you write, manipulate, and correct. Your computer, on the other hand, can understand only *machine language*, a compact series of computer-readable instructions that make no sense to people. They make sense to some advanced computer gurus, but my general assertion stands that they don't make sense to people.

Listing 1.1 shows machine language. Can you decipher any of it? Your computer can. Your computer loves machine language. Actually, it's the only language your computer understands. And different computers understand their own versions of machine language, so what works on one type of computer will not necessarily work on another. It's best to stay away from machine language and let products such as Python convert your higher-level language into machine language's cryptic 1s and 0s.

LISTING 1.1 **Machine language is extremely difficult for people to decipher**

```
01100100
10111101
10010011
10010100
00001111
01010101
11111110
```

All programs you run on your computer, phone, or tablet, including Microsoft Word, Internet Explorer, and programming languages, are already converted into machine language. That's why you can click a program's icon, and the program begins immediately. No interpretation or compilation is required. By providing you with the machine language only, software vendors serve two purposes:

▶ They give you programs that execute quickly, without the intervening compiling step.

▶ They ensure that you don't change the source code, thereby protecting their intellectual property.

Your First Program

The first program that you write will be simple. You may not understand much of it, and that's fine. The goal here is not to explain the program details but to walk you through the entire process of the steps that are typical of computer programming:

1. Type a program's source code and save it.

2. Run the program in whatever Python environment you choose to use (see Appendix A, "Installing Python," for more about this topic). This book was written with the use of Jupyter notebooks (https://jupyter.org). Others use pycharm, Visual Studio, and others. Some just write code in text editors, but for beginners, you are best served picking an IDE and working with it. It's ultimately a personal preference, and the code examples in this book will work on any IDE.

3. If the page is not doing what you want and has errors, called *bugs*, you need to fix those bugs in your source code and repeat these steps. Hour 7, "Debugging Tools," explains how to locate and fix common bugs. You may need to do some bug hunting earlier than Hour 7 if you experience problems with your programs in these first few hours. If a program does not work as described, you will need to compare your source code very carefully to the code in the book and fix any discrepancies before saving it again.

Starting with Python

You can write your Python code in a number of different environments, and you can also choose between the latest version, Python 3, or Python 2. This book uses the latter, but for basic programming topics, there is little to worry about in terms of difference between the two. If you end up working on some existing Python projects, they may be incompatible with Python 3, but the newer version is still the better learning option. No matter which version of Python you choose, it is best to write your program in that version's IDE or a text editor. (Not to scare you with another three-letter acronym right off the bat, but IDE stands for *integrated development environment*, which is ultimately just a fancy phrase that refers to the Python program that you download; again, see Appendix A.) You can write your programs in a word processor if you really want, but you have to save them as text-only files, or they will not work as intended. Documents written in word processors have additional unseen characters that give the files their formatting, and when you attempt to convert a program written in such a file to machine code, as discussed earlier in the chapter, it will not work because of these extra unseen characters.

NOTE

Unlike word processors, your editor will not wrap the end of a line down to the subsequent line. It's important that programming instructions (called *statements*) remain separate and stay on their own lines in many cases. Even if a programming language allows multiple program statements per line, you'll find that your programs are more readable and easier to debug if you keep your statements one per line. Sometimes, a single statement can get lengthy, and you may span long statements over two or three lines, but rarely would you want multiple statements to appear on the same line.

Also, while many programming languages ultimately do not care about spaces and line breaks, the spacing is very important to how a Python program is written. If you follow the spacing in the programs as written in this book, you will be fine, and you will soon find yourself following the pattern automatically.

Clarifying Comments

The program presented in Figure 1.2 has not only program statements but also some lines that do not do anything when the program is run; however, these lines have great value to anyone reading your code. These lines, which start with a pound sign (#), are known as *comments*. Python ignores all text to the right of the pound sign. As soon as you press Return, Python starts paying attention to the code again. So if you want to keep commenting, you need to start the next line with a fresh pound sign. Consider an example:

```
# The next five lines ask users for their favorite
# movie and flavor of gelato
```

In this example, if you left off the pound signs, Python would assume that you were either typing The or calling a function named The, and you might not get the results you were expecting.

All languages support comments, which are also called *remarks*, although some languages use slashes instead. Although you'll find many comments in programs, and you should put many comments in the programs you write, comments are not for the interpreter or for the computer. Comments are for people. In Python, for example, the interpreter ignores all text to the right of pound sign. The computer knows that comments are for you and not for it.

Reasons for Comments

Comments help produce more understandable program listings. The programming industry considers including comments to be one of the most important good programming habits you can develop. Here are common reasons programmers put comments in their programs:

- ▶ Comments can identify programmers. If you develop programs with others or write programs for a company, you should put your name and contact information in comments at the top of your programs. Later, anyone who has a question about the program or wants you to change the program will know that you wrote the program and will be able to contact you.

- ▶ Before a section of tricky code, you can use comments to include your explanation of the code's purpose. Later, if you or someone else needs to change the program, the change will be easier; reading the comments is much simpler than trying to figure out the goals of the tricky code from uncommented code.

Placement of Comments

When you use the pound sign (#), a comment can appear on the same line as code. The following code shows comments to the right of lines of other program instructions:

```
if hours > 12:              # Test the hour for AM/PM indicator
    hours = hours - 12   # Convert 24-hour time to 12-hour
    amOrPm$ = " PM"   # Set indicator that will print
```

TIP

While most programming languages are *free-form*, meaning that you can indent lines and add as many spaces and blank lines as you like, Python does have some rules around indentation and *whitespace* (extra spaces and lines in code). Following these rules makes your program more readable. In Hour 7, you'll learn how to use *whitespace* to improve your programs' readability by separating one program section from another, thereby making it easier for programmers to understand your code.

Sure, as a programmer, you will often understand code without the need to put a remark to the right of each line. But at the time you write a program, the program is clearest to you. When you later go back to edit a program, what may have been clear before may no longer be so clear because time has passed. A few comments will go a long way toward reminding you of your original intent.

However, do not overdo comments. Some comments are redundant, as the following shows:

```
print("Martha")    # Prints the word Martha
```

Such a comment is not helpful and serves only to cloud an already-understandable instruction. Don't overuse comments but do use them generously when needed to clarify your code.

Entering Your Own Program

You're now ready to type and run your own simple program from scratch. The goal here is to get you used to using the editor or IDE you selected in Appendix A.

TRY IT YOURSELF ▼

Follow these steps to create your own program:

1. In your text editor or IDE, select File and then New File to create a brand-new document.

2. Type the program in Listing 1.2 into the editor. Be careful that you type the program exactly as you see it in the listing. If you make a typing mistake, you will not be able to run the program. The program is a little bit complicated, but if you type it as is, you should have a working program.

LISTING 1.2   **Type your first program into the editor**

```
# Teach Yourself Beginning Programming in 24 Hours
# Listing 1.2


ProgLang = "Python"
Hours = 24
Name = "Reader" #If you want you can change this to your name!

print("We are learning programming basics in what language?")
print(ProgLang,"!")
print(Name,"will soon be programming after", Hours, "Hours!")
```

3. If you are using the Jupyter Notebook, you can change the name of your program by clicking on the name in the highlighted box show in Figure 1.3. I named mine TYCode2. The program should autosave. When you have finished typing the program, click the Run button, highlighted in Figure 1.4. If you have typed everything correctly, you should see the output shown in Figure 1.5.

FIGURE 1.3
Double-clicking the name at the top (usually it starts as untitled) enables you to enter whatever name you want. *(© 2019 Project Jupyter)*

FIGURE 1.4
After you've typed in your code, click the Run button to run the program and see the results.

```
We are learning programming basics in what language?
Python!
Reader will soon be programming after 24 Hours!
```

FIGURE 1.5
The results of your programming!

If your program contained an error, the results would not look the same as the output shown in Figure 1.5. You would have to work through your version line by line to find the error and fix it.

Summary

Now that you know a bit more about the computer industry as a whole, you have a better idea of where programmers fit into the picture. Computers can do nothing without programs, and programmers are responsible for providing those programs.

You have already gotten a taste of programming this hour by typing your first Python program and viewing the results. As you saw by typing your own program into an editor, entering and running a code is not painful at all. As a matter of fact, the quick feedback that programming offers is a rewarding experience. Programmers often like their profession very much because they can see the results of their work quickly.

Q&A

Q. When I finish writing a program, is my job finished?

A. It is said that a program is written once and modified many times. Throughout this 24-hour tutorial, you will learn the importance of maintaining a program after it is written. As businesses change and computing environments improve, the programs that people use must improve as well. Companies provide upgrades to software as new features are needed. The programs that you write today will have to change in the future to keep up with the competition as well as with new features that your users require.

Q. Can I enter other programming language listings in my editor as well?

A. The Jupyter Notebook, suggested in Appendix A, is specific to Python. If you chose to use a text editor, you can write programs in other programming languages, such as C, C++, and Java, in your text editor. However, you would need a compiler or an interpreter (depending on the language) to convert the programming language's code to machine language. A machine language program is your program's instructions compiled to a language your computer can understand. You can also find IDEs specific to those languages.

Workshop

The quiz questions are provided for your further understanding.

Quiz

1. What is the difference between data and information?

2. What is a program?

3. What is a programming language?

4. True or false: Computers never make mistakes.

5. Why should people not fear computers replacing their jobs?

6. What do programmers use editors for?

7. What does IDE stand for?

8. True or false: There's no problem writing your programs in a typical word-processing program.

9. Tweak the program in Listing 1.2 so that the `Name` is set to the name of someone else you know.

Answers

1. Data consists of raw facts and figures, and information is processed data that has more meaning.

2. A program is a set of detailed instructions that tells the computer what to do.

3. A programming language is a set of commands and grammar rules with which you write programs that give computers instructions.

4. False. A computer might make a mistake, but it's rare that it does so. In the vast majority of cases where a computer is blamed, a person entered bad data or typed a bad program.

5. Computers increase jobs rather than replacing them. The information industry has had a large impact on the economic growth of the past several decades.

6. Programmers use editors to type programs into the computer.

7. Integrated development environment.

8. False. The default method of saving files in word processors adds formatting codes that generate errors when you try to run your program. You can still use a word processor, but you must always remember to save your files as plain text.

9. Here is one possible solution:

```
'''
Teach Yourself Beginning Programming in 24 Hours
Listing 1.2
'''

ProgLang = "Python"
Hours = 24
Name = "Maggie" #If you want you can change this to your name!

print("We are learning programming basics in what language?")
print(ProgLang,"!")
print(Name,"will soon be programming after", Hours, "Hours!")
```

HOUR 2
Process and Techniques

The words *program* and *programmer* are mentioned throughout each of these 24 lessons, and you undoubtedly heard them before you picked up this book. Before going back into specifics of Python and other programming languages, this hour explains what a program really is. A firm grasp of this hour's material is a prerequisite for moving on to the more advanced programming concepts introduced throughout this book.

As you read this hour's lesson, keep in mind that programming is rewarding—not only financially but also mentally and emotionally. Programmers often feel the same sense of creative rush that artists and skilled craftspeople feel while honing their projects. Writing a program, however, can be tedious. It is often a detail-oriented task, and ample frustration comes with the territory. The computer's quick feedback on your mistakes and results, however, often provides a sense of accomplishment that keeps you programming until you get it right.

The highlights of this hour include the following:

- ▶ Directing a computer with programs
- ▶ Putting enough details in a program that a computer can follow the instructions
- ▶ Executing programs in memory rather than from the hard drive
- ▶ Looking at whether programming is an art or a science
- ▶ Learning why computers cannot yet understand a human language

Understanding the Need for Programs

When individuals and companies need a program or an app, they can obtain it in one of three ways:

- ▶ Buy a program that's already written
- ▶ Buy a program and modify it so that the customized version does exactly what they need
- ▶ Write their own program

There are advantages and disadvantages to each option (see Table 2.1). The first two options are much quicker than the third and are much less expensive.

TABLE 2.1 Advantages and disadvantages of obtaining programs

Option	Advantages	Disadvantages
Buy	The program can be obtained quickly and relatively inexpensively.	The program may not be exactly what is needed.
Buy and customize	A usable program that does what is needed can be obtained fairly quickly. Also, the program is relatively inexpensive, depending on the changes needed.	It isn't always possible to modify the program.
Write	The program (after proper design and testing) does exactly what you want it to do.	This option can be very expensive and can take a lot longer than the other options.

Most computer users (of PCs, Macs, tablets, and smartphones) choose the first option because the programs are fairly inexpensive, given their power. Because companies such as Apple, Microsoft, and Adobe sell so many of the same programs or apps, they can do so at reasonable prices. Individual computer users simply don't have the resources that companies have to write the many programs they need.

Companies, on the other hand, do not always choose the first option, and you might wonder why. The reason is that companies spend many years developing products and services to distinguish themselves from other companies, and they learn to keep records in specific ways so that they can manage those services effectively. When a company computerizes any of its record keeping, it is vital that new programs reflect exactly what the company already does. The company should not have to change the way it does business just so it can use programs found in app stores or online. On the other hand, programs that can be purchased off the shelf have to be generic so that the producers of the programs can sell them to more than one customer.

The second option—buy a program and customize it—might seem like the smartest option, but it is chosen least often. If companies could buy a program that is already written, they would have a framework in which to quickly adapt the program to their specific needs. The problem is that software is rarely sold, as you learned in the previous hour; software is *licensed*. When you buy a program, you do not own the program; you only own the right to use it. You often cannot legally change it, sell it, or copy it (except for backup purposes). Some software does come with a license to revise the code, but most software that you purchase off the shelf does not allow the modification of code.

NOTE

There is a class of software and operating systems that not only allows modification of code but encourages it. Open-source software makes the code available with the program so that improvements to the program can be made by the public in a collaborative manner. The Linux operating system is a famous example of open-source software.

Not only are there legalities involved, but also sometimes you cannot physically change the software. Programs come in two formats:

▶ Source code, such as the Python program you created in the previous hour

▶ Compiled, executable code, such as apps you purchase for your phone or tablet

Once a program is written and compiled, programmers can no longer modify the program. Programs that are sold in stores do not usually include the source code. Therefore, companies cannot modify the programs they buy to make the programs conform to their specific businesses. (Of course, you can modify and re-compile programs that you write and compile because you have access to your own source code.)

So, although it is expensive and time-consuming to write programs from scratch, many businesses prefer to do so, and they keep large programming departments on hand to handle the programming load. A company might have several members of its data-processing staff spend a full year writing a program that is close, but not identical, to one that the company could buy. Companies also might utilize contract programmers for specific projects.

Despite the cost and effort involved, it is worth it to some companies not to have to conform to a program they buy from someone else. The program, once written, conforms to the company's way of doing business.

NOTE

Some companies have found that they can sell programs they develop to other firms doing similar business, thereby recapturing some of their development costs. As you write programs for your company or for individuals, keep in mind the possible subsequent sale of your program to others.

Companies often measure the amount of time it takes to write programs in *people-years*. If it takes 2 people-years to write a single program, it is estimated that 2 people could write it in a single year, or 1 person would take 2 years. A 20-people-year project would take 20 people 1 year, or 1 person 20 years, or 10 people 2 years, and so forth. This measurement is only an estimate, but it gives management an idea of how it should allocate people and time for programming projects.

If you become a contract programmer, the people-years measurement is a great tool to use when pricing your service. You might give a customer an estimate of the price per people-year (or, for smaller projects, perhaps you would estimate the job in people-months or people-weeks). If you hire programmers to help you finish the program, you might finish early, but you can still charge fairly for each person's labor because you priced the programming job in people-years rather than in calendar time.

NOTE

Recently, a lot of attention has been given to the idea of people-years. Critics of this measurement state that computer firms do not generally estimate people-year measurements properly and that such measurements are rarely meaningful. That may be, but just because people misuse the measurement does not make the measurement a bad way to gauge a project's completion when it is estimated correctly.

Programs, Programs Everywhere

Why aren't all the programs ever needed already written? Search the Internet today, and you'll see hundreds of programs for sale or free to download. There are programs for everything: word processing, accounting, drawing, playing games, editing and manipulating photos and videos, and so much more. In addition, Apple, Amazon, Android, and many other sites contain thousands of apps you can download and run on your tablet or other mobile device. Some of these programs are free, and some are for sale. It seems as if any program you need is within reach. Because computers have been around more than half a century, you would think that everybody would be about done with all the programming anyone would need for a long time.

If all the programs needed were already written, you would not see the large listings of "Programmer Wanted" ads on job-listing websites. The fact is that the world is changing every day, and businesses and people must change with it. Programs written five years ago are not up to date with today's practices. Also, they were written on computers much slower and more limited than today's machines. Finally, earlier programs were written just for personal computers, while companies must now interact with users who access resources via tablets and smartphones. As hardware advances are made, the software must advance with it.

There is a tremendous need for good programmers today more than ever before. As computers become easier to use, some people believe that programmers will become relics of the past. What they fail to realize is that it takes top-notch programmers to produce those easy-to-use programs. More importantly, it takes programmers to modify and improve upon the vast libraries of programs in use today. Even with economic slumps, the world is becoming more digitized daily, and the demand for programmers will increase as more people use computers more often.

Programs as Directions

If you have ever followed your GPS into unfamiliar territory, you know what it is like for your computer to follow a program's instructions. With only the instructions being called out, you can feel blind as you move from place to place, turning left and right, until you reach your destination or find that you made a wrong turn somewhere. Your computer, as the previous hour explained, is a blind and dumb machine waiting for you to give it directions. When you do, the computer acts out the instructions you give it without second-guessing your desires. If you tell your PC to do something incorrectly, it does its best to do so. Recall this definition of a program (from Hour 1, "Hands-On Programming"):

> A program *is a list of detailed instructions that the computer carries out.*

The term *detailed* in this definition is vital to making a machine follow your orders. Actually, the job of programming is not difficult; what is difficult is breaking the computer's job into simple and detailed steps that assume nothing.

Practice with Detailed Instructions

To get an idea of the thinking involved in programming, consider how you would describe starting a car to someone from the past. Suppose a cowboy named Heath, from the Old West, appears at your doorstep, bewildered by the sights around him. After getting over the future shock, Heath wants to adapt to this new world. Before learning to drive your car, Heath must first learn to start it. When he is comfortable doing that, you will teach him to drive. Unlike a 16-year-old learning to drive, Heath has not grown up seeing adults starting cars, so he really needs to master this process before going any further. Being the busy programmer you are, you leave him the following set of instructions taped to the car key:

1. Use this key.

2. Start the car.

How far would Heath get? Not very far. You gave correct instructions for starting a car, but you assumed too much knowledge on his part. You must remember that he knows nothing about these contraptions called automobiles, and he is relying on you to give him instructions that he can understand. Instead of assuming so much, these might be better instructions:

1. Attached is the key to the car. You need it to start the car.

2. With the key in hand, go to the car door that is closest to the front door of our home.

3. Under the door's black handle, you will see a round silver-dollar-sized metal place into which you can insert the key (with its rough edge pointing down).

4. After sticking the key into the hole as far as it will go, turn it to the right until you hear a click.

5. Turn the key back to the left until it faces the same way as it did when you inserted it and remove the key.

6. Pull up on the black handle to open the door and get into the car. Be sure to sit in front of the round wheel (called a *steering wheel*) on the left-hand side of the front seat.

7. Close the door.

8. On the right side of the column holding the steering wheel, you will see a slot in which you can put the key.

Are you beginning to get the idea? This list of eight items is very detailed, and Heath hasn't even started the car yet. You still have to describe the brake pedal that he might have to press while he turns the key, in the correct direction of course. You also don't want to assume that Heath will turn *off* the car when he is done practicing, so you have to give him directions about that as well. (Perhaps you should also warn your neighbors to stay off the streets for a while!)

If you are beginning to think this car-starting analogy is going a little too far, consider what you must do to tell a nonthinking piece of electronic equipment—a computer—to perform your company's payroll. A payroll program cannot consist of only the following steps:

1. Get the payroll data.

2. Calculate the payroll and taxes.

3. Print the checks.

To the computer, these instructions lack thousands of details that you might take for granted. It is the detailing of the program's instructions that provides for the tedium and occasional frustration of programming. Programming computers isn't difficult, but breaking down real-world problems into lots of detailed steps that a computer can understand is hard.

TIP

A typical payroll program might contain 20,000 or more lines of instructions. Don't let this deter you from learning to program, however. Large programming projects are written by teams of programmers; you will have plenty of help if you ever write such programs for a living. Also, new programming techniques and programming environments for today's computer languages make programming, even for an individual programmer working alone, much easier than ever before.

Closer to Home: A Python Example

Consider the program output window shown in Figure 2.1. A Python program produced this output.

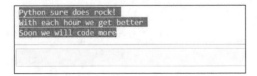

FIGURE 2.1
It takes detailed instructions to produce simple output.

What does it take to produce the three simple lines of output? It takes detailed instructions in the Python programming language. The computer cannot read your mind to know what you want. You must specifically tell Python to print those three lines and even tell Python that you want each line of the poem to start on a new line. Listing 2.1 shows the program that produced this output.

LISTING 2.1   You must supply detailed instructions when you want the computer to do something

```
# Teach Yourself Beginning Programming in 24 Hours
# Listing 2.1


# This is a a three-line poem printed by Python


print("Python sure does rock!")
print("With each hour we get better")
print("Soon we will code more")
```

Even though you don't yet know the Python programming language, you've got to admit that the program in Listing 2.1 is rather simple to understand. Three `print` statements tell the computer to print three lines of output. Each new print call starts printing on a new line, which is something that other programming languages do not always do.

Sure, if you want to see the words in Figure 2.1, all you need to do is start WordPad or some other word processor and type the text into the document window. Nevertheless, a lot of programming work went into that word processor to allow you to put text in the document so easily. The idea in these early hours is to focus on creating programs that produce results.

Tools That Help

Many design tools exist to help you break down large problems into detailed components that translate into programming elements. Hour 3, "Designing a Program," explains many of the methods that programmers use to get to a program's needed details. You'll find that programming is simple as long as you approach it systematically, as this text attempts to do. By learning theory and getting as much early, hands-on examples as possible, you'll understand what you're doing and learn how to program faster. If programming were truly difficult, there is no way so many computer advances could have been made over the past 70 years.

Programs Are Saved Instructions

The nice thing about programs you write is that you save them to disk after you write them. As with word-processed text, you store the programs you write in disk files, as you did in the previous hour's lesson with the TYcode2 program. A program is to a computer as a recipe is to a cook. When a cook wants to make a certain dish, he or she finds the correct recipe and follows the instructions. When someone wants to execute a program, she or he instructs the computer to load the program from disk into memory and then run the program's instructions.

The computer's internal memory (*random access memory*, or *RAM*) is vital for holding program execution. Your computer's CPU cannot execute a program's instructions directly from the disk. Just as you cannot know what is in a book lying on a table until you read the book's contents into your memory (using your own CPU—your mind), your CPU cannot process a program's instructions until it loads the program from disk into main memory. Figure 2.2 shows the process of loading a program from the computer's disk (or disk-like storage, such as a flash drive) into memory. As the figure shows, the CPU has direct access to memory but has no access to the disk drive. The disk is the long-term storage, and the memory is the short-term storage, where programs temporarily reside while the CPU executes them.

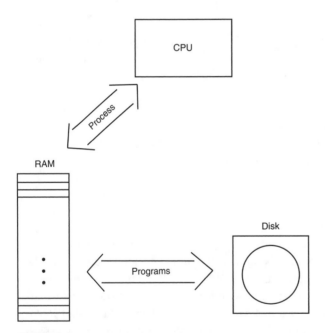

FIGURE 2.2
A program must be in memory before the CPU can execute the program's instructions.

As you already know, a program differs greatly from the output. The program is a set of instructions, and the *output* is the result of those instructions. A recipe's output is the finished dish, and the program's output is the printed output that results when the instructions run.

Perhaps a specific example will further clarify what it means to a programmer for a user to use a program. If you use a word processor, then you probably follow steps similar to these:

1. You load the word-processing program from your hard drive into the computer's main memory. When you select the word-processing program's name from the menu or select its icon, you are instructing the computer to search the disk drive for the program and load it into main memory.

2. What you see onscreen is output from the program. You can produce more output by typing text on the screen. Everything that appears onscreen throughout the program's execution is program output.

3. After you type text, you may interact with other devices. You will probably issue a command to print the document (more than likely using the standard Windows File, Print menu option) to the printer and save the document in a data file on the disk.

4. When you exit the word processor, your operating system regains control. The word-processing program is no longer in memory, but it is still safely tucked away on disk.

As you can see, the results of a program's execution make up the output. The instructions produce those results. Figure 2.3 gives an overview of the program-to-output process. Modern-day programs produce output in many different ways. Programs play music, talk to other computers over Wi-Fi, and control external devices. Output sent to the screen and printer still makes up the majority of today's program output.

FIGURE 2.3
The program comes from disk, executes, and then sends its results to any of the many output devices, such as the disk, screen, or printer (or more than one of them from within the same program).

When a program is in memory, it is not there alone. Your operating system always resides in memory. If it did not, you could neither load a program from disk nor run it because the operating system is what actually loads programs to and from memory when you issue the correct command. Limited memory often poses a problem for larger programs. Recall that a program processes data, and the data and the program must be in memory before the program can easily process the data.

Figure 2.4 shows what a typical computer installation's memory looks like when a program is running. The operating system takes a big chunk, the program must be there, too, and finally there must be room for data.

Memory

FIGURE 2.4
A typical memory layout shows that the operating system shares memory with executing programs.

The more memory your PC has, the faster your programs run. The extra memory means that the operating system will have to swap less to and from disk as the program operates. A program may even be contained in memory in its entirety the whole time that the program runs. As a programmer, you should run with ample memory, as much as 256MB or 512MB, so that you can properly test your running programs while still keeping your programming environment loaded.

Art or Science?

A debate that you often see in computer literature is whether programming is an art or a science. Through the years, there have been advances made in programming that, if followed, improve a program's accuracy, readability, and *maintainability* (the ability to change the program later to perform a different or additional set of tasks). Most of these advances are nothing more than suggestions; that is, programmers don't have to use them to write programs that work.

Two of the most important advances in programming have been more philosophically based than engineered. They are *structured programming* and *object-oriented programming*. This book explores these two programming advances thoroughly in the hours that follow. They both offer ways that a programmer can write a program to make it better. Again, though, these are just suggested approaches to programming; programmers can (and many do) ignore them.

There are many ways to write even the smallest and simplest programs. Just as authors write differently and musicians play differently, programmers each have a unique style. Therefore, you would think that programming is more of an art than a science. On the continuum of science to art, you would be closer to being correct than those few who argue that programming is more of a science.

Nevertheless, as more advances are made in developing programming approaches, as has already been done with structured programming and object-oriented programming, you should see a shift in thinking. With the proliferation of computers in today's world, there is a massive educational effort in process to train tomorrow's programmers. Because programming is still a young industry, many advances are still left to be made.

Some of the biggest proponents of moving away from the artful approach to a more scientific approach, using structured and object-oriented programming, are the companies paying the programmers. Companies need to react quickly to changing business conditions, and they need programs written as quickly and as accurately as possible. As advances in computer programming are discovered, more companies are going to adopt policies that require their programmers to use more scientific and time-proven methods of writing better programs.

Speak the Language

The instructions you give in your programs must be in a language the computer understands, which, as you learned in Hour 1, is machine language. At its lowest level, a computer is nothing more than thousands of switches flipping on and off—lightning fast. A switch can have only one of two states; it can be *on* or *off*. Because either of these two states of electricity can be controlled easily with switches, many thousands of them control what your computer does from one microsecond to another.

If it were up to your computer, you would have to give it instructions using switches that represent on and off states of electricity. Actually, that is exactly the way that programmers programmed early computers. A panel of switches, such as the one shown in Figure 2.5, had to be used to enter all programs and data. The next time you find yourself cursing errors that appear in programs you write, think of what it would have been like programming 60 years ago.

FIGURE 2.5
Programmers used a panel of switches to program early computers.

The on and off states of electricity are represented as 1s and 0s at the computer's lowest level. This representation has a name: *binary*. You can control what your computer does if you know the correct pattern of 1s and 0s required to give it commands. You can program a computer simply by issuing 1s and 0s if you have the correct system tools. Of course, programming in the binary digits of 1s and 0s is not much better than flipping switches up and down on the switch panel, so there has to be a better way.

Computers Cannot Handle Ambiguity

Spoken languages are too ambiguous to computers. People's brains can decipher sentences intuitively—but a nonthinking machine can't. Some inroads are being made into *artificial intelligence*, which is the science of programming computers so that they can learn on their own. It also includes programming them to understand a spoken language such as English. Despite recent advancements, artificial intelligence is many years away (if it is even possible for computers to understand simple English commands).

Consider the following sentence:

> *Time flies like an arrow.*

Your mind has no trouble understanding the parts of this sentence. You know that it is an analogy, and the parts of speech make total sense to you. *Time* is a noun, and the verb describes the action that time performs: It *flies*, and it does so *like an arrow*. If you teach the computer to accept these descriptions of this sentence, it will work fine until it runs into something like this:

> *Fruit flies like an orange.*

Think about this for a moment. Again, you have no problem understanding this sentence, even though it is completely different from the other one. The computer taught to decipher the first sentence, however, is going to throw its cables up in frustration at the second sentence because none of the parts of the sentence are the same. The word *flies* is now a noun and not an action verb. The phrase *like an orange* is no longer a description of the action but rather both the verb (*like*) and the object receiving the action (*an orange*). As you can see from these two sentences alone, understanding simple sentences that most people take for granted poses a tremendous problem for programmers trying to "teach" a computer to understand a language such as English.

Here's another example.

> *The pop can has a lid.*

Computers have extreme problems with statements such as this one because the sentence appears to have a subject/verb agreement problem. Does the sentence state that the can of pop has a lid or that the pop can have a lid? If it's the latter, then *has* should be *have*. The human mind can easily distinguish these problems and knows that the can of pop has a lid, but given today's technology, machines simply cannot easily do so.

Therefore, computers and people are at opposite ends of the spectrum. People want to speak their own language, but computers want to stick to their language comprised of 1s and 0s. There has to be some kind of go-between. Programming languages were created to try to appease both the computer and the person programming the computer. You've seen from Python that programming languages use words similar to those that people use, but programming languages have a highly specific syntax that allows little room for the ambiguity that is so prevalent in spoken languages. The computer can take a programming language and translate it to its machine language of 1s and 0s; the human programmer can learn, remember, and use the programming languages more effectively than 1s and 0s because programming languages appear similar to spoken languages, although they are more precise and simple.

Computers Speak Many Languages

You are going to learn a lot about several programming languages in this 24-hour course. You may have heard of some of the languages before. Over the years since the first computer language was invented, hundreds of programming languages have been written, but only a handful of them have prevailed to dominate the rest. Table 2.2 lists several programming languages that have gained more than obscure notoriety through the years.

TABLE 2.2 Many programming languages have appeared through the years

Algol	PL/I
PROLOG	LISP
COBOL	Forth
RPG	RPG II
Pascal	Object Pascal
Go	Ada
C	C++
C#	FORTRAN
SmallTalk	Eiffel
BASIC	Visual Basic
APL	Java
Python	PHP
JavaScript	Ruby

The computer is like a modern-day tower of Babel, indirectly responsible for more programming languages than were ever needed. Most people considered to be computer experts might know only a handful of programming languages—from three to five—and they probably know only one or two very well. Don't let the large number of languages deter you from learning to program.

There are lots of reasons there are so many programming languages. Different people have different preferences, some languages are better than others for different tasks, and some people have access to only one or two of the languages. For example, HTML is a language that programmers use for developing websites. FORTRAN was used in the past for highly mathematical applications, although other languages have supplanted FORTRAN in many programming departments. Java, JavaScript, and PHP, combined with HTML, are great languages for putting interaction on web pages. The emergence of agile development methodology has resulted in an increase in the use of Ruby programming.

Summary

There are several ways to obtain programs for computers, but to really make computers do what you want, you have to write programs yourself. Most programs that you purchase are merely licenses to use but not customize the programs. Companies need programs that enable them to do business the way they prefer and that do not force them to change their practices to conform to the programs.

Before you can program, you must learn a programming language. You may want to learn several languages, but your work and interest goals will determine which languages you learn. Perhaps you want to specialize in Internet languages, or perhaps you have a long-term Python contract. You'll find that the more languages you learn, the easier it will be for you to pick up additional languages.

The next hour describes some of the background needed for proper program design.

Q&A

Q. Why do programs have to be so detailed?

A. Programs are detailed because computers are machines. Machines do not have intelligence. A computer blindly follows your instructions, step by step. If you do not give detailed instructions, the computer can do nothing.

Workshop

The quiz questions are provided for your further understanding.

Quiz

1. What are the three ways to acquire a new program?

2. Why do businesses often write their own programs, despite the extra expense required?

3. Why must programmers know a programming language?

4. Why do computers not understand human language?

5. Which is more ambiguous: human language or computer language?

6. True or false: To be useful, a programmer should know at least five programming languages.

7. Why is RAM-based internal memory so important to a running program?

8. Which languages from Table 2.2 do you think are derived from the C programming language?

9. Why might a programmer specialize in only one programming language?

10. What is open-source software?

Answers

1. You can buy a program that's already written, buy a program with source code and modify the program, or write your own program from scratch.

2. Companies want their programs to conform to the way they do business.

3. Programmers must use programming languages to create programs.

4. Computers only understand a very low-level machine language and are not advanced enough to recognize higher languages.

5. Human language has more ambiguity than computer language.

6. False. A programmer might only know one or two languages and still be extremely useful and productive.

7. The more RAM your computer contains, the more of your program and data can fit into memory at the same time and the faster your program executes.

8. C++ and C# are derived from the C language.

9. A programmer might specialize in only one programming language because the programmer's company may use only one language. Also, the more specialized the programmer is, the better the programmer will be in that skill. Nevertheless, most programmers are familiar with several languages and prosper more because of that knowledge.

10. Open-source programs are distributed with their source code along with the executable files. Users are encouraged to alter the code and improve the program, as long as they share their code changes with the community.

HOUR 3
Designing a Program

Programmers learn to develop patience early in their programming careers. They learn that proper design is critical to a successful program. Perhaps you have heard the term *systems analysis and design*. This is the name given to the practice of analyzing a problem and then designing a program from that analysis. Complete books and college courses have been dedicated to systems analysis and design. Of course, you want to get back to hands-on programming—and you'll be doing that very soon. However, to be productive at hands-on programming, you need to understand the importance of design. This chapter covers program design highlights, letting you see what productive computer programmers go through before writing programs.

The highlights of this hour include the following:

▶ Understanding the importance of program design

▶ Mastering the three steps required to write programs

▶ Using output definition

▶ Comparing top-down and bottom-up designs

▶ Seeing how flowcharts and pseudocode are making room for RAD

▶ Preparing for the final step in the programming process

The Need for Design

A builder who begins to build a house doesn't pick up a hammer and begin on the kitchen's frame. A designer must design the new house before anything can begin to be built. As you will soon see, a program should also be designed before it is written.

A builder must first find out what the purchasers of the house want. Nothing can be built unless the builder has an end result in mind. Therefore, the buyers of the house must meet with an architect. They tell the architect what they want the house to look like. The architect helps the buyers decide by telling them what is possible and what isn't. During this initial stage, the price is always a factor that requires the designers and the purchasers to reach compromise agreements.

After the architect completes the plans for the house, the builder must plan the resources needed to build the house. Only after the design of the house is finished, the permits are filed, the money is in place, the materials are purchased, and the laborers are hired can any physical building begin. As a matter of fact, the more effort the builder puts into these preliminary requirements, the faster the house can actually be built.

The problem with building a house before it is properly designed is that the eventual owners may want changes made after it is too late to change them. It is very difficult to add a bathroom in the middle of two bedrooms *after* the house is completed. The goal is to get the owners to agree with the builder on the design of the house prior to construction. When the specifications are agreed on by all the parties involved, there is little room for disagreement later. The clearer the initial plans are, the fewer problems down the road because all parties agreed on the same house plans.

Sure, this is not a book on house construction, but this example provides a good analogy for writing programs of any great length. You should not go to the keyboard and start typing instructions into the editor before designing the program any more than a builder should pick up a hammer before the house plans are finalized.

TIP

The more up-front design work that you do, the faster you will finish the final program.

Thanks to computer technology, a computer program is easier to modify than a house. If you leave out a routine that a user wanted, you can add it later more easily than a builder can add a room to a finished house. Nevertheless, adding something to a program is never as easy as designing the program correctly the first time.

User–Programmer Agreement

Suppose you accept a job as a programmer for a small business that wants to create sales and inventory software. (After you've gone through these 24 hours, you'll understand programming better, and you'll even learn how to write programs in Python or be able to switch to another language.) The changes that the owners want sound simple. They want you to write some interactive Python routines that enable them to look at existing inventory and to print what products have sold in the past day, week, month, or year.

So, you listen to what they want, you agree to a price for your services, you get an advance payment, you plan out the software, and you go to your home office to begin the work. After some grueling months of work, you bring your masterpiece program back to show the owners.

"Looks good," they say. "But where is the report that breaks down credit card versus cash purchases? Where can we check in-store versus warehouse inventory? Where does the program list the products we've back-ordered and that are unavailable? Why can't the program total sales tax we've collected anywhere?"

You've just learned a painful lesson about user–programmer agreements. The users did a lousy job at explaining what they wanted. In fairness to them, you didn't do a great job at pulling out of them what they needed. Both of you thought you knew what you were supposed to do, and neither knew in reality. You realize that the price you quoted them originally will pay for about 10% of the work this project requires.

Before you start a job and before you price a job, you must know what your users want. Learning this is part of the program design experience. You need to know every detail before you'll be able to price your service accurately and before you'll be able to make customers happy.

NOTE

Proper user–programmer agreement is vital for all areas of programming, not just for contract programmers. If you work for a corporation as a programmer, you also will need to have detailed specifications before you can begin your work. Other corporate users who will use the system must sign off on what they want so that everybody knows up front what is expected. If the user comes back to you later and asks why you didn't include a feature, you will be able to answer, "Because we never discussed that feature. You approved specifications that never mentioned that feature."

The program maintenance that takes place after the program is written, tested, and distributed is one of the most time-consuming aspects of the programming process. Programs are continually updated to reflect new user needs. Sometimes, if the program is not designed properly before it is written, the user will not want the program until it does exactly what the user wants it to do.

Computer consultants learn early to get the user's acceptance—and even the user's signature—on a program's design before the programming begins. If both the user and the programmers agree on what to do, there is little room for argument when the final program is presented. Company resources are limited; there is no time to add something later that should have been in the system all along.

Steps to Design

There are three fundamental steps you should perform when you have a program to write:

1. Define the output and data flows.

2. Develop the logic to get to that output.

3. Write the program.

Notice that writing the program is the *last* step in writing the program. This is not as silly as it sounds. Remember that physically building the house is the last stage of building the house; proper planning is critical before any actual building can start. You will find that writing and typing in the lines of a program is one of the easiest parts of the programming process. If your design is well thought out, the program practically writes itself; typing it in becomes almost an afterthought to the whole process.

Step 1: Define the Output and Data Flows

Before beginning a program, you must have a firm idea of what the program should produce and what data is needed to produce that output. Just as a builder must know what the house should look like before beginning to build it, a programmer must know what the output is going to be before writing the program. Anything that the program produces and the user sees is considered output that you must define. You must know what every screen in the program should look like and what will be on every page of every printed report.

Some programs are rather small, but without knowing where you're heading, you might take longer to finish the program than you would if you first determined the output in detail. Suppose you wanted to add a Python-based program that allowed a small business to record and store customer contact information. To start, you should make a list of all fields that the program is to produce onscreen. You would not only list each field but also describe the fields. Table 3.1 details the fields on the program's window.

TABLE 3.1   Fields that your contact management program might display

Field	Type	Description
Contacts	Scrolling list	Displays the list of contacts
Name	Text field	Holds contact's name
Address	Text field	Holds contact's address
City	Text field	Holds contact's city
State	Text field	Holds contact's state
Zip	Text field	Holds contact's zip code
Home Phone #	Text field	Holds contact's phone number
Cell Phone #	Text field	Holds contact's mobile number
Email	Text field	Holds contact's email address
Stage	Fixed, scrolling list	Displays a list of possible stages this contact might reside in, such as being offered a special follow-up call or perhaps the initial contact
Notes	Text field	Miscellaneous notes about the contact, such as whether the contact has bought from the company before

Field	Type	Description
Filter Contacts	Fixed, scrolling list	Enables the user to search for groups of contacts based on the stage the contacts are in so that the user can see a list of all contacts who have been sent a mailing
Edit	Function	Enables the user to modify an existing contact
Add	Function	Enables the user to add a new contact
Delete	Function	Enables the user to delete an existing contact

Many of the fields you list in an output definition may be obvious. The field called `Name` obviously will hold and display a contact's name. Being obvious is okay. Keep in mind that if you write programs for other people, as you often will do, you must get approval of your program's parameters. One of the best ways to begin is to make a list of all the intended program's fields and make sure that the user agrees that everything is there. Perhaps your client has specific interests, like wanting the Twitter handle of contacts as well. By communicating with your client, you will get a better idea of what you need to add to the program.

As you'll see later this hour, in the section "Rapid Application Development," you'll be able to use programs to put together a model of the actual output screen that your users can see. With the model and with your list of fields, you have double verification that the program contains exactly what the user wants.

Input windows such as the Contacts program data-entry screen are part of your output definition. This may seem contradictory, but input screens require that your program place fields on the screen, and you should plan where these input fields must go.

The output definition is more than a preliminary output design. It gives you insight into what data elements the program should track, compute, and produce. Defining the output also helps you gather all the input you need to produce the output.

CAUTION

Some programs produce a huge amount of output. Don't skip this first all-important step in the design process just because there is a lot of output. With more output, it becomes more important for you to define it. Defining the output is relatively easy—sometimes even downright boring and time-consuming. The time you need to define the output can take as long as typing in the program. You will lose that time and more, however, if you shrug off the output definition at the beginning.

The output definition consists of many pages of details. You must be able to specify all the details of a problem before you know what output you need. Even command buttons and scrolling list boxes are output because the program will display these items.

In Hour 1, "Hands-On Programming," you learned that data goes into a program, and the program outputs meaningful information. You should inventory all the data that goes into a program. If you're using Python to make a customer contact program, you need to know what specific data the owners want to collect from the users. Define what each piece of data is. Perhaps the owners want to ask customers whether they want to submit a name and email address for the weekly sales email blast. Does the company want any additional data from the user, such as physical address, age, and income?

Object-Oriented Design

Throughout this 24-hour tutorial, you will learn what *object-oriented programming* (OOP) is all about. Basically, OOP turns data values, such as names and prices, into objects that can take on a life of their own inside programs. Part III, "Java and Object-Oriented Programming," covers the basics of OOP.

A few years ago, some OOP experts developed a process for designing OOP programs called *object-oriented design* (OOD). OOD made an advanced science out of specifying data to be gathered in a program and defining that data in a way that was appropriate for the special needs of OOP programmers. Grady Booch was one of the founders of OOD. His specifications from almost three decades ago continue to help OOP programmers collect data for the applications they are about to write and to turn that data into objects for programs.

In Hour 4, "Getting Input and Displaying Output," you'll learn how to put these ideas into a program. You will learn how a program asks for data and produces information on the screen. This *I/O* (*input/output*) process is the most critical part of an application. You want to capture all data required and in an accurate way.

Something is still missing in all this design discussion. You understand the importance of gathering data. You understand the importance of knowing where you're headed by designing the output. But how do you go from data to output? That's the next step in the design process: You need to determine what processing will be required to produce the output from the input (data). You must be able to generate proper data flows and calculations so that your program manipulates that data and produces the correct output. The final sections of this hour discuss ways to develop the centerpiece—the logic for your programs.

All output screens, printed reports, and data-entry screens must be defined in advance so you know exactly what is required of your programs. You must also decide what data to keep in files and the format of your data files. As you progress in your programming education, you will learn ways to lay out data files in appropriate formats.

When capturing data, you want to gather data from users in a way that is reasonable, requires little time, and has prompts that request the data in a friendly and unobtrusive manner. Prototyping (discussed next) and rapid application development can help.

Prototyping

In the days of expensive hardware and costly computer usage time, the process of system design was, in some ways, more critical than it is today. The more time you spent designing your code, the smoother the costly hands-on programming became. This is far less true today because computers are inexpensive, and you have much more freedom to change your mind and add program options than before. Yet the first part of this hour was spent in great detail explaining why up-front design is critical.

The primary problem many new programmers have today is that they do absolutely no design work. That's why many problems take place, such as the one mentioned earlier this hour about the company that wanted far more in its program than the programmer ever dreamed of.

Although the actual design of output, data, and even the logic in the body of the program itself is much simpler to work with, given the power and low cost of today's computing tools, you still must maintain an eagle eye toward developing an initial design with agreed-upon output from your users. You must also know all the data that your program is to collect before you begin your coding. If you don't, you will have a frustrating time as a contract programmer or as a corporate programmer because you'll constantly be playing catch-up with what the users actually want and failed to tell you about.

One of the benefits of the Windows operating system is its visual nature. Before Windows, programming tools were limited to text-based design and implementation. Designing a user's screen today means starting with a programming language such as Visual Basic, drawing the screen, and dragging to the screen objects that the user will interact with, such as an OK button. Therefore, you can quickly design *prototype screens* that you can send to the user. A prototype is a model, and a prototype screen models what the final program's screen will look like. After the user sees the screens that he or she will interact with, the user will have a much better feel for whether you understand the needs of the program.

Many Windows programming languages, such as Visual C++ and Visual Basic, include prototyping tools. For comparison, Figure 3.1 shows the Visual Basic development screen. The language covered in these early chapters, Python, is more likely to help you behind the scenes, working with the data and analyzing it as needed. You can certainly perform input and output functions with Python, but if you are developing a Windows application, other languages are more appropriate, such as what you see in Figure 3.1. The screen looks rather busy, but the important things to look for are the Toolbox and the output design window. To place controls such as command buttons and text boxes on the form that serves as the output window, the programmer only has to drag that control from the Toolbox window to the form. So, to build a program's output, the programmer only has to drag as many controls as needed to the form and does not have to write a single line of code in the meantime.

Toolbox   Drag controls here   Already-placed controls

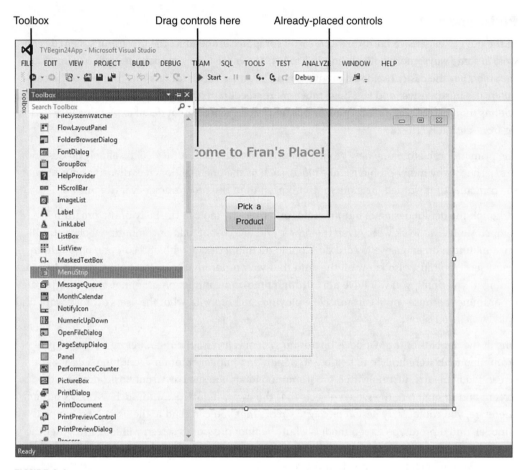

FIGURE 3.1
Program development systems such as Visual Basic provide tools that you can use to create output definitions visually.

Once you place controls on a form window with a programming tool such as Visual Basic, you can do more than show the form to your users. You actually can compile the form, just as you would a program, and let your user interact with the controls. When the user is able to work with the controls, even though nothing happens as a result, the user is better able to tell if you understand the goals of the program. The user often notices if there is a missing piece of the program and can also offer suggestions to make the program flow more easily from a user's point of view.

CAUTION
_____

A prototype is often only an empty shell that cannot do anything except simulate user interaction until you tie its pieces together with code. Your job as a programmer has only just begun once you get approval on the screens, but the screens are the first place to begin because you must understand what your users want in order to know how to proceed.

Rapid Application Development

A more advanced program design tool used for defining output, data flows, and logic itself is called *rapid application development*, or *RAD* for short. RAD is the process of quickly placing controls on a form—not unlike you just saw done with Visual Basic—connecting those controls to data, and accessing pieces of prewritten code to put together a fully functional application without writing a single line of code. In a way, programming systems such as Visual Basic are fulfilling many goals of RAD. When you place controls on a form, as you'll see done in far more detail in Hour 20, "Programming with Visual Basic 2012," the Visual Basic system handles all the programming needed for that control. You don't ever have to write anything to make a command button act like a command button should. Your only goal is to determine how many command buttons your program needs and where they are to go.

But these tools cannot read your mind. RAD tools do not know that, when the user clicks a certain button, a report is supposed to print. Programmers are still needed to connect all these things to each other and to data, and programmers are needed to write the detailed logic so that the program processes data correctly. Before these kinds of program development tools appeared, programmers had to write thousands of lines of code, often in the C programming language, just to produce a simple Windows program. At least now the controls and the interface are more rapidly developed. Perhaps someday a RAD tool will be sophisticated enough to develop the logic also. But in the meantime, don't quit your day job if your day job is programming, because you're still in demand.

TIP

Teach your users how to prototype their own screens! Programming knowledge is not required to design the screens. Your users, therefore, will be able to show you exactly what they want. The prototyped screens are interactive as well. That is, your users will be able to click the buttons and enter values in the fields even though nothing happens as a result of that use. The idea is to let your users try the screens for a while to make sure they are comfortable with the placement and appearance of the controls.

Top-Down Program Design

For large projects, many programming staff members find that a top-down design helps them focus on what a program needs and helps them detail the logic required to produce the program's results. *Top-down design* is the process of breaking down a problem into more and more detail until you finalize all the details. With top-down design, you produce the details needed to accomplish a programming task.

The problem with top-down design is that programmers tend not to use it. They tend to design from the opposite direction (called *bottom-up design*). When you ignore top-down design, you impose a heavy burden on yourself to remember every detail that will be needed; with top-down design, the details fall out on their own. You don't have to worry about the petty details if you follow a strict top-down design because the process of top-down design takes care of producing the details.

TIP
One of the keys to top-down design is that it forces you to put off the details until later. Top-down design forces you to think in terms of the overall problem for as long as possible. Top-down design keeps you focused. If you use bottom-up design, it is easy to lose sight of the forest for the trees. You get to the details too fast and lose sight of your program's primary objectives.

Top-down design involves a three-step process:

1. Determine the overall goal.

2. Break that goal into two, three, or more detailed parts. Don't add too many details, or you might leave things out.

3. Keep repeating steps 1 and 2—and put off the details as long as possible—until you cannot reasonably break down the problem any further.

You can learn about top-down design more easily by relating it to a common real-world problem before looking at a computer problem. Top-down design is not just for programming problems. Once you master top-down design, you can apply it to any part of your life that you must plan in detail. Perhaps the most detailed event that a person can plan is a wedding. Therefore, a wedding is the perfect place to see top-down design in action.

What is the first thing you must do to have a wedding? First, find a prospective spouse. (You'll need a different book for help with that.) When it comes time to plan the wedding, the top-down design is the best way to approach the event. The way *not* to plan a wedding is to worry about the details first, yet this is the way most people plan a wedding. They start thinking about the dresses, the organist, the flowers, and the cake to serve at the reception. The biggest problem with trying to cover all these details from the beginning is that you lose sight of so much; it is too easy to forget a detail until it's too late. The details of bottom-up design get in your way.

What is the overall goal of a wedding? Thinking in the most general terms possible, "Have a wedding" is about as general as it can get. If you were in charge of planning a wedding, the general goal of "Have a wedding" would put you right on target. Assume that "Have a wedding" is the highest-level goal.

The overall goal keeps you focused. Despite its redundant nature, "Have a wedding" keeps out details such as planning the honeymoon. If you don't put a fence around the exact problem you are working on, you'll get mixed up with details and, more importantly, you'll forget some details. If you're planning both a wedding and a honeymoon, you should do two top-down designs or include the honeymoon trip in the top-level general goal. This wedding plan includes the event of the wedding—the ceremony and reception—but doesn't include any honeymoon details. (Leave the honeymoon details to your spouse so you can be surprised. After all, you have enough to do with the wedding plans, right?)

Now that you know where you're heading, begin by breaking down the overall goal into two or three details. For instance, what about the colors of the wedding, what about the guest list, what about paying the officiant...*oops,* too many details! The idea of top-down design is to put off the details for as long as possible. Don't get in a hurry. When you find yourself breaking the current problem into more than three or four parts, you are rushing the top-down design. Put off the details. Basically, you can break down "Have a wedding" into the following two major components: the ceremony and the reception.

The next step of top-down design is to repeat the same process with the new components. The ceremony is made up of the people and the location. The reception includes the food, the people, and the location. The ceremony's people include the guests, the wedding party, and the workers (officiant, organist, and so on—but those details come a little later).

Don't worry about the time order of the details yet. The goal of top-down design is to produce every detail you need (eventually), not to put those details into any order. You must know where you are heading and exactly what is required before considering how those details relate to each other and which ones come first.

Eventually, you will have several pages of details that cannot be broken down any further. For instance, you'll probably end up with the details of the reception food, such as peanuts for snacking. (If you start out listing those details, however, you could forget many of them.)

Now move to a more computerized problem; assume that you are assigned the task of writing a payroll program for a company. What would that payroll program require? You could begin by listing the payroll program's details, such as:

▶ Print payroll checks.

▶ Calculate federal taxes.

▶ Calculate state taxes.

What is wrong with this approach? If you said that the details were coming too early, you are correct. The perfect place to start is at the top. The most general goal of a payroll program might be "Perform the payroll." This overall goal keeps other details out of this program (no general ledger processing will be included, unless part of the payroll system updates a general ledger file) and keeps you focused on the problem at hand.

Consider Figure 3.2. This might be the first page of the payroll's top-down design. Any payroll program has to include some mechanism for entering, deleting, and changing employee information such as address, city, state, zip code, number of exemptions, and so on. What other details about the employees do you need? At this point, don't answer that question. The design is not ready for all those details.

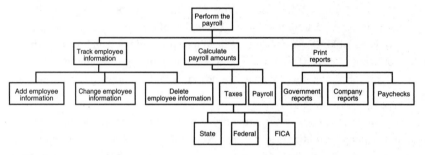

FIGURE 3.2
The first page of the payroll program's top-down design would include the highest level of details.

There is a long way to go before you finish with the payroll top-down design, but Figure 3.2 is the first step. You must keep breaking down each component until the details finally appear.

Only when you and the user gather all the necessary details through top-down design can you decide what is going to comprise those details.

Step 2: Develop the Logic

After you and the user agree to the goals and output of the program, the rest is up to you. Your job is to use that output definition to decide how to make a computer produce the output. You have broken down the overall problem into detailed instructions that the computer can carry out. This doesn't mean you are ready to write the program—quite the contrary. You are now ready to develop the logic that produces that output.

The output definition goes a long way toward describing *what* the program is supposed to do. Now you must decide *how* to accomplish the job. You must order the details that you have so they operate in a time-ordered fashion. You must also decide which decisions your program must make and the actions produced by each of those decisions.

Throughout the rest of this 24-hour tutorial, you'll learn the final two steps of developing programs. You will gain insight into how programmers write and test a program after developing the output definition and getting the user's approval on the program's specifications.

CAUTION

Only after learning to program can you learn to develop the logic that goes into a program, yet you must develop some logic before writing programs to be able to move from the output and data definition stage to the program code. This "chicken before the egg" syndrome is common for newcomers to programming. When you begin to write your own programs, you'll have a much better understanding of logic development.

In the past, users would use tools such as *flowcharts* and *pseudocode* to develop program logic. A flowchart is shown in Figure 3.3. It is said that a picture is worth a thousand words, and the flowchart provides a pictorial representation of program logic. The flowchart doesn't include all the program details but represents the general logic flow of the program. If your flowchart is correctly drawn, writing the actual program becomes a matter of rote. After the final program is completed, the flowchart can act as documentation for the program.

Flowcharts are made up of industry-standard symbols. Plastic flowchart symbol outlines, called *flowchart templates*, are still available at office supply stores to help you draw better-looking flowcharts instead of relying on freehand drawing. There are also some programs that guide you through the creation of a flowchart and enable you to print flowcharts on your printer.

Although some still use flowcharts today, RAD and other development tools have virtually eliminated flowcharts except for depicting isolated parts of a program's logic for documentation purposes. Even in its heyday in the 1960s and 1970s, flowcharting did not completely catch on. Some companies preferred another method for logic description called *pseudocode*, sometimes called *structured English*, which involves writing logic using sentences of text instead of the diagrams used in flowcharting.

Pseudocode doesn't have any programming language statements in it, but it also is not free-flowing English. It is a set of rigid English words that allow for the depiction of logic you see so often in flowcharts and programming languages. As with flowcharts, you can write pseudocode for anything, not just computer programs. A lot of instruction manuals use a form of pseudocode to illustrate the steps needed to assemble parts. Pseudocode offers a rigid description of logic that tries to leave little room for ambiguity.

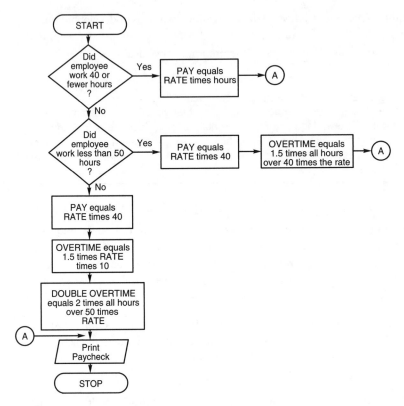

FIGURE 3.3
The flowchart depicts the payroll program's logic graphically.

Here is the logic for the payroll problem in pseudocode form. Notice that you can read the text, yet it is not a programming language. The indention helps keep track of which sentences go together. The pseudocode is readable by anyone, even by people unfamiliar with flowcharting symbols:

```
For each employee:
  If the employee worked 0 to 40 hours then
    net pay equals hours worked times rate.
  Otherwise,
    if the employee worked between 40 and 50 hours then
    net pay equals 40 times the rate;
    add to that (hours worked -40) times the rate times 1.5.
  Otherwise,
    net pay equals 40 times the rate;
    add to that 10 times the rate times 1.5;
    add to that (hours worked -50) times twice the rate.
  Deduct taxes from the net pay.
Print the paycheck.
```

Step 3: Writing the Code

The program writing takes the longest to learn. After you learn to program, however, the actual programming process takes less time than the design if your design is accurate and complete. The nature of programming requires that you learn some new skills. The next few hourly lessons will teach you a lot about programming languages and will help train you to become a better coder so that your programs will not only achieve the goals they are supposed to achieve but also will be simple to maintain.

Summary

A builder doesn't build a house before designing it, and a programmer should not write a program without designing it either. Too often, programmers rush to the keyboard without thinking through the logic. A badly designed program results in lots of bugs and maintenance. This hour describes how to ensure that your program design matches the design that the user wants. After you complete the output definition, you can organize the program's logic using top-down design, flowcharts, and pseudocode.

The next hour focuses on training you in your first computer language, Python.

Q&A

Q. At what point in the top-down design should I begin to add details?

A. Put off the details as long as possible. If you were designing a program to produce sales reports, you would not enter the printing of the final report total until you had completed all the other report design tasks. The details fall out on their own when you can no longer break a task into two or more other tasks.

Q. Once I break the top-down design into its lowest-level details, don't I also have the pseudocode details?

A. The top-down enables you to determine all the details your program will need. The top-down design doesn't, however, put those details into their logical execution order. The pseudocode dictates the executing logic of your program and determines when things happen, the order in which they happen, and when they stop happening. The top-down design simply determines everything that might happen in the program. Instead of using pseudocode, however, you should consider getting a RAD tool that will help you move more quickly from the design to the finished, working program. Today's RAD systems are still rather primitive, and you'll have to add much of the code yourself.

Workshop

The quiz questions are provided for your further understanding.

Quiz

1. Why does proper design often take longer than writing the program code?

2. Where does a programmer first begin determining the user's requirements?

3. True or false: Proper top-down design forces you to put off details as long as possible.

4. How does top-down design differ from pseudocode?

5. What is the purpose of RAD?

6. True or false: You do not have to add code to any system that you design with RAD.

7. Which uses symbols: a flowchart or pseudocode?

8. True or false: You can flowchart both program logic as well as real-world procedures.

9. True or false: Your user will help you create a program's output if you let the user work with an output prototype.

10. What is the final step of the programming process (before testing the final result)?

Answers

1. The more thorough the design, the more quickly the programming staff can write the program.

2. A programmer often begins defining the output of the proposed system.

3. True

4. Top-down design enables a program designer to incrementally generate all aspects of a program's requirements. Pseudocode enables you to specify the logic of a program once the program's design has been accomplished using tools such as top-down design.

5. RAD provides a way to rapidly develop systems and move quickly from the design stage to a finished product. RAD tools are not yet advanced enough to handle most programming tasks, although RAD can make designing systems easier than designing without RAD tools.

6. False. RAD requires quite a bit of programming in many instances once its work is done.

7. A flowchart uses symbols.

8. True

9. True

10. The final step of programming is writing the program code.

HOUR 4
Getting Input and Displaying Output

Input and output are the cornerstones that enable programs to interact with the outside world. In the previous hour, you learned how important the output process is to programming because through output, your program displays information. A program must get some of its data and control from the user's input, so learning how to get the user's responses is critical as well.

The highlights of this hour include the following:

- Displaying output in Python
- Printing multiple occurrences per line
- Separating output values
- Using variables to hold information
- Getting data in Python
- Prompting for data input
- Sending output to your printer

Printing to the Screen with Python

In Python, the primary method for displaying output on the screen is to use the `print()` function. You've already seen the `print()` function in action in the programs presented in the first two hours of the book. Almost every program you write will output some data to the screen. Your users must be able to see results and read messages from the programs that they run.

NOTE

In programming, a *function* is a collection of programming statements that perform a specific task. When programming, if you find yourself needing to do the same thing over and over again, you will save time by creating a function. Most programming languages include a series of predefined functions for output, input, and many mathematical operations. Some of Python's built-in functions are covered in this book, but there are many more available. The Python functions that you learn in this book generally have comparable functions in other programming languages; once you learn one, it should be pretty easy to understand other similar functions in other languages.

The output to the screen in most programs is a combination of unchanging and changing information. Luckily, the `print()` function can handle both. The following statements show some examples:

```
print('2 + 3 = ',2+3)
print('Math is fun!')
```

These statements produce the following output:

```
2 + 3 = 5
Math is fun!
```

Remember that with the `print()` function in Python, you need to put what you plan to print in the parentheses. Without that, you will not get a result; instead, your code will generate an error message. You may be wondering about the information between the parentheses in the lines of code. There's a string of characters between the two single quote marks in both, and that first single quote tells Python "print all characters you see from here on out until you get to the second, closing single quote mark." The quotation marks are not printed; they mark the string to be printed. But what if you want to print quotation marks? Python has an easy solution. If you enclose your string to be printed in double quote marks, you can then include the single quotation mark as something to print. For example, if you changed the second line to the line:

```
print("Isn't math fun?")
```

the output would be:

```
Isn't math fun?
```

Whether you use single or double quotation marks, understand that numbers and mathematical expressions will print as is inside the string. Python will not do any math within a string. If you write:

```
print('2 + 3')
```

Python doesn't print 5 (the result of 2 + 3). Because quotation marks enclose the expression, the expression prints exactly as it appears inside the quotation marks. However, as you can see in the second half of the first statement, if you print an expression without the quotation marks, Python prints the result of the calculated expression:

```
print(5 + 7)
```

prints 12.

Consider the program in Listing 4.1. It prints the radius of a circle, as well as the area of the entire circle and half of the circle.

LISTING 4.1 Printing results of calculations

```
# Filename: AreaHalf.py
# Program that calculates and prints the area
# of a circle and half circle


print("The area of a circle with a radius of 3 is ");
print(3.1416 * 3 * 3);
print("The area of one-half that circle is ");
print((3.1416 * 3 * 3) / 2);
```

NOTE

Don't worry too much about understanding the calculations in this hour's programs. Hour 5, "Data Processing with Numbers and Words," explains how to form calculations in Python.

Here is the output you see if you run the program in Listing 4.1:

```
The area of a circle with a radius of 3 is
28.2744
The area of one-half that circle is
14.1372
```

Note that in Python, each time you call the print() function, it begins its output on a new line. You can also force the output to a second line by using the newline character (\n). For the newline character to work, it must be typed as the backlash character immediately followed by an n. For example, in the previous code, if you wanted the output in the first statement to span two lines but didn't want to write two print() statements, you could alter the code to:

```
print("The area of a circle \nwith a radius of 3 is ");
```

and the output of that line of code would be:

```
The area of a circle
with a radius of 3 is
```

Storing Data

As its definition implies, *data processing* refers to a program processing data. That data must somehow be stored in memory while a program processes it. In Python programs, as in most other languages' programs, you must store data in *variables*. You can think of a variable as if it were a box inside your computer holding a data value. The value might be a number, a character, or a string of characters.

NOTE

Data is stored inside memory locations. Variables keep you from having to remember which memory locations hold your data. Instead of remembering a specific storage location (called an *address*), you only have to remember the name of the variables you create. The variable is like a box that holds data, and the variable name is a label for that box that lets you know what's inside.

Your programs can have as many variables as you need. Variables have names associated with them. You don't have to remember which internal memory location holds data; you can attach names to variables to make them easier to remember. For instance, `Sales` is much easier to remember than the 4,376th memory location.

You can use almost any name you want, provided that you follow these naming rules:

- Variable names must begin with an alphabetic character such as a letter.
- Variable names can be as long as you need them to be.
- Uppercase and lowercase variable names differ; `MyName` and `MYNAME` refer to two different variables.
- After the first alphabetic character, variable names can contain numbers and underscores.

CAUTION

Avoid strange variable names. Try to name variables so that their names help describe the kind of data being stored. `Balanc19` is a much better variable name for an accountant's 2019 balance value than `X1y96a`, although Python doesn't care which one you use.

Here are some examples of valid and invalid variable names:

Valid	Invalid
Sales04	Sales-04
MyRate	My$Rate
ActsRecBal	5ActsRec
row	if

CAUTION

Don't assign a variable the same name as a Python statement, or Python will issue an invalid variable name error message.

Variables can hold numbers or *character strings*. A character string usually consists of one or more characters, such as a word, a name, a sentence, or an address. Python lets you hold numbers or strings in your variables.

Assigning Values

Many Python program statements use variable names. Often, Python programs do little more than store values in variables, change variables, calculate with variables, and output variable values.

When you are ready to store a data value, you must name a variable to put it in. You must use an assignment statement to store values in your program variables. The assignment statement includes an equal sign (=). Here are two sample assignment statements:

```
sales = 956.34

salesperson = "Tina Grant"
```

TIP

If you learn another language, it may require that you use a keyword to first declare a variable, so keep that in mind.

Think of the equal sign in an assignment statement as a left-pointing arrow. Whatever is on the right side of the equal sign is sent to the left side to be stored in the variable there. Figure 4.1 shows how the assignment statement works.

A=23

Variable

FIGURE 4.1
The assignment statement stores values in variables.

If you want to store character string data in a variable, you must enclose the string inside either single or double quotation marks. Here is how you store the phrase Python programmer in a variable named `myJob`:

```
myJob = "Python programmer" # Enclose strings in quotation marks
```

After you put values in variables, they stay there for the entire run of the program or until you put something else in them. A variable can hold only one value at a time. Therefore, the two statements:

```
age = 67;
age = 27;
```

result in `age` holding 27 because that was the last value stored there. The variable `age` cannot hold both values.

You can also assign values of one variable to another and perform math on the numeric variables. Here is code that stores the result of a calculation in a variable and then uses that result in another calculation:

```
pi = 3.1416;
radius = 3;
area = pi * radius * radius;
halfArea = area / 2;
```

▼ TRY IT YOURSELF

When you are looking to print the values stored in variables, print the variable names without quotes around them. Listing 4.2 contains code similar to Listing 4.1, but instead of printing calculated results directly, the program first stores calculations in variables and prints the variables' values.

LISTING 4.2   Calculating the area of a circle with variables

```
# Filename AreaHalf2.py
# program that calculates and prints the area
# of a circle and half circle


pi = 3.14159; # mathematical value of PI
radius = 3; # radius of the circle
```

```
# calculate the area of the whole circle
area = pi * radius * radius;

print("The area of a circle with a radius of 3 is ", area);

print("The area of a half circle is ", area/2);
```

Getting Keyboard Data with `input()`

So far, the programs you've created have used specific pieces of information and data coded right into the programs. Even variables have been defined with specific values, such as the radius of the circle in Listing 4.1. While this is interesting, it's ultimately limiting. To make programs more valuable, you need to get information from your user.

The `input()` function is sort of the opposite of `print()`. The input function receives values from the keyboard. You can then assign the values typed by the user to variables. In the previous section, you learned how to assign values to variables. You used the assignment statement because you knew the actual values. However, you often don't know all the data values when you write a program.

Think of a medical reception program that tracks patients as they enter the doctor's office. The programmer has no idea who will walk in next and so cannot assign patient names to variables. The patient names can be stored in variables only when the program is run.

When a program reaches a prompt call, it creates a dialog box that stays until the user types a value and clicks or taps the OK button. Here is an input:

```
input("What is your favorite color?");
```

When program execution reaches this statement, the computer displays a dialog box or prompt with the message you type in the quotation marks. The dialog box is a signal to the user that something is being asked, and a response is desired. The more clear you make the statement you send to the prompt, the easier it will be for the user to enter the correct information.

TRY IT YOURSELF ▼

The program in Listing 4.3 is a third attempt at the area of a circle program, but this time the user gets to enter the radius of the circle. Now that the user can enter the radii of different-sized circles, this program has far more value.

NOTE

It might start to get a little dull to keep writing variations of the same program, but making just subtle changes to your code to achieve the same or slightly different results is a great way to understand new commands and techniques.

LISTING 4.3   Using `input` to get the value of a circle's radius

```
# Filename AreaHalf3.py
# program that calculates and prints the area
# of a circle and half circle
pi = 3.14159 # mathematical value of PI
radius = float(input("Enter a circle's radius: ")) # get radius
# calculate the area of the whole circle
area = pi * radius * radius
print("The area of a circle with a radius of", radius, "is %.2f" % area);
print("The area of a half circle is %.2f" % (area/2));
```

If the user runs this program, the prompt statement produces the dialog box featured in Figure 4.2.

```
Enter a circle's radius: |
```

FIGURE 4.2
The program will not advance until the user enters a value and then presses Enter.

The statement to get the input needs to be examined a bit:

```
radius = float(input("Enter a circle's radius: "))
```

You are using the `input()` function to get the value the user wants and will be assigning it to the variable `radius`. But when users enter information, the computer makes no assumptions that what they have entered is a string of letters or a number. So, you have to tell Python to treat the information as a number—in this case, by putting `float()` around the input statement. This tells Python to treat whatever is inside the `()` as a floating-point number, a concept known as *casting*. This concept will be covered in more detail in later hours, but remember from Hour 1 that computers are dumb machines that do exactly what you tell them to do, so you have to tell them this specific variable is a number.

Once the user enters a value for the radius, the program proceeds as it did before, with a few differences. First, it shows the area of an entire circle and then the area of a half circle. But the `print()` function looks a little different than it did before:

```
print("The area of a circle with a radius of that radius is %.2f" % area);
print("The area of a half circle is %.1f" % (area/2));
```

Now the output is a little different. Rather than just ending the two strings with `is` and then printing the number, you have ...`%.2f` at the end of the first string and `%.1f` at the end of the second one. These are specific formatting instructions for Python. In the first case, you are telling Python to take the value after the second `%`—the one outside the string (the area)—and put it inside the string. However, the `.2` is telling Python to include only two places after the decimal point. So if you entered 2 as the radius, the area output would be `12.57`. Without the `.2` in the `%.2f` (that is, if your string ended with `%f`) the area output would be `12.566360`. It's a more exact answer, but it's also more awkward. Using this kind of formatting is useful for cleaner-looking output, especially when you are dealing with money. If you were trying to figure out how much sales tax you'd pay if the tax rate were 7% and the amount were $56.76, without this type of formatting help, you'd get an answer of $3.9732. But $3.97 is not only cleaner looking but correct. So sometimes you need to do this type of formatting.

The second line shows the same type of formatting, but with only one value to the right of the decimal place, showing that you can be as exact as you want. Without formatting, Python defaults to using six digits, but you can actually use formatting to print more than (or less than) six.

Inputting Strings

Unlike in many programming languages, a variable in Python can hold either a number or a string. Any type of variable, numeric or string, can be entered by the user through a prompt dialog box. For example, this line waits for the user to enter a string value:

```
fname = input("What is your first name");
```

When the user types a name in response to the question, the name is put into the `fname` variable.

CAUTION

If the user only clicks or taps OK, without entering a value in response to the prompt, Python puts a value called *null* into the variable. A null value is a zero for numeric variables or an empty string for string variables. An empty string—a string variable with nothing in it—is literally zero characters long.

TRY IT YOURSELF ▼

Listing 4.4 is a simple program that once again takes user input and again stores the information in variables. This time, you are prompting the user for strings (two of them).

LISTING 4.4   **Using input to get a user's first and last names**

```
# Filename entername.py
# program that asks the user's first and last
```

```
# name and then displays it in a last, first format

# Ask the user for their first name
fname = input("What is your first name? ")

# Ask the user for their last name
lname = prompt("What is your last name? ")

print("First name first: ", fname, lname);
print("Last name first: ", lname, ",", fname);
```

TIP

Python's ability to combine the string asking the user to enter information and the prompt for the data itself is not a feature all programming languages share. When you use other languages (such as C), you may have to have a separate output statement telling the user what you need and an input statement to receive the information.

This program gets two strings from the user—a first name and a last name—and then combines them in two different formats in print() statements. There are other ways to combine strings, as discussed in the next lesson. The other issue is that there is no checking to ensure that the user entered the correct information. With strings, the program accepts numbers and treats them as strings. So if your user enters Helga as their first name and 11 as their last name, Python will set the full name as Helga 11.

While numbers can be treated as strings, the opposite is not true (for strings being entered as numbers). In Listing 4.3, if the user enters a series of letters for the radius, the program returns an error. When you are writing programs that take input, you often need to ensure that the user has entered the expected value. This is known as *data validation*, and this topic is covered in more detail in Hour 6, "Controlling Your Programs."

▼ TRY IT YOURSELF

Listing 4.5 shows a program that a small store might use to compute totals at the cash register. The input functions in this program are required; only at runtime will the customer purchase values be known. As you can see, getting input at runtime is vital for real-world data processing.

LISTING 4.5   You can use `Input` to simulate a cash register program for a small store

▼

```
# Filename: Storereg.py
# A more practical use of input and output
# Asks users for specific info on sold items

print("Welcome to Fran's Place!\n\n")
print("Let's proceed to checkout!")
# A series of statements to find out how much of each
# item has been purchased

candy = int(input("How many candy bars did they buy? "))
drinks = int(input("How many energy drinks did they buy? "))
gas = int(input("How many gallons of gas did they buy? "))

# This section will take each value and
# multiply it by the current cost per item
candytotal = candy * 1.25
drinktotal = drinks * 2.25
gastotal = gas * 2.879
subtotal = candytotal + drinktotal + gastotal

# Don't forget sales tax! 7.25% in this example
tax = subtotal * .0725;
#Finally print the itemized receipt

print("\n\nItem      Qnt     Total")
print("----------------------------")
print("Candy ", candy, "    $%.2f" % candytotal)
print("Drinks ", drinks, "    $%.2f" % drinktotal)
print("Gas    ", gas, "     $%.2f" % gastotal)
print("----------------------------")
print("Subtotal      $ %.2f" % subtotal)
print("Tax           $ %.2f" % tax)
print("Total         $ %.2f" % (subtotal+tax))
print("\n\nHAVE A GREAT DAY!")
```

Figure 4.3 shows the output of this program. As you can see, this type of program could be helpful for a small store. Obviously, it is unlikely that a store would only have three items, but once you learn some additional features of Python (such as dictionaries), you can quickly and easily build a more robust set of data for any need you have, personally or professionally.

You might be wondering about the \t character that appears in several of the last 10 lines that print out the receipt. This is another example of a formatting character you can use in Python. When Python encounters a \t in a string, it tabs over (as in a word processor) before continuing to print. This can be extremely useful if you are looking to line up columns when printing out output, as this program does for the quantities and totals of items purchased. The print() statements also perform formatting you have seen before, including using \n to jump down a line and %.2f to limit the digits to the right of the decimal points to two, which is all you should see in a financial transaction. When asking for purchase amounts, this program has lines for each item in inventory. While this works, it can be inefficient. Later on, in Hour 6, you will learn some tricks to loop through identical or similar code lines with fewer total lines. This might not seem like a big deal when you're only dealing with 3 products, but what if you had 20 or more? In such situations, you can really improve your coding efficiency by taking advantage of loops.

```
Welcome to Fran's Place!


Let's proceed to checkout!
How many candy bars did they buy?4
How many energy drinks did they buy?6
How many gallons of gas did they buy?12


Item    Qnt    Total
------------------------------
Candy   4      $5.00
Drinks  6      $13.50
Gas     12     $34.55
------------------------------
Subtotal       $ 53.05
Tax            $ 3.85
Total          $ 56.89


HAVE A GREAT DAY!
```

FIGURE 4.3
Running the cash register program produces this output.

NOTE

Again, there is a lot you can do with input and output in Python, but this lesson just covers programming basics. If you want to learn more, please pick up a tutorial devoted to the language; your programs will thank you if you do!

Summary

Proper input and output can mean the difference between a program that your users like to use and one they hate to use. If you properly label all input that you want so that you prompt your users through the input process, the users will have no questions about the proper format for your program.

The next hour describes in detail how to use Python to program calculations using variables and the mathematical operators, as well as some handy string-manipulation tricks.

Q&A

Q. How can I ensure users enter information in the proper format for my program?

A. As mentioned earlier in the hour, techniques known as data validation can check to make sure the information entered is expected. If it isn't you can either generate an error message or give the user another chance to enter the information. Data validation is covered more in later hours, but it will become an important consideration of any program that features user interaction.

Q. Why don't I have to tell Python what type of variable I want to use?

A. Python is just that smart! Actually, for most programming languages, you need to specify the type of variable, and if you try to put a different type of data in that variable, you can get an error or unpredictable results. Python changes the variable type on-the-fly, so you can use the same variable as a string in the beginning of the program and then a number later. This is not the best idea, however. You should keep your variables focused on a specific type and a specific job.

Workshop

The quiz questions are provided for your further understanding.

Quiz

1. What is a function?

2. How would you write a `print()` statement that prints the sum of 10 and 20?

3. Declare a variable named `movie` and assign to it the last movie you saw in theaters.

4. What character is used in `print()` statements to force a new line?

5. What is a variable?

6. What function is used to get information from a program's user?

7. What is a prompt?

8. Write a simple program that asks the user for his or her birthday in three separate prompts—one for month, one for day, and one for year—and then combine the three into a *Month date*, *year* format that you print on the screen.

9. In Python, what does the /t character do?

Answers

1. A function is a collection of statements that perform a specific task.

2. `print(10 + 20)`

3. (Obviously, this should vary based on your most recent cinema-viewing experience.) For me:

   `movie = "Once Upon a Time in Hollywood"`

4. The newline character is \n.

5. A variable is a named storage location.

6. The `input()` function

7. A prompt describes the information that a user is to type.

8. Here is one possible solution:

```
# Answer to Chapter 4, Question 8


bYear = input("What year were you born? ")
bMonth = input("What month were you born? ")
bDay = input("What day were you born? ")

print("You were born on", bMonth, bDay, ",", bYear, "!")
```

9. It tabs over the input.

Data Processing with Numbers and Words

Without an in-depth knowledge of characters, strings, and numbers, you won't be able to understand any programming language. This doesn't mean that you must be a math whiz or an English major. You must, however, understand how languages such as Python represent and work with such data.

In this hour, you will learn more about how Python performs its mathematical calculations. In addition, you will learn how Python represents and works with strings. Along the way, you will discover functions and powerful built-in routines that perform many programming chores for you.

The highlights of this hour include the following:

▶ Merging strings together

▶ Understanding internal representation of strings

▶ Mastering the programming operators

▶ Digging into Python's functions

Strings Revisited

Like most other programming languages, Python has excelled in supporting strings. Hardly any programming language before BASIC was created (in the 1960s) supported string data except in a rudimentary form. BASIC was created for beginners, but it offered advanced support for strings.

Even since the first BASIC language, programming languages have been slow to adopt string support beyond a rudimentary level. C++, one of the most used programming languages in the past 50 years, did not directly support strings. To work with strings in C++ (and its earlier rendition, C), programmers had to do some fancy footwork to get around the fact that the fundamental string data type was not supported.

Merging Strings

You can merge, or *concatenate* (programmers rarely use a simple word when a longer word will confuse more people), two strings together simply by placing a plus sign between them.

▼ TRY IT YOURSELF

To see the concept in more detail, consider the short program in Listing 5.1. This program asks the user for his or her hometown and home state names, using two prompt methods, then prints the full location by concatenating them together with a comma and a space between them to separate the names.

LISTING 5.1   Merging two strings together is simple

```
# Filename mergetown.py
# program that asks the user's hometown and state
# and then displays it in a town, state format


# Ask the user for their hometown
town = input("What town are you from? ")

# Ask the user for their state
state = input("In what state were you born? ")

# Make a comma-separated variable for
# city, state format

fullLocation = town + ', ' + state

print("So you are from ", fullLocation)
```

Figure 5.1 shows the final output of the program, after the user has entered a town and stxate.

```
What town are you from? Winterville
In what state were you born? North Carolina
So you are from  Winterville, North Carolina
```

FIGURE 5.1
String concatenation enables you to build one larger string by combining any number of smaller strings.

When using concatenation, you can either combine variables or string literals, as demonstrated in Listing 5.1. Two variables are joined with a literal comma plus a space in the middle. This example also demonstrates that users don't have to limit input in a prompt to a single word. After all, state names (such as North Carolina), and city names (such as Salt Lake City) can be made up of one or more words.

The ASCII Table

To fully understand strings, you must understand how your computer represents characters internally. A concept that will come into major play while you program in any language is the *ASCII* (pronounced *ask-ee*) *table*. Although the reason for the ASCII table and how to take advantage of your knowledge of the ASCII table will increase as you hone your programming skills, you should take a few moments for an introduction to this important character-based table.

Years ago, somebody wrote all the various combinations of 8 binary 1s and 0s, from 00000000 to 11111111, and assigned a unique character to each one. The table of characters was standardized and is known today as the ASCII table. Table 5.1 shows a partial listing of the ASCII table, which contains 256 entries in total. ASCII stands for *American Standard Code for Information Interchange*. Some ASCII tables use only the last 7 *bits* (called the *7-bit ASCII table*) and keep the far-left bit off. As you might surmise, a bit is a 1 or a 0. Eight bits form a *byte,* which is a *character* in computer terminology—due to the ASCII table. 7-bit ASCII tables cannot represent as many different characters as can today's 8-bit ASCII tables.

TABLE 5.1 Every possible character has its own unique ASCII value

Character	ASCII Code	Decimal Equivalent
Space	00100000	32
0	00110000	48
1	00110001	49
2	00110010	50
3	00110011	51
9	00111001	57
?	00111111	63
A	01000001	65
B	01000010	66
C	01000011	67
A	01100001	97
B	01100010	98

Each ASCII value has a corresponding decimal number associated with it. These values are shown at the right of the 8-bit values in Table 5.1. Therefore, even though the computer represents the character ? as 00111111 (two *off* switches and six *on* switches), you can refer, through programming, to that ASCII value as 63, and your computer will know you mean 00111111. One of the advantages of high-level programming languages is that many of them let you use the easier (for people) decimal values, and the programming language converts the value to the 8-bit binary value used inside the computer.

As you can tell from the ASCII values in Table 5.1, every character in the computer, both upper-case and lowercase letters, and even the space, has its own unique ASCII value. The unique ASCII code is the only way that the computer has to differentiate characters.

Every microcomputer uses the ASCII table. Large mainframe computers use a similar table called the *EBCDIC* (pronounced *eb-se-dik*) *table*. EBCDIC stands for *Extended Binary Coded Decimal Interchange Code*. The ASCII table is the fundamental storage representation of all data and pro-grams that your computer manages. A coding scheme called *Unicode* is now a popular alternative to ASCII. Unicode spans far more than the 256-character limit of the ASCII or EBCIDIC tables, taking into account languages such as the Japanese-based *kanji*, and other languages that require numerous characters. Unicode assigns hundreds of numbers to hundreds and even thousands of possible characters, depending on the language being represented.

When you press the letter *A* on a keyboard, that *A* is not stored in your computer; rather, the ASCII value of the letter *A* is stored. As you can see from the ASCII values in Table 5.1, the letter *A* is represented as 01000001; this means that all eight switches except two are *off* in every byte of memory that holds a letter *A*.

TIP

The ASCII table is not very different from another type of coded table you may have heard of. Morse code is a table of representations for letters of the alphabet. Instead of 1s and 0s, the code uses combinations of dashes and dots to represent characters.

As Figure 5.2 shows, when you press the letter *A* on your keyboard, the *A* does not go into memo-ry, but the ASCII value 01000001 does. The computer keeps that pattern of *on* and *off* switches in that memory location as long as the *A* is to remain there. As far as the user is concerned, the *A* is in memory as the letter *A*, but now you know exactly what happens.

FIGURE 5.2
The letter A is not an A after it leaves the keyboard.

As Figure 5.2 illustrates, when you print a document from your word processor, the computer prints each "character" stored in that memory location; the computer's CPU sends the ASCII code for the letter *A* to the printer. Just before printing, the printer knows that it must make its output readable to people, so it looks up 01000001 in its own ASCII table and prints the *A* to paper. From the time the *A* left the keyboard until right before it printed, it was not an *A* at all but just a combination of eight 1s and 0s representing an *A*.

Performing Math with Python

Python performs mathematical calculations in the same way as most other programming languages. Therefore, when you understand the way Python calculates, you'll understand how virtually every other computer language calculates. Table 5.2 lists the Python math operators with which you should familiarize yourself.

TABLE 5.2   Python math operators are simple

Operator	Description
()	Groups expressions together
**	Exponent
*, /, %	Multiplication, division, and modulus
+, -	Addition and subtraction

The order of the operators in Table 5.2 is important. If more than one of these operators appears in an expression, Python doesn't always calculate the values in a left-to-right order. In other words, the expression:

```
v = 5 + 2 * 3
```

stores the value 11 in v, not 21, as you might first guess. Python doesn't perform calculations in a left-to-right order but rather in the order given in Table 5.2. Because multiplication appears before addition in the table, Python computes the 2 * 3 first, resulting in 6; it then computes the answer to 5 + 6 to get the result 11.

TIP

The order in which operators are evaluated is often called *operator precedence*. Just about every programming language computes expressions based on a precedence table. Different programming languages might use different operators from the ones shown in Table 5.2, although almost all of them use parentheses and the primary math operators (*, /, +, and −) in the same way as Python does.

Parentheses have the highest operator precedence. Any expression enclosed in parentheses is calculated before any other part of the expression. The statement:

```
v = (5 + 2) * 3
```

does assign the value 21 to v because the parentheses force the addition of 5 and 2 before its sum, 7, is multiplied by 3.

Python also has an exponentiation operator to raise a number to a particular power, although some programming languages, such as JavaScript, do not have an exponent operator and instead use a built-in function. Instead you can use ** in Python. If you use a ** b in a Python expression, a is the number multiplied by itself b times. For example, if you wanted to know 4 × 4 × 4, sometimes written as 4^3, you would use 4 ** 3 in Python, which would return the answer 64.

You can also raise a number to a fractional power with this operator. For example, the statement:

```
x = 81 ** 0.5
```

raises 81 to the one-half power, in effect taking the square root of 81. If this math is getting deep, have no fear; some people program in Python for years and never need to raise a number to a fractional power. But if you need to, you can thank Python for doing the heavy lifting for you.

The forward slash (/) divides one number into another. For example, the statement:

```
d = 3 / 2 ;
```

assigns 1.5 to d.

▼ TRY IT YOURSELF

To sum up (pardon the pun) math operators, Listing 5.2 contains a program that prints the result of calculations that use many of the Python operators described in this lesson. The output of the program is shown in Figure 5.3.

LISTING 5.2 Sampling Python math operators

```
# Filename mathcheck.py
# Program that asks for two numbers
# and then performs various math operations on them

# Two input statements to get the numbers and covert the entries
# into floating-point numbers
a = float(input("Enter the first num: "))
b = float(input("Enter the second num: "))
```

```
#Create a third variable, c, that will store the calculations
c = a + b
print(a, '+', b, '=', c)
c = a - b
print(a, '-', b, '=', c)
c = a * b
print(a, '*', b, '=', c)
c = a / b
print(a, '/', b, '=', c)
c = a % b
print(a, '%', b, '=', c)
c = a ** b
print(a, '^', b, '=', c)
```

```
Enter the first num: 4
Enter the second num: 3
4.0 + 3.0 = 7.0
4.0 - 3.0 = 1.0
4.0 * 3.0 = 12.0
4.0 / 3.0 = 1.3333333333333333
4.0 % 3.0 = 1.0
4.0 ^ 3.0 = 64.0
```

FIGURE 5.3
Viewing the output of the calculations.

Without using the `%.2f` formatting in your code, you can see that some calculations result in a long string of digits after the decimal place. While Python converts entered numbers from strings into floating-point (aka decimal) numbers, it can't convert an incorrectly entered value. So, if your user enters a letter like `r` for one of the two numbers, the program will not proceed and will instead generate an error message, telling you that it cannot convert the string to a number. Again, as you become a more seasoned programmer, you need to never assume that the user will enter the correct type of data, and you need to enter some code to check input and perform data validation to prevent your program from breaking.

How Computers Really Do Math

At their lowest level, computers cannot subtract, multiply, or divide. Neither can calculators. The world's largest and fastest supercomputers can only add—that's it. They perform the addition at the bit level. Binary arithmetic is the only means by which any electronic digital-computing machine can perform arithmetic.

The computer makes you think it can perform all sorts of fancy calculations because it is lightning fast. The computer can only add, but it can do so very quickly.

Suppose you want a computer to add together seven 6s. If you ask the computer (through programming) to perform the calculation:

```
6 + 6 + 6 + 6 + 6 + 6 + 6
```

the computer returns the answer 42 immediately. The computer has no problem performing addition. The problems arise when you request that the computer perform another type of calculation, such as this one:

```
42 - 6 - 6 - 6 - 6 - 6 - 6 - 6
```

Because the computer can only add, it cannot do the subtraction. However (and this is where the catch comes in), the computer can *negate* numbers. That is, the computer can take the negative of a number. It can take the negative of 6 and represent (at the bit level) negative 6. After it has done that, it can *add* –6 to 42 and continue doing so seven times. In effect, the internal calculation becomes this:

```
42 + (-6) + (-6) + (-6) + (-6) + (-6) + (-6) + (-6)
```

Adding seven –6s produces the correct result, 0. In reality, the computer is not subtracting. At its bit level, the computer can convert a number to its negative through a process known as *two's complement*. The two's complement of a number is the negative of the number's original value at the bit level. The computer has in its internal logic circuits the ability to rapidly convert a number to its two's complement and then carry out the addition of negatives, thereby seemingly performing subtraction.

NOTE

Here's another kind of two's complement: *That's a very fine two you have there.*

Because the computer can add and simulate subtraction (through successive addition of negatives), it can simulate multiplying and dividing. To multiply 6 by 7, the computer actually adds 6 together seven times and produces 42. Therefore:

```
6 * 7
```

becomes this:

```
6 + 6 + 6 + 6 + 6 + 6 + 6
```

To divide 42 by 7, the computer subtracts 7 from 42 (well, it adds the *negative* of 7 to 42) until it reaches 0 and counts the number of times (6) it took to reach 0, like this:

```
42 + (-7) + (-7) + (-7) + (-7) + (-7) + (-7)
```

The computer represents numbers in a manner similar to characters. As Table 5.3 shows, numbers are easy to represent at the binary level. After numbers reach a certain limit (256 to be exact), the computer uses more than 1 byte to represent the number, taking as many memory locations as it needs to represent the extent of the number. The computer, after it is taught to add, subtract, multiply, and divide, can then perform any math necessary as long as a program is supplied to direct it.

TABLE 5.3   The first 20 numbers can be represented in their binary equivalents

Number	Binary Equivalent
0	00000000
1	00000001
2	00000010
3	00000011
4	00000100
5	00000101
6	00000110
7	00000111
8	00001000
9	00001001
10	00001010
11	00001011
12	00001100
13	00001101
14	00001110
15	00001111
16	00010000
17	00010001
18	00010010
19	00010011
20	00010100

NOTE

The first 255 binary numbers overlap the ASCII table values. That is, the binary representation for the letter A is 01000001, and the binary number for 65 is also 01000001. The computer knows by the context of how your programs use the memory location whether the value is the letter A or the number 65.

To see an example of what goes on at the bit level, follow this example to see what happens when you ask the computer to subtract 65 from 65. The result should be 0, and as you can see from the following steps, that is exactly the result at the binary level:

1. Suppose you want the computer to calculate the following:

   ```
    65
   -65
   ```

2. The binary representation for 65 is 01000001, and the two's complement for 65 is 10111111 (which is –65 in *computerese*). Therefore, you are requesting that the computer perform this calculation:

   ```
    01000001
   +10111111
   ```

3. Because a binary number cannot have the digit 2 (there are only 0s and 1s in binary), the computer carries 1 any time a calculation results in a value of 2; 1 + 1 equals 10 in binary. Although this can be confusing, you can make an analogy with decimal arithmetic. People work in a base-10 numbering system. Binary is known as base-2. There is no single digit to represent 10; we have to reuse two digits already used to form 10, namely 1 and 0. In base 10, 9 + 1 is 10. Therefore, the result of 1 + 1 in binary is 10, or "0 and carry 1 to the next column." The next column has a 0 and 1, which would add up to one, but you need to include the 1 carried over to the next column, so you are actually adding 1+0+1, which again is 10. So, you would place a zero in that column, and carry the 1 over to the next column. Continue this until you have added all 8 columns. (as you can see in the answer below).

   ```
     01000001
   +10111111
   100000000
   ```

4. Because the answer should fit within the same number of bits as the two original numbers (at least for this example—your computer may use more bits to represent numbers), the ninth bit is discarded, leaving the 0 result. This example shows that binary 65 plus binary negative 65 equals 0, as it should.

TIP

While many programming languages use the ASCII table (which you can see at http://www. AsciiTable.com/), Python uses the Unicode table (which you can see at https://en.wikipedia.org/wiki/List_of_Unicode_characters). The difference between the two is covered in the next section.

Using Unicode Characters

The ASCII and Unicode tables have a number of characters in common—specifically the first 128 characters, which correspond to available English letters, both lowercase and uppercase, as well as the 10 single digits and common characters and punctuation marks. For instance, the capital letter *A* is number 65. The lowercase *a* is 97. Since you can type letters, numbers, and some special characters on your keyboard, the ASCII table is not needed much for these. However, you cannot use the keyboard to type the Spanish Ñ or the cent sign (¢), under normal circumstances. For this reason, programmers soon expanded the ASCII table to an additional 128 characters—the extended ASCII table. As mentioned earlier this hour, many programming languages allow you to print these characters with built-in methods and functions. Python also has a built-in function—the `chr()` function—to print these characters, but it uses Unicode instead of ASCII. What's the difference between the two? With Unicode, you are not limited to 256 characters, which means you can print significantly more characters, which is great as you can support more languages, as well as additional math and scientific symbols. (Again, see the website above for the possibilities). You will probably never use the bulk of these characters, but it's nice to have the option available.

Why talk about the ASCII table when Python uses Unicode? Because while the first 128 characters are similar (for example, lowercase *a* is character 97 in both), there are differences in the extended characters (for example, a lowercase *n* with a tilde over it is 164 in the extended ASCII table, but 164 is a currency symbol in Unicode, and the lowercase *n* with a tilde over it is 241 in Unicode).

Back to the `chr()` function. To use the function, you use this format:

```
chr(A number)
```

You would then either assign the result to a variable or print it directly. The following `print()` statement prints a capital *N* with a tilde over it, followed by a lowercase *n*, also with a tilde, and then the upside-down question mark that begins questions in Spanish:

```
print(chr(209),chr(241),chr(191))
```

These characters would come in handy if you decided to translate your website to Spanish. Here is the output:

```
Ñ ñ ¿
```

The first 31 ASCII and Unicode codes represent *nonprinting* characters. Nonprinting characters cause an action to be performed instead of producing characters.

Overview of Functions

Functions are built-in routines that manipulate numbers, strings, and output. You have already used several Python functions, including `print()`, `input()`, and `chr()`, but you will soon see that Python has a number of other valuable functions. You can accomplish some pretty cool goals with string functions, but before you do, you need to understand a bit about arrays, as they will help you better to use Python's available functions.

TIP

Other programming languages have built-in methods instead of functions. There are some technical differences between the two, but don't worry about that at this point.

Understanding Arrays

Just as words and sentences are collections of single letters, strings are collections of characters, including words, spaces, letters, and any other special characters you choose to type or add using the ASCII functions discussed earlier in this lesson. When you assign a string to a variable, such as:

```
hometown = "Salt Lake City, Utah"
```

Python considers this an array of characters and lets you access either the whole name or individual elements of that name. If you write a `print()` statement and send `hometown` to it:

```
print(hometown)
```

as you can probably guess, your output will be:

```
Salt Lake City, Utah
```

What is probably not obvious is what would happen if you wrote a `print()` statement and sent `hometown[3]` to it, as in this example:

```
print(hometown[3])
```

If you did this, you would get a single letter in the dialog box:

```
t
```

Now you may have figured out that the number in brackets would refer to a specific letter or character in the string. (Good job if you did!) But even then, you might think, why not the letter *l*? After all, it is the third character in the name of the city. While that is true, Python and most other programming languages start their counting with 0 instead of 1. So the *S* is `hometown[0]`, the *a* is `hometown[1]`, and the *t* is `hometown[3]`. You might be wondering what character corresponds to `hometown[4]`. It is the space, and the *L* is `hometown[5]`. When figuring arrays,

Python counts every character, including spaces. In this `hometown` variable, spaces are the 4, 9, and 15 spots in the array, and the comma is the 14.

This might seem confusing, but understanding arrays is important for almost every programming language. (It is more important with some than with others; C, for example, does not have a string data type, so to work with strings in C, you need to create an array of characters.) For now, just know that every single character in a string corresponds to a specific number and that if you're counting characters to figure it out, you need to start with 0 and include all spaces, characters, letters, and numbers.

The next sections cover some of Python's string and math functions.

String Functions

Once you've defined a string, you can access some built-in Python functions to alter your strings. This section does not cover all the string functions, just some of the more interesting ones. Feel free to explore online or use a Python tutorial to cover some of the others.

Making Strings All Capital or All Lowercase Letters

Two functions can be used to change the case of all the letters in a string. Any non-letter characters are just ignored. The two methods, `lower()` and `upper()`, create a new string and leave the original string untouched. Taking the previous example, if the variable `hometown` is equal to `"Salt Lake City, Utah"`, the following two calls:

```
newtown1 = hometown.lower();
newtown2 = hometown.upper();
```

will result in `newtown1` holding the string `"salt lake city, utah"` and `newtown2` holding the string `"SALT LAKE CITY, UTAH"`. The original string remains the same.

If you want to change the case of the original string permanently, just set the new string equal to the old name. For example, the statement:

```
hometown = hometown.upper()
```

permanently changes `"Salt Lake City, Utah"` to `"SALT LAKE CITY, UTAH"`.

The string methods discussed in this section must always be called with a period (`.`) between the name of the string and the specific method.

Replacing Part of a String

Another valuable string function is one that lets you replace part of a string. Say the good folks of Utah decide to be more health-conscious and rename their capital Blue Lake City. You can use the `replace()` method to create a new string that switches words in a string. You can either make a new string, as demonstrated in the previous section, or overwrite your existing string. If `hometown` is still equal to `"Salt Lake City, Utah"`, the code line:

```
hometown = hometown.replace("Salt", "Blue");
```

results in `hometown` now being equal to `"Blue Lake City, Utah"`. You don't have to replace entire words, either. For example:

```
hometown = hometown.replace("lt", "lty");
```

results in `hometown` now being equal to `"Salty Lake City, Utah"`. One additional note about `replace`. It changes every instance it finds of the substring you were trying to replace. So if your hometown is `"New York, New York"`, calling:

```
hometown = hometown.replace("New", "Old");
```

results in `hometown` being equal to `"Old York, Old York"`. If you want to change `New` only in the city, and not in the state, you wouldn't want to call `replace`. These methods are powerful and useful, but you should experiment with them to ensure that you get the intended results.

Other valuable string functions include `len`, which returns the number of characters in a string (so with `len(hometown)`, if hometown is `New York, New York`, the function returns `18`); `index`, which finds where a specific value occurs in a string for the first time; `split`, which breaks a string into several smaller strings (which is useful for breaking a sentence at spaces, so you get each individual word); and `swapcase`, which makes the capital letters lowercase and vice versa (for example, if you provided `"Salt Lake City, Utah"`, the method would return `"sALT lAKE cITY, uTAH"` as the new string). Some of these may seem to have little value, but as you develop scripts and programs, you'll find them more useful than you'd initially guess.

Numeric Functions

Several of the functions supplied by Python perform math routines, and this section introduces you to some of them. However, to run these functions, you need to first add a line of code to the programs that plan to use them:

```
import math
```

When Python sees the `import` statement, it looks for a module with the name included after the `import`. Then the collection of functions and methods in that module are available for you to use in your program. You might be wondering why you need to perform this step. Why aren't the modules already included? It's a way to make your programs run faster; if you are not going to use those math functions, then they shouldn't be loaded into memory. Programmers are always looking to make their code run as fast as possible, and shaving time by not including too many built-in functions (or *overhead*) helps. You might not think it matters in the small programs you are writing, but when a robust program uses millions of lines of code (which some programs do), every shortcut can help.

Once you have imported the `math` module, you can run the functions included by typing `math.NameOfTheFunction`. One common numeric function is the `math.floor()` method. `math.floor()` returns the integer whole value of the numbers you put in the parentheses. If you put a decimal number inside the parentheses, `math.floor()` converts it to an integer. For example,

```
print(math.floor(8.93)
```

prints an 8 (the method's return value) on the screen. `math.floor()` returns a value that is equal to or less than the argument in the parentheses. It does not round numbers up. If you would like to round off to the nearest integer, use the `round()` method. (This is going to seem a little confusing, but `round()` is called just as round; you do not call `math.round()`.) If you were to create the following statement:

```
print(round(8.51));
```

you would get 9 as an answer.

TIP

With all math functions, you can use a variable or an expression as the function argument.

`math.floor()` and `round()` work for negative arguments as well. The following line of code:

```
print(math.floor(-7.6));
```

prints −8. This might surprise you until you learn that the complete definition of `math.floor()`. It returns the highest integer that is less than or equal to the argument in parentheses. The highest integer less than or equal to −7.6 is −8.

You don't have to be an expert in math to use many of the mathematical functions available with Python. Often, even in business applications, the following method, which is not in the `math` module, comes in handy:

```
abs(numeric value)
```

The `abs()` method, which is the *absolute value* method, can be used in many programs. `abs()` returns the absolute value of its argument. The absolute value of a number is simply the positive representation of a positive or negative number. Whatever argument you pass to `abs()`, its positive value is returned. For example, the line of code:

```
print(abs(-5), abs(-5.75), abs(0), abs(5.7))
```

produces the following output:

```
5 5.75 0 5.7
```

The `math` module includes a lot of advanced math methods, including the following:

```
math.atan(numeric value);
math.cos(numeric value);
math.sin(numeric value);
math.tan(numeric value);
math.exp(numeric value);
math.log(numeric value);
```

These are probably some of the least-used functions in Python. Scientific and mathematical programmers are the ones most likely to need them. Thank goodness Python supplies these functions, so programmers don't have to write their own versions.

The `math.atan()` function returns the arctangent of the argument in radians. The argument is assumed to be an expression representing an angle of a right triangle. If you're familiar with trigonometry (and who isn't, right?), you might know that the result of an arctangent calculation always falls between $-\pi/2$ and $+\pi/2$, and the `math.atan()` function requires that its argument also fall within this range. `math.cos()` always returns the cosine of the angle of the argument, expressed in radians. `math.sin()` returns the sine of the angle of the argument, expressed in radians. `math.tan()` returns the tangent of the angle of the argument, expressed in radians.

TIP

If you need to pass an angle expressed in degrees to these functions, convert the angle to radians by multiplying it by $(\pi /180)$. (π is approximately 3.141592654.)

If you understand these trigonometric functions, you should have no trouble with `math.exp()` and `math.log()`. You use them the same way. If you do not understand these mathematical functions, that's okay. Some people program in Python for years and never need them.

`math.exp()` returns the base of the natural logarithm (*e*) raised to a specified power. The argument to `math.exp()` can be any constant, variable, or expression less than or equal to 88.02969. *e* is the mathematical expression for the value 2.718282. The following program shows some `math.exp()` statements:

```
print(math.exp(1))
print(math.exp(2))
print(math.exp(3))
print(math.exp(4))
print(math.exp(5))
```

Here is the output produced by these five `print()` statements:

```
2.718281828459045
7.38905609893065
20.085536923187668
54.598150033144236
148.4131591025766
```

Notice the first number; *e* raised to the first power does indeed equal itself.

`math.log()` returns the natural logarithm of the argument. The argument to `math.log()` can be any positive constant, variable, or expression. The following program line demonstrates the `math.log()` function in use:

```
print(math.log(3))
```

Here is the output:

```
1.0986122886681098
```

Summary

You now understand how Python calculations work. By utilizing the math operators and by understanding the math hierarchy, you will know how to compose your own calculations.

By understanding the ASCII and Unicode tables, you not only better understand how computers represent characters internally but also understand how to access those Unicode values by using the `chr()` method. Many of Python's methods are universal; similar functions exist in many languages that you'll learn throughout your programming career.

Q&A

Q. In Python, do I have to know all the values that I will assign to variables when I write a program?

A. Data comes from many sources. You will know some of the values that you can assign when you write your programs, but much of your program data will come from users or from data files.

Q. What kinds of data can variables hold?

A. Variables can hold many kinds of data, such as numbers, characters, and character strings. As you learn more about programming, you will see that numeric data comes in all formats and that to master a programming language well, you must also master the kinds of numeric data that are available. As you advance in your Python studies, you will see that Python can also create collections of data known as lists, tuples, and dictionaries.

Workshop

The quiz questions are provided for your further understanding.

Quiz

1. What is the result of the following expression?

```
(1 + 2) * 4 / 2
```

2. What is the result of the following expression?

```
(1 + (10 - (2 + 2)))
```

3. What is a function?

4. What is the output from the following `print()` statement?

```
print(math.floor(-5.6))
```

5. What is the output from the following `print()` statement?

```
print(abs (-2.1) + math.floor(45.1))
```

6. Write a `print` statement call that replaces the "Beginning Programming" in "Teach Yourself Beginning Programming" with "Basic Python."

7. Name three of the trigonometric functions mentioned in this hour.

8. What is the difference between `math.round()` and `math.floor()`?

9. What does the following statement print?

```
print(chr(65),chr(67),chr(69))
```

Answers

1. 6

2. 7

3. A function is a section of code designed to perform a specific task.

4. −6

5. 47.1

6. BookName = 'Teach Yourself Beginning Programming'
print(BookName.replace('Beginning Programming','Basic Python'))

7. Three trigonometric functions are `sin()`, `cos()`, and `tan()`.

8. `math.floor()` returns the integer value of a number passed to it. `math.round()` returns the integer value of the number if the decimal portion is less than .5 or the next highest integer if the decimal portion is .5 or higher.

9. ACE

HOUR 6
Controlling Your Programs

This hour's lesson extends your knowledge of Python by showing you how to compare values and repeat sections of Python programs. A user's responses or calculated data can control the flow of your program. This lesson teaches you how to write programs that make decisions. The code sometimes needs to repeat sections in order to complete the processing of several data values. You'll learn how to create a loop to do just that.

With the concepts that you learn in this lesson, you can write powerful programs to do what you need done. You will find yourself thinking of new ideas and new ways to use your computer.

The highlights of this hour include the following:

▶ Making decisions with Python

▶ Using the `if` statement

▶ Changing decisions with the `elif` and `else` statements

▶ Repeating sections of code

▶ Using the `for` loop

▶ Using `while` loops

Comparing Data with `if`

Python provides the ability for a program to make a choice and to perform one action or another action, depending on a condition. A Python decision statement has two possibilities. To decide which path to take in a Python program, you must use the `if` statement. Most programming languages have an `if` statement that works exactly like Python's. Therefore, once you learn how Python supports the `if` statement, you will be able to apply the same principles for most other computer languages as well.

▼ TRY IT YOURSELF

Listing 6.1 shows an example of a program that contains an `if` statement. Even though you have never seen a Python `if` statement before, you will probably have little trouble figuring out what this program does.

LISTING 6.1 Use an `if` statement when you want your program to make a decision

```
# Filename ifbranch.py

# Program that decides how much of a bonus
# to pay a salesperson

# Get the name and sales of the salesperson
salesname = input("What is the salesperson's name?")
salestotal = int(input("What were their sales?"))
if (salestotal < 5000):
    bonus = 0
    daysOff = 0
else:
    bonus = 100
    daysOff = 2
print(salesname," earned a bonus of", bonus)
print('as well as', daysOff, 'Days off!')
```

Look at the following two sample runs of the program. Pay attention to the fact that the program calculates a different bonus depending on the salesperson's total sales. The first sample run follows:

```
What is the salesperson's name? John Ray
What were their sales? 4560
John Ray earned a bonus of 0
as well as 0 Days off!
```

The salesperson did not get a bonus because the sales were not high enough. Consider the difference in the following:

```
What is the salesperson's name? Alice Jayne
What were their sales? 5600
Alice Jayne earned a bonus of 100
as well as 2 Days off!
```

The program offers complete control over one of two options via the `if` statement. Figure 6.1 provides a flowchart that shows how this program works. As explained in Hour 3, "Designing a Program," although programmers rarely use flowcharts to design programs anymore, flowcharts are helpful in illustrating how statements logically work. The diamond in the flowchart is a *decision symbol* and shows the operation of Python's `if` statement.

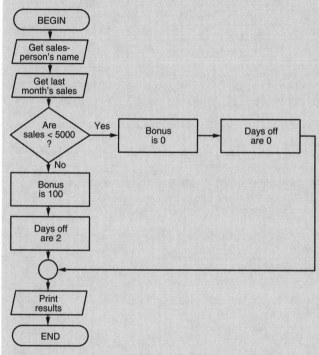

FIGURE 6.1
The flowchart's decision symbol illustrates the nature of the salesperson program's `if` statement.

The `if` statement works just like it reads: If the statement to the right of the `if` is true, the block of statements following `if` executes. If the statement to the right of `if` is not true, the block of statements following the `if` is ignored. If an `else` statement block follows the `if` and the statement to the right is not true, the `else` block executes instead. The `else` is optional; without it, you are testing to see whether you will execute a single block of statements. For example, the following is an `if` statement that prints a message only if the statement to the right of `if` is true. If it is not, and there is no `else`, the program continues on. Although you do not need to put punctuation at the end of most Python statements, you do need to place a colon (`:`) at the end of an `if` or `else` statement. In addition, you need to indent each of the statements you want Python to execute if the `if` or `else` is true. In fact, Python will continue to execute all indented statements until it reaches a statement that isn't indented. If you don't include the colon after the if or else statement or indent the statements you want to run if the if statement is true, your program will not run the way you want. So in the following example, the print statement will only execute if age is less than 18. However, if you did not indent the statement, it would print even if the age was greater than or equal to 18.

```
if (age < 18):
    print("You are not old enough")
```

NOTE

The parentheses around the statement to the right of the if are not required, but they clarify what exactly is being tested. This statement to the right of if, typically enclosed within parentheses, is called a *relational test*.

You can also test more than two cases with the elif statement, which is short for *else if*. In the previous sales program, imagine if there were three levels of bonus program—$100 and 2 days off for sales over $5,000, $250 and 3 days off for sales over $7,500, and $400 and 4 days off for sales over $10,000. You can use Python's if, elif, and else statements to make that happen, as in this example:

```
if (sales > 10000):
        bonus = 400
        daysOff = 4
elif (sales > 7500):
        bonus = 250
        daysOff = 3
elif (sales > 5000):
        bonus = 100
        daysOff = 2
else:
        bonus = 0
        daysOff = 0
```

When testing multiple possibilities, think about the order in which you want to list things. What would happen if you made the (sales > 5000) test the first test? Someone who had $11,000 in sales would pass that test and get the smaller bonus and days off, when you wanted to give that salesperson the maximum bonus and days off. This is an example of how flowcharts and testing your programs can ensure that you get the result you want. The next section includes a program that tests multiple cases.

Writing the Relational Test

The `if` statement reads just as it does in plain English: *If something is true, do one thing; otherwise, do something else.* You do not always add an *else* after a spoken *if*, and you do not have to have one in Python, either. Consider the following statements:

If I make enough money, I'll retire early.

If you're out late, call me, or you'll get in trouble.

If you're in town, we'll eat dinner together.

As a programming language, Python is fairly strict about how you make the `if` test. The relational test—the statement to the right of the `if`—usually includes one of the symbols from Table 6.1.

TABLE 6.1   `if` statement relational operators determine how the `if` behaves

Operator	Description	Example
<	Less than	`if (sales < maxSales)`
>	Greater than	`if (amount > 100.00)`
==	Equal to	`if (age == 21)`
>=	Greater than or equal to	`if (grade >= 90)`
<=	Less than or equal to	`if (price <= 1.00)`
!=	Not equal to	`if (year != 2004)`

You learned about math operators in Hour 5, "Data Processing with Numbers and Words." Python supplies these relational operators so you can test certain conditions with `if` statements. There are always two possibilities with the relational operators. Something is either less than something else, or it is not. Something is either greater than something else, or it is not. Something is either equal to something else, or it is not.

TIP

The two possibilities that the relational operators enable provide the means for duplicating the two-legged decision symbol in a flowchart. A decision symbol has two possible outcomes, and so does the `if`. `if` is either `true` or `false`.

▼ TRY IT YOURSELF

The statements following `else` can be any Python statement or multiple statements. A program can even contain one or more `if` statements within `else` clauses in its block. Listing 6.2 contains a set of `if` and `elif` statements that print different messages, depending on when in the month the user was born, based on the day the user enters.

LISTING 6.2 You can nest several `if` statements to check a series of conditions

```
# Filename ifbranch2.py


# Program that demonstrates multiple
# if, elif and else statements



# Get the day of the month someone was born

bdate = int(input('What day were you born? '))

if (bdate <=7):
    print("The first week of the month")
elif (bdate <= 18):
    print("The middle of the month")
elif (bdate <= 31):
    print("The end of the month")
else:
    print("I don't think that's right")
```

As Listing 6.2 demonstrates, you can validate some input values to make sure the user enters what you expect. If the user enters a day of the month higher than 31, the last `else` executes and tells the user that she or he probably entered invalid data.

NOTE

Most languages, like Python, allow for multiple `if...else if...else if` layers, but some also offer another way to handle several possible conditions or values to a single variable: the `switch` statement. The `switch` statement is not an option for Python, but you will encounter it in other languages, like C and JavaScript.

Looping Statements

Looping statements are another important feature of any programming language. Python supplies two statements that control loops. Your computer will never get bored. It will loop over and over, quickly repeating statements as long as you need it to.

Loops have many uses. You might need a loop to ask the user for several people's data, to calculate a combined total, or to print several lines of data. Python's two primary looping statements are:

- `for` loops
- `while` loops

The following sections describe these looping statements.

Using the `for` Loop

The `for` loop is actually a block of statements indented following the initial `for` statement. Before you look at a `for` loop, an analogy to things in everyday life might be helpful. As with `if`, a `for` loop is a natural way of expressing an idea. Consider the following description:

```
For each of today's invoices:
        check the accuracy of the invoice,
        add the total amount to the daily sales total.
```

You can sense from this description of invoice totaling that a repetitive process happens. If there are five invoices, the process repeats for each invoice.

The computer's `for` loop works just like the `for-each` concept in the invoice description (that's why it's called `for`). To ease you into the use of `for` loops, Listing 6.3 shows a simple loop that explains the `for` statement.

LISTING 6.3   Use `for` to control a counting loop

```
# Filename: firstforloop.py

# A program that goes through the first 10 numbers and
# prints the number and the number times itself
for x in range(10):
    print(x, x*x)
```

Here is the output from the program in Listing 6.3:

```
0 0
1 1
2 4
3 9
```

```
4  16
5  25
6  36
7  49
8  64
9  81
```

The `for` statement can save a programmer time and effort by repeating a line or a block of code. The `for` statement in Python is a little different than the versions you see in other programming languages. In Python, you generally use the `for` statement to iterate (loop) through something. In this example, you are working through a set of numbers—specifically the numbers 0 through 9. As noted in the discussion of strings in the previous hour, your list of numbers starts with 0 and ends at 9, the last number before the 10 in the `range()` function. So the first time the loop runs, it assigns 0 to the variable x. It proceeds to the `print()` statement and prints both x (0) and x * x (also 0). As with the `if` statements earlier, Python considers any indented line of code part of the `for` loop. Once it reaches the last indented line (in this case, the only indented line), Python returns to the `for` statement and increments the variable x by 1. Once again, it proceeds to the `print()` statement and prints both x (1) and x * x (also 1). This continues until the last number in the loop that is less than the number specified in the `range()` function (10). (If you wanted to print up through 10, you'd have to put 11 in the `range()` function.) Python then departs the `for` loop.

Listing 6.4 shows a program that does exactly the same thing as Listing 6.3 but without using a `for` loop. You can see that the `for` loop makes repetitive statements much easier to code. (Consider how much easier it would be to use a `for` statement to print the numbers from 1 to 200 than to write 200 lines of code to print those numbers if you used the method in Listing 6.4.)

LISTING 6.4   **Printing without a `for` loop gets tedious**

```
# Filename: noforloop.py

# A program that prints the first 10 numbers
# and prints the number times itself, but
# doesn't use a for loop

x = 0
print(x, x*x)

x = 1
print(x, x*x)

x = 2
print(x, x*x)

x = 3
```

```
print(x, x*x)

x = 4
print(x, x*x)

x = 5
print(x, x*x)

x = 6
print(x, x*x)

x = 7
print(x, x*x)

x = 8
print(x, x*x)

x = 9
print(x, x*x)
```

You do not have to print the value of the loop variable the way it's done in Listing 6.4; often, a loop variable just serves as a counter and is not printed at all.

Often, a `for` loop controls a set of statements, determining the number of times those statements repeat, without using the control variable for anything else. Listing 6.5, controlled by a `for` loop, prints a message 15 times.

LISTING 6.5   **Printing a message several times in a loop is efficient**

```
# Filename formessage.py

# Program that prints a message
# 15 times


for i in range (0,15,1):
    print("Happy birthday!")
```

Another example will make this clearer. Look at the program in Listing 6.6. A teacher might use it to print a grade sheet. The program asks the teacher how many test scores are to be entered. It uses that answer to loop through a series of statements, asking for the next child's name and grade. As the teacher enters the data, the values are printed to the printer. At the end of the program, there is a complete listing of names and grades. (Later, in Listing 6.8, you will see how to program an accumulator to add all the grades together and to print a class average.)

LISTING 6.6   A teacher's grade-printing program is easy to follow when you use a loop

```python
# Filename gradingpapers.py

# Program asks how many students are in a class
# and then gets their names and grades


# Get the number of students in the class
students = int(input('How many students? '))

# Set up two lists
# One for names and one for grades
studentnames = []
studentscores = []

# Get the test scores for each student
for x in range (students):
    studentnames.append(input("Name: "))
    studentscores.append(int(input("What was their test score? ")))

# Print all the names and grades
for x in range (students):
    print(studentnames[x], "got a", studentscores[x])
```

Now after running the program, the user gets a prompt box, asking for a number of students in the class (for this example, 5 was entered). The program loops through a series of additional prompts, asking for name and grade of each student. After the data entry is complete, the following output appears (though yours will match the data you enter):

```
Andrew got a 87
Benjamin got a 88
Chris got a 91
Katie got a 86
Maddie got a 98
```

A quick note about the method of data collection used in this program: In the last lesson, you learned that a word or phrase is an array of characters. With Python, you have additional ways to collect similar data under a single name, including lists, sets, tuples, and dictionaries. The program in Listing 6.6 uses two lists: one for the names of the students (studentnames) and one for their test scores (studentscores). Lists come in handy when you need a collection of similar numbers, like grades in this program or monthly expense totals. You could obviously create a separate variable for each item, but one variable name with multiple numbered versions is much easier to handle, particularly if you face a larger set of data to collect. What if you had 5,000 customers and needed to keep a balance for each? Would you prefer to create 1 name with

5,000 copies or 5,000 different variables? The former, right? In Python, if you want to create a list of any type of data, you can create it with a statement such as:

```
studentnames = []
```

This sets up a list named `studentnames`. With nothing between the brackets, the set is currently empty. It will be filled later with input from the user. You could also fill the list when you define it by putting the items in between the brackets. For example, if you already knew the names of the students, you could use a statement like:

```
NewStudents = ['Anna', 'Thomas', 'Julian', 'Maria']
```

This would create a list of four students, with Anna being `NewStudents[0]`, Thomas being `NewStudents[1]`, Julian being `NewStudents[2]`, and Maria being `NewStudents[3]`. Lists are extremely flexible: You can add or delete items as your needs change.

This program then creates a second list, one for the grades. The program then runs through two `for` loops, the first one to get the input and the second to print out the data. The two `for` statements show the use of the `range()` function, but instead of passing a specific number, you are passing a variable—the number of students the teacher entered. If the teacher has 5 students, the program loops 5 times. If the teacher inputs that there are 10 students, the program loops 10 times.

Another new function is used twice in the first `for` loop. When you create a new list, you need to use the `append()` function to add a new item to the end of the list. So in the new student list example, if you write the statement:

```
NewStudents.append('Hector')
```

the list now has a fifth element, with `NewStudents[4]` being equal to `'Hector'`. There are a number of functions associated with lists that you can use to add, delete, copy, and sort lists. They cannot all be covered here, but if you're interested, look for a more comprehensive Python reference.

With just six lines of Python, you've managed to create a pretty powerful piece of code. (The program is longer, but the rest of the lines are comments or blank lines for readability; you only had to write *six* lines of code.)

Controlling the `for` Loop

The `range()` function can be used in a variety of ways. In Listing 6.3, you saw it take a single number and count from 0 to right up to the top number by 1s. That's a great technique, and many of your programs will be able to use it. But what if you didn't want to start at 0? What if you wanted to count up by 2s or 5s? What if you wanted to count down? The `range()` function can do all of these types of counting; you just need to pass it three values instead of one:

```
range(a, b, c)
```

where:

>   *a* is the starting number
>
>   *b* is the ending number
>
>   *c* is the increment

So if you wanted to count from 25 to 100 by 5s, you would use this `for` statement:

```
for (x in range(25,100,5))
```

Or if you wanted to print the odd numbers between 1 and 100, you would use this `for` statement:

```
for (x in range (1,100,2))
```

You could even count down from 10 to 1 by using this `for` statement:

```
for(x in range(10,0,-1))
```

This last one is a little tricky at first, but it just tells you that if you start with your highest number and your ending number is smaller, you must use a negative number as the increment (which is then called a decrement).

Listing 6.7 shows a program that counts down from 10 to 1 and then prints `Blast Off!` at the end of the loop. To carry out the countdown, a negative value has to be used in the third part of the `range()` function. Each time through the loop, –1 is added to `i` to create the descending count.

LISTING 6.7 Counting down from 10 to 1 is simple with a `for` loop

```
# Filename countdown.py
# Program uses a for loop to
# count down instead of up


for i in range(10,0,-1):
    print(i,'...')
print("Blastoff!")
```

Here is the output from the program:

```
10...
9...
8...
7...
6...
5...
4...
3...
```

```
2...
1...
Blast Off!
```

The `for` loop offers a lot of loop control, but it is designed to count through the control loop's value. You don't have to increase or decrease your counter variable by 1 in the third part of the `for` loop. Finally, the last line of code executes when the `for` loop has completed, so you print 10 countdown numbers but print the `Blast Off!` message only once.

You can nest one loop inside another. Such nested constructs can seem rather advanced to beginning programmers, but the nested loops are simple to understand if you consider what happens when you need to perform a loop more than once. You *could* write the loop twice, back to back, or you could enclose the loop inside another loop that executes its body twice. Hour 9, "Programming Algorithms," explains nested loops in more detail.

Not all loops can be determined by a counting variable. Sometimes you need loops that loop while a certain condition is true or until a certain condition is met. The loops described in the next section often prove more effective for such programming goals.

Using the `while` Loop

The `while` loop provides a way to control loops through a relational test. A loop's relational test uses the same relational operators used with `if` statements. (Refer to Table 6.1 for a complete list of relational operators.)

Suppose the teacher with the grade-printing program doesn't know exactly how many students took the test and doesn't want to take the time to count them. Because the total number of tests must be specified to control the `for` loop properly, another method is required. Listing 6.8 shows the same program but controlled by a `while` loop. Notice that the `while` continues looping while a certain condition is true. The condition in this case is the teacher's answer in response to having more tests to enter.

LISTING 6.8   You can control the grade program with a `while` loop

```python
# Filename gradingpapers2.py

# Program uses a while loop to
# get students names and grades
# until the teacher is done

# Set up two lists
# One for names and one for grades
studentnames = []
studentscores = []

answer = 'Y'
```

```
students = 0
totalscore = 0

# Get the names and test scores for each student
while (answer == 'Y'):
    studentnames.append(input("Name: "))
    studentscores.append(int(input("What was their test score? ")))
    totalscore = totalscore + studentscores[students]
    students += 1
    answer = input("Do you have another score to enter (Y/N)? ")


# Print all the names and grades
for x in range (students):
    print(studentnames[x], "got a", studentscores[x])

print("The average score was %.1f." % (totalscore/students))
```

This program keeps looping until the teacher indicates that there are no more grades to enter. Notice that the `while` is followed by a relational test, the result of which (`true` or `false`) determines whether the loop repeats again or quits. So if the conditional statement is `false` the first time, the block of code does not run at all. In this program, we've guaranteed the code will run one time by setting the `answer` variable to `'Y'` to trigger the first pass through the loop.

Note that this is a rather limited form of data entry as only a capital `Y` answer will continue the loop. If a teacher enters `y` or `Yes` or `1 more` or anything other than `Y`, the test will return `false`, and the loop will end. (There are better ways to ensure that data entry is complete, but this is just a general method to introduce the concept to you.)

One added bonus to this program is the addition of a `totalscore` variable, which gets the value of all grades and then is divided by the number of students that took the test in order to get an average grade. It's an extra piece of information your program calculates for the teacher to add some additional programming value.

TIP

When using a `while` loop, make sure that, somewhere in the block of code, you are altering the variable you are testing in the relational statement. Otherwise, you might get yourself caught in an infinite loop, and your program will not end.

Summary

Congratulations! You can now enter data into a Python program and format the resulting output. You have also mastered the true power of any programming language—looping. The programs you saw in this lesson are getting to be powerful, yet you have seen that programming is easy. You have learned how the relational operators are used with the `if` statement so that a Python program can make decisions based on the data. In addition, the looping constructs enable sections of your program to repeat as long as necessary.

The next hour shows you how to analyze your programs to locate errors that might appear in them. You'll learn bug-catching secrets so that you can write more accurate programs more quickly.

Q&A

Q. Does it matter whether I select `while` or `for` statements when I'm writing loops?

A. Generally, `for` loops are useful when you must count values or iterate the loop's body a specified number of times. The `while` loop is useful for iterating until or while a certain condition is met. If you are counting up or down, a `for` loop is easier to write and is slightly more efficient than an equivalent `while` loop. Ultimately, though, you can use whatever style of loop you prefer.

Q. How does `if` compare to `for`?

A. Both the `if` statement and the `for` statement, as well as the `while` statements, rely on conditional values to do their jobs. Nevertheless, an `if` statement is never considered to be a loop. Always keep in mind that an `if` statement executes its body of code at most one time—and possibly never if the `if` is `false` to begin with. Even if the `if` condition is `true`, the `if` statement never executes its body more than one time, whereas the looping statements can repeat their code bodies many times.

Workshop

The quiz questions are provided for your further understanding.

Quiz

1. How does a conditional operator differ from a mathematical operator?
2. What is a loop?
3. True or false: Code inside an `if` statement might never execute.
4. True or false: Code inside `for` loops always executes at least once.
5. How can you make a `for` loop count down?

6. How many times does the following `for` loop print?

```
for (i in range (2,19;3)):
    print i
```

7. Which loop, `while` or `for`, is best to use when you want to execute a loop a fixed number of times?

8. Where does the conditional appear in a `while` loop?

9. What function do you use to add a new element to a list?

10. What are the four techniques that Python uses to collect data under a single variable name?

Answers

1. A conditional operator tests how two values compare, whereas a mathematical operator calculates an answer based on values.

2. A loop is a set of instructions that repeat.

3. True. If the conditional tested by the `if` statement is `false`, the code inside the `if` statement is skipped.

4. False. If the `for` loop's counter variable is already past the limit before the loop begins, the `for` loop does not execute, and control passes to the statement that follows the loop's next statement.

5. Use a negative increment to make a `for` loop count down.

6. The loop executes six times.

7. Use the `for` loop when you want to execute a loop a fixed number of times.

8. The conditional appears after the `while` command.

9. `append()`

10. Lists, sets, tuples, and dictionaries

Debugging Tools

Programs are easy to write. Writing *correct* programs is a different story. Locating program bugs can be difficult. When you are working with tools that compile or interpret your programs, debugging tools are built in to the compilation or interpretation process, which makes your life much easier. Although the compiler or interpreter locates syntax errors for you, locating logic errors often takes extra time, and you must be the one to locate such problems before your users locate the problems. For example, when a payroll amount comes out incorrectly due to a bug, you need to locate the problem as quickly as possible.

Although your debugging skills will improve as your programming skills improve, you can help reduce bugs that appear and make debugging simpler by learning to write programs in a way that will make them easier to maintain and update. When you write clear and concise code, you'll debug your programs more quickly. Many sophisticated debugging tools exist in today's programming languages. This hour shows you how to access debugging tools available to Python developers so that you can try them yourself.

The highlights of this hour include the following:

▶ Looking in the past to the first computer bug

▶ Learning the difference between logic errors and syntax errors

▶ Seeing the importance of writing clear and concise code

▶ Using Python debugging tools

▶ Stepping through a program one line at a time

The First Bug

The term *bug* has an interesting origin. The late U.S. Navy Admiral Grace Hopper was one of the early pioneers of computer hardware and software. She helped to design and write the first COBOL compiler for the military. *COBOL* (Common Business-Oriented Language) was a language later used by most business programmers of the 1960s and 1970s. Admiral Hopper was working on a military computer system in the early 1950s and, while she was printing a report, the printer stopped working. Admiral Hopper and her coworkers set out to find the problem.

After spending a lot of time and not finding any problems in the program or in the data, Admiral Hopper looked inside the printer and noticed that a moth had lodged itself in a printer's relay switch, keeping the printer from operating properly. As soon as the *bug* (get it?) was removed, the printer worked perfectly. The moth did not fare as well, but it did go down in computer history as the first computer bug.

NOTE

Michael Crichton may have used Admiral Hopper's true story as the basis for his nail-biting suspense novel *Andromeda Strain*, a story that had a small printer problem that almost caused disaster.

Accuracy Is Everything

You are now aware that a computer is a machine that cannot deal well with ambiguity. A programmer's plague is the collection of errors that show up in code. Perhaps as you've entered Python programs in the earlier hours, you've run across problems that occurred as you mistyped a character or two. Bugs can creep into code. Programmers must ensure that they do not write programs that contain errors, although this is not always as easy as it might seem.

When breaking the programming problem into detailed instructions, programmers often leave things out or code the wrong things. When a program runs, errors may appear because the programmer didn't plan for a particular event, used an incorrect calculation, or typed a line of code incorrectly.

TIP

Some of the most common bugs you will encounter—and those that are often the most difficult to spot—involve mistyping or omitting punctuation marks, including forgetting that second quotation mark, brace, or parenthesis, or not ending a Python `if`, `while`, or `for` statement with a colon. If your program doesn't run the way you intended (or if it doesn't run at all), double-checking all your special characters like these is often a good place to start.

A programmer goes through the debugging process to exterminate the bugs from a program. As a programmer writes a program, he or she often runs the program in its unfinished state (as much as it can be run) to catch as many bugs as possible during the program's development. Incrementally running the program as more and more of the code is completed helps eliminate bugs from the finished program. Still, the majority of the bugs can be found only after the program is completely written.

Beginning programmers often fail to realize how easy it is for bugs to creep into code. Expect them, and you will not be surprised. Many early programming students have taken a program to an instructor saying, "The computer doesn't work right," when in reality, the program has a bug or two. When you begin to write programs, expect to have problems you will have to correct. Nobody writes a perfect program every time.

Depending on the length of a program, the time it takes the programmer (or programmers) to correct problems is often almost as long as the time taken to write the program originally. Some errors are very difficult to find.

There are two categories of computer bugs: syntax errors and logic errors. To learn the difference, take a few moments to find the two errors in the following statement:

There are two errrors in this sentence.

TIP
_____
Found only one problem? Need a clue? Not yet; look again for two mistakes before going further.
_____

The first error is obvious. The word *errrors* is misspelled; it should be spelled *errors*. The second problem is much more difficult to find. The second problem with the statement is that the entire premise of the statement is incorrect. There is only *one* error in the statement, and that error is the misspelled word *errrors*. Therefore, the logic of the statement itself is in error.

This problem demonstrates the difference between a *syntax error* and a *logic error*. The syntax error is much easier to find. As you learned in Hour 1, "Hands-On Programming," syntax errors often appear as misspelled programming language commands and grammatical problems with the way you use the programming language. Logic errors occur when your program is syntactically correct, but you told it to do something that is not what should really be done.

Compilers and interpreters locate your program's syntax errors when you try to compile your program. This is another reason syntax errors are easier to spot than logic errors: Your computer tells you where they are. When a computer runs into a syntax error, it halts and refuses to analyze the program further until you correct the syntax error. Listing 7.1 shows a Python program that does not work because of a syntax error. It's one of the first programs you wrote, one to compute the area of a circle. However, a character has been removed from the original code to create the error. Figure 7.1 shows the how the code runs.

LISTING 7.1 Even a simple program can have an error in it
_____
```
# Filename AreaHalf2.py
# program that calculates and prints the area
# of a circle and half circle

pi = 3.14159 # mathematical value of PI
radius = 3 # radius of the circle
```

```
# calculate the area of the whole circle
area = pi * radius * radius

print("The area of a circle with a radius of 3 is ", area)
pint("The area of a half circle is ", area/2)
```

```
# Filename AreaHalf2.py
# program that calculates and prints the area
# of a circle and half circle


pi = 3.14159 # mathematical value of PI
radius = 3 # radius of the circle

# calculate the area of the whole circle
area = pi * radius * radius

print("The area of a circle with a radius of 3 is ", area)

pint("The area of a half circle is ", area/2)

The area of a circle with a radius of 3 is  28.274309999999996

---------------------------------------------------------------------
NameError                         Traceback (most recent call last)
<ipython-input-3-bee9200c5225> in <module>
     12 print("The area of a circle with a radius of 3 is ", area)
     13
---> 14 pint("The area of a half circle is ", area/2)

NameError: name 'pint' is not defined
```

FIGURE 7.1
Running a Python program in the Jupyter Notebook gives you clear information on what went wrong with
the program.

If you review the output, you'll see how helpful an IDE can be when running code. The program
prints the first statement in the program because no errors have occurred yet. The typo was introduced in the last line, and the Jupyter Notebook reprints the offending line of code, points it out
with a handy arrow, and then gives an explanation of the problem.

Some of the time, it can be a little difficult to translate what went wrong based on the message
received, but this one is very clear: "Pint" is not defined. The error in the code is that print is
misspelled, and Python has no idea what you are trying to do with the term pint.

You could actually get a different error with this same code. Imagine that you had defined a
string variable named pint to be equal to the message My favorite beer. If you misspelled
print as pint in this case, you would still get an error, but it would be a different one, as reflect-
ed in Figure 7.2.

```
In [5]:  # Filename AreaHalf2.py
         # program that calculates and prints the area
         # of a circle and half circle


         pi = 3.14159 # mathematical value of PI
         radius = 3 # radius of the circle
         pint = "My favorite beer"

         # calculate the area of the whole circle
         area = pi * radius * radius

         print("The area of a circle with a radius of 3 is ", area)

         pint("The area of a half circle is ", area/2)

         The area of a circle with a radius of 3 is  28.274309999999996

         -------------------------------------------------------------------
         TypeError                          Traceback (most recent call last)
         <ipython-input-5-1aeb4c45388f> in <module>
              13 print("The area of a circle with a radius of 3 is ", area)
              14
         ---> 15 pint("The area of a half circle is ", area/2)

         TypeError: 'str' object is not callable
```

FIGURE 7.2
The error message has changed! Now `pint` is defined, but it can't do what you are trying to make it do.

These are just two of the possible errors that could arise from a single typo. In the next lesson, you will learn how to create your own custom functions. If you had created a function named `pint` (perhaps one that takes a number in ounces and returns how many pints that amount would be), your program would still probably generate an error, but the message would be different.

Look back at the original program shown in Figure 7.1, and you'll see another advantage of using an IDE. Most integrated development environments use color-coding of terms and phrases to help you differentiate between items. In the program from Figure 7.1, the Jupyter Notebook uses five different colors. The term `print` (a defined function in Python) is in green. Comments (the pound sign and anything after them) are in blue. Operators like the multiplication and equal signs are in purple. Strings are in red. Everything else is in black. If you follow along when writing your program, you can use these colors to get context clues that something may not work as expected. When originally writing the program, if you saw that what you expected to be the second `print` statement is in a different color from the first, you might catch your spelling error before you even tried to run the program. And catching errors as soon as possible is vitally important.

Suppose you're writing a program to print invoices for your company's accounts receivable department. Because of an error, the computer prints all the invoices with a balance due of –$1,000. In other words, according to the invoice, every customer has a $1,000 credit. Your computer did its job, acting out your program's instructions. The program obviously contained no syntax errors because it ran without stopping. The logic errors, however, kept it from working properly.

Extensive testing is critical. A programmer wants to get all the errors out so the program will work correctly when the user finally uses it. The larger the program, the more difficult this is. Exterminating program bugs is just part of the daily job programmers tackle.

NOTE

There is a third kind of error, called a *runtime error*. Runtime errors are almost always caused by logic mistakes because the programmer failed to predict and therefore handle a potential problem. Runtime errors can occur if a program attempts to write to a disk without first checking to ensure that the disk is mounted. A runtime error can occur, for instance, if the program divides by zero (division by zero is undefined mathematically). The more you program, the more you will learn about heading off potential runtime errors that can occur.

Some errors will not show up until you use the program. Consider the simple code in Listing 7.2.

LISTING 7.2   Taking two user-entered variables and dividing them by each other

```
a = int(input("What value would you like to assign a? "))
n = int(input("What value would you like to assign n? "))
print("n divided by a is ", n/a)
print("a divided by n is ", a/n)
```

It's a pretty straightforward program without any visible bugs, right? You can even run it to check for bugs, as demonstrated in Figure 7.3, where the user enters 1 and 3 at the two prompts.

```
a = int(input("What value would you like to assign a? "))
n = int(input("What value would you like to assign n? "))


print("n divided by a is ", n/a)
print("a divided by n is ", a/n)

What value would you like to assign a? 1
What value would you like to assign n? 3
n divided by a is  3.0
a divided by n is  0.3333333333333333
```

FIGURE 7.3
The division worked exactly as expected, giving you the two answers you figured you would see.

But what if a user enters 3 and 0 at the two prompts? Now you get an error, and again the IDE shares information with you that is going to help you debug the program and get to the root of the issue (see Figure 7.4).

```
a = int(input("What value would you like to assign a? "))
n = int(input("What value would you like to assign n? "))


print("n divided by a is ", n/a)
print("a divided by n is ", a/n)
```
```
What value would you like to assign a? 3
What value would you like to assign n? 0
n divided by a is  0.0

---------------------------------------------------------------------------
ZeroDivisionError                         Traceback (most recent call last)
<ipython-input-13-61a6ca79ee8f> in <module>
      4
      5 print("n divided by a is ", n/a)
----> 6 print("a divided by n is ", a/n)

ZeroDivisionError: division by zero
```

FIGURE 7.4
You can't divide by 0, so the program can't give you an answer.

It can get even worse. What if the user enters 20 and x for the two prompts (see Figure 7.5)?

```
a = int(input("What value would you like to assign a? "))
n = int(input("What value would you like to assign n? "))


print("n divided by a is ", n/a)
print("a divided by n is ", a/n)
```
```
What value would you like to assign a? 20
What value would you like to assign n? x

---------------------------------------------------------------------------
ValueError                                Traceback (most recent call last)
<ipython-input-12-61a6ca79ee8f> in <module>
      1 a = int(input("What value would you like to assign a? "))
----> 2 n = int(input("What value would you like to assign n? "))
      3
      4
      5 print("n divided by a is ", n/a)

ValueError: invalid literal for int() with base 10: 'x'
```

FIGURE 7.5
Entering a non-number when a number is expected can make the program extremely cranky.

This brings up an important consideration when debugging your programs: You must also have users test the program, almost to the point of trying to break it. This is what is going to happen to your programs in the real world, and most of the time it isn't even malicious. What if someone were running the code in Listing 7.2 and typed out the word for a specific number (such as one instead of 1)? You would get the same error message in Figure 7.5 because Python was expecting a number and got a string.

Testing and debugging your programs generally takes at least as much time as writing the original code. But don't get down; it is only with this level of commitment to writing bulletproof code that you can create top-notch applications.

Write Clear Programs

As you write programs, keep in mind the future maintenance that will be required. Sometimes, a program might be in use for a long time before a bug appears because a certain combination of factors must occur to bring the bug to light. Perhaps an unexpected data value appears, such as a negative value in an age field that should never be negative. Perhaps an operating system update causes a program to stop working.

Not only might bugs appear down the road, but programs often need to be modified as the needs of the program change. When you write your programs, write clear and concise code. Every time you write a new line of code, consider whether a comment is needed to explain that line or to introduce a new section. Add extra whitespace characters to your program.

Consider the C program shown in Listing 7.3. The program is a valid, legal, C program that works on many C compilers that you might use. However, the program is horribly written. The program works and contains no syntax or logic errors, but the program is virtually impossible to maintain easily. The program is rather short, but even advanced C programmers will have to hesitate to decipher the code if they are to make changes to it.

LISTING 7.3   This C program contains no errors but is extremely difficult to maintain

```
/* Filename: CFIRST.C Initial C program that
demonstrates the C comments and shows a few variables
    and their declarations */
#include <stdio.h>
main() {int i,j;/* These 3 lines declare 4 variables */
char c;float x;i=4;/* i and j are assigned integer values */
j=i+7;c='A';/* All character constants are enclosed in
single quotes */x=9.087;/* x requires a floating-point
value since it was declared as a floating-point variable */x=
x*4.5;/*Change what was in x with a formula */
/* Sends the values of the variables to the screen */printf("%d %d %c %f",i,
j,c,x);return 0;/* End programs and functions this way*/}
```

Whether you know C or not, you must admit that Listing 7.3 is bunched together and difficult to read. By adding whitespace and extra lines, the program automatically becomes easier to understand even for non–C programmers, as Listing 7.4 demonstrates.

TIP

You'll find that much of C programming is clear to you, thanks to your Python experience. If you want to learn C, you still have to learn about some of the ways C works, including some of the lines in Listings 7.3 and 7.4, but you'll certainly have a head start.

LISTING 7.4 This C program with better spacing is far clearer and easier to understand

```c
/*   Filename: CFIRST.C
     Initial C program that demonstrates the C comments
     and shows a few variables and their declarations */
#include <stdio.h>

main()
{
    int i, j;                /* These 3 lines declare 4 variables */
    char c;
    float x;

    i = 4;                   /* i and j are assigned integer values */
    j = i + 7;
    c = 'A';             /* All character constants are
                             enclosed in single quotes */
    x = 9.087;       /* x requires a floating-point value since it
                         was declared as a floating-point variable */
    x = x * 4.5;     /* Change what was in x with a formula */

 /* Sends the values of the variables to the screen */
    printf("%d %d %c %f", i, j, c, x);

    return 0; /* End programs and functions with return */
}
```

Additional Debugging Techniques

No matter how you program Python (or any other language you choose), you are going to find robust debugging tools and add-ons. It's not possible to cover all of them in an introductory chapter like this, so instead, it makes sense to cover some of the techniques that are universal across almost all debugging tools and modules.

The following is a partial list of some of the features you'll find in most of today's debugging systems:

- ▶ You can analyze variables at runtime and view those variables in a window separate from the output.

- ▶ You can change contents of variables during the execution of the program so that the rest of the program acts as though the code had assigned those values.

- ▶ You can set *breakpoints* throughout the program so that the program runs at normal speed until your preset breakpoint is reached. At that time, you can single-step through the rest of the code.

- ▶ You can set *watch variables* that halt the program's execution when the watch variables receive a specific value or range of values.

- ▶ You can skip statements that you don't want to execute during debugging.

In addition to the usual debugging features, many tools allow you to retrace your steps through a program. When you need to see exactly which parts of a program have executed up to a breakpoint, you can look at the *call stack*. The call stack appears in a dialog box and shows all procedures that have executed in the program to that point. If you double-click a procedure name, the code window opens to that procedure, and all variable values are still intact so that you can see what values have been computed.

Be sure to explore the development tools available to you for your programming language and development environment of choice. They are numerous!

Summary

This hour showed how you can use debugging tools to locate problems in your programs. You used the Python IDE to learn skills related to debugging, and those same skills will transfer rapidly to other languages and tools. Learning how to debug pays dividends when you need to track bugs. Although the debugging tools cannot locate specific logic bugs on their own, they make locating logic bugs easier for you to do.

Q&A

Q. **How can single-stepping help me debug a program when it takes so long to step through a large application?**

A. By executing a program one line at a time, you can analyze variable and control values at your pace. Remember that you don't have to single-step through every statement, but only the statements that you want to analyze. After you view values, you can run the rest of the program or set a breakpoint later in the code and run the program at normal speed to that set breakpoint. Single-stepping helps you ensure that data values are correct, and it also enables you to monitor the execution of a program to make sure that the program's statements execute in the order that you intended.

Q. **Can I debug a compiled program?**

A. Unfortunately, the debugging tools only work with source code. The source code is needed to display variable names and locate program statements. As a good programmer, you will keep a copy of all source code you compile into user's programs so you can locate and fix bugs that you or the user find later.

Workshop

The quiz questions are provided for your further understanding.

Quiz

1. True or false: The first bug in a computer program was literally a bug.

2. What is one of the most common causes of bugs?

3. What are the two main categories of bugs?

4. What are the differences between the two main categories of bugs?

5. What does single-stepping mean?

6. What are watch variables?

7. If your program compiles without errors and executes without stopping at a runtime error, are you assured that the program is bug free?

Answers

1. True (a moth, to be precise)

2. Mistyping a bit of punctuation in your code, such as a semicolon

3. The two types are syntax errors and logic errors.

4. A logic error is a mistake in program logic, whereas a syntax error is a mistake in program grammar or spelling.

5. To single-step means to walk through a program's execution one statement at a time, analyzing the results of each statement.

6. Watch variables are variables you set up to monitor during a program's debugging session.

7. Just because a program compiles and runs does not mean that you have fully debugged it. Sometimes, an error appears long after the program has been in use because a special set of circumstances occur together.

HOUR 8
Structured Techniques

Now you are familiar with the steps to take before programming. You also know how to do some programming, and you have a little Python in your programming bag of tricks. In this hour's lesson, you'll begin honing your programming skills. From Hour 3, "Designing a Program," you now know that two steps must always precede writing the program: defining the output and data as well as developing the logic. After you develop the logic, you can write the program, using one of the many available programming languages.

This hour guides you into being a more structured programmer, writing clearer code, and writing code that is maintainable. Your future as a programmer depends on your being able to write code that others can change and manage.

The highlights of this hour include the following:

▶ Understanding the importance of structured programming

▶ Analyzing the three structured-programming constructs

▶ Testing a program

▶ Checking a program in stages

▶ Using parallel testing to eliminate downtime

Structured Programming

Structured programming is a philosophy stating that programs should be written in an orderly fashion without a lot of jumping to and fro. If a program is easy to read, the program is easier to change. People have known for many years that clear writing style is important, but it became obvious to computer people only after nearly 20 years of using nonstructured techniques.

In the late 1960s, programming departments began to wallow in programming backlogs that grew at tremendous rates. More people were writing more programs than ever, but many programmers had to be hired to maintain the previously written programs.

TIP

You cannot hear the importance of writing readable and maintainable programs too often. By using a conscientious approach (instead of the old "throw a program together" approach that some programmers use), you help ensure your future as a programmer. Companies save money when a programmer writes code that is easily maintained.

When you finish a program, you are finished only for the time being. The program's assumptions about the job it performs will change over time. Businesses never remain constant in this global economy. Data processing managers began to recognize that the programming maintenance backlog was beginning to take a toll on development. Programmers were pulled away from new projects in order to update older projects. The maintenance was taking too long.

By the way, the programming backlog of the 1960s has never really gotten better. Companies all around the world keep contract programmers and programming staff on hand to develop the new systems that they need. A backlog of computer projects seems to be the norm in the computer world. Constant change in the world means that an organization's data processing has to change as well.

Roots of Structured Programming

During the maintenance crisis of the 1960s, data processing people began looking for new ways to program. They weren't necessarily interested in new languages but in new ways to write programs that would make them work better and faster and, most importantly, make them readable so that others could maintain the programs without too much trouble. Structured-programming techniques were developed during this time.

There is some debate about exactly when beginning programmers should be introduced to structured programming. Some people feel that programmers should be trained in structured programming from the beginning. Others feel beginners should learn to program any way that gets the job done, and then they should adapt to structured programming.

You've seen what flowcharts are, and the rest of this hour uses those tools to show you what structured programming is all about. As mentioned in Hour 3, flowcharts are not used much anymore to design complete programs, but they are used for showing small logic flows. It is a good idea to incorporate structured-programming techniques into your code-writing process. Many of today's languages naturally lend themselves to structured-programming techniques because their commands and structure mirror the structured-programming rules you'll learn in the next sections.

Looking at Structure

Just because a program is well written and easily read doesn't necessarily mean it's structured. Structured programming is a specific approach to programming that generally produces well-written and easily read programs. Nothing can make up for a programmer rushing to finish a program by proceeding in what he thinks is the fastest way. You often hear, "Later, I'll make it structured, but for now, I'll leave it as it is." *Later* never comes. People use the program until one day, when changes have to be made, the changes turn out to take as long as or longer than it would take to scrap the entire program and rewrite it from scratch.

Structured programming includes the following three constructs:

▶ Sequence

▶ Decision (also called *selection*)

▶ Looping (also called *repetition* or *iteration*)

A *construct* (from the word *construction*) is a building block of a language and one of a language's fundamental operations. As long as a programming language supports these three constructs (most modern languages do), you can write structured programs. The opposite of a structured program is known as *spaghetti code*. Like spaghetti that flows and swirls all over the plate, an unstructured program—one full of spaghetti code—flows all over the place with little or no structure. An unstructured program contains lots of *branching*. A branch occurs when a program goes this way and that with no particular order.

Jumping Around

Many programming languages enable you to branch with a `goto` statement. The `goto` works just as it sounds: It tells the computer to go to another place in the program and continue execution there. Python does not include the `goto` statement, so you don't have to worry about learning what it does and then avoid using it. However, if you work with other languages, you will see this technique used; keep in mind that it should be avoided whenever possible.

The three structured-programming constructs aren't just for programs. You will find that you can use them for flowcharts, pseudocode, and any other set of instructions you write for others, whether those instructions are computer related or not. The three structured-programming constructs ensure that a program doesn't branch all over the place and ensure that any execution is controlled and easily followed.

The following three sections explain each of the three structured-programming constructs. Read them carefully, and you'll see that the concept of a structured program is easy to understand. Learning about structure before learning a language should help you think of structure as you develop your programming skills.

Sequence

Sequence is nothing more than two or more instructions, one after the other. The first few programs you wrote in Python use sequence. The sequential instructions are the easiest of the three structured-programming constructs because you can follow the program from the first statement to the last within the sequence. Figure 8.1 shows a flowchart that illustrates sequence.

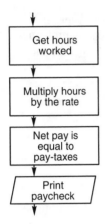

FIGURE 8.1
The sequence structured-programming construct executes the program in order.

To show that you can represent any kind of logic using pseudocode as well as a flowchart, here is pseudocode that matches the sequence shown in the flowchart:

```
Get the hours worked.
Multiply the hours by the rate.
Subtract taxes to compute net pay.
Print paycheck.
```

NOTE

Some programmers prefer to see pseudocode when looking at logic instead of flowcharts because of pseudocode's compact nature and its closeness to actual computer code.

Because computers must have the capability of making decisions and performing repetitive tasks, not all your programs can consist of straight sequential logic. When sequence is available, however, it makes for straightforward program logic.

Decision (Selection)

You have seen the *decision* construct before. In Hour 6, "Controlling Your Programs," when you wrote an `if` statement in Python, you were using the structured-programming decision construct. At the point of such a decision, the program must take off in one of two directions. Obviously, a decision is a break from the sequential program flow, but it's a controlled break.

By its nature, a branch must be performed based on the result of a decision; in effect, the code must skip the code that is not to execute. Based on new data, the program might repeat a decision and take a different route the second time, but again, you can always assume that the decision code not being executed at the time is meaningless to the current loop.

Figure 8.2 shows a flowchart that contains part of a teacher's grading program logic. The flow-chart illustrates the use of the decision construct.

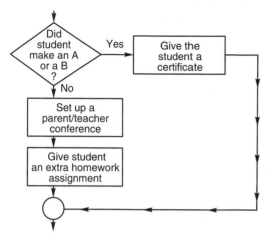

FIGURE 8.2
The decision structured-programming construct offers one of two choices.

Here is the pseudocode for the decision shown in the flowchart:

```
If the student makes an A or B,
    give the student an achievement certificate.
Otherwise:
    set up a parent-teacher conference;
    give the student extra homework.
```

Looping (Repetition and Iteration)

Perhaps the most important task of computers is *looping* (the term for repeating or iterating through lines of program code, as you did in Hour 6). Computers repeat sections of a program millions of times and never become bored. Computers are perfect companions for workers who have lots of data to process because a computer can process the data, repeating the common cal-culations needed throughout all the data, and the person can analyze the results.

Looping is prevalent in almost every program written. Rarely do you write a program that is a straight sequence of instructions. The time it takes to design and write a program isn't always worth the effort when a straight series of tasks is involved. Programs are most powerful when they can repeat a series of sequential statements or decisions.

Figure 8.3 shows a flowchart that repeats a section in a loop. Loops only temporarily break the rule that says flowcharts should flow down and to the right. Loops within a flowchart are fine because eventually the logic will stop looping.

CAUTION

Be aware of the dreaded *infinite loop*. An *infinite loop* is a never-ending loop. If your computer goes into an infinite loop, it continues looping without finishing, and sometimes it's difficult to regain control of the program without rebooting the computer. Loops should always be prefaced with a decision statement so that eventually the decision triggers the end of the loop, and the rest of the program can finish.

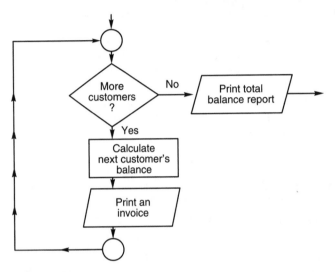

FIGURE 8.3
The looping structured-programming construct repeats parts of the program.

Here is the pseudocode for the flowchart:

```
while there are more customers,
      calculate the next customer's balance;
      print an invoice.
Otherwise,
print the total balance report.
```

As you can see, eventually there won't be any customers, and the loop (beginning with while) will stop looping so that the rest of the logic can take over.

None of these structured-programming constructs should be new to you because you have already worked with them in Python programs. As long as you keep these three constructs in mind while you develop your program's logic, and as long as you resist the temptation to start branching all over the program, you will write well-structured, easy-to-maintain programs and secure your position as a programmer for many years to come.

Packaging Your Python Code into Functions

When writing programs, you often need to perform specific jobs repeatedly. To save time, you can create a function and then reuse it in any Python program you write. These reusable bits of code are similar to the functions you have seen so far, like the `print()` and `input()` functions. Writing functions is not limited to Python either; it is a fundamental practice of structured programs in most other languages as well.

Creating Functions

Suppose you realize that you always need to cut your variable values in thirds (perhaps you have three kids and need to divide everything equally among them). Rather than constantly write the code needed to divide your variables in three, you decide to create a function to do it for you. The following code would do the trick:

```
def thirds(target):
    "This function will take a number and return 1/3 of it"
    third = target/3
    return (third)
```

The `target` in the parentheses can be any value. You can replace it with an actual number (such as 6) or a variable. The function will take that number, divide it by 3, and then return the new value. The line in quotation marks is a docstring that describes what the function does. A docstring is optional but can be useful to anyone reviewing your code after you've written it. (It can also be good for you as once you start writing code, it is unlikely that you will remember every function you write, so having the docstring will serve as an effective reminder.)

The keyword `return` is probably new to you. If your function is going to perform some operation on a variable, you need to get the new value back to your original code. The `return` keyword tells your program to send some value back to the calling function. To use the function in your code, you could call it in the following manner:

```
candy = int(input("How many pieces of candy in the bag?"))
candyperkid = thirds(candy)
print("Each kid gets ", candyperkid, "pieces")
```

So in this case you've created a new variable, `candyperkid`, and set it to the value that your function calculates. You can then call the function as often as you want, just as you can call any `string` or `math` method as often as you want.

▼ TRY IT YOURSELF

The value of writing functions that you will use repeatedly is that you can use them in multiple files. To do this, you need to create two files—one containing the functions (Listing 8.1) and one that uses the functions (Listing 8.2).

LISTING 8.1   Collect multiple function definitions in a single file you can reuse.

```python
# Filename: Functions3.py


# Program that defines a new function that
# divides an item in thirds.


def thirds(target):
    B = target/3
    return (B)

def fourths(target):
    C = target/4
    return(C)

def SayHi(message):
    print("Time to print a message...")
    print(message)
```

This file contains the definitions of three different functions: two that return a value, and one that prints a standard line and passes the message.

Typing your functions in the same file that uses them doesn't really save you any time. However, you can create files that collect your functions in organized groups that make sense, which is what Listing 8.1 is attempting. Listing 8.2 is used to call the three functions defined in Listing 8.1.

LISTING 8.2   **A separate file can call your functions.**   ▼

```
# Filename: Test3.py


# Program that calls the functions
# in the Function3 file


import Functions3

checker = float(input("Enter a number: "))
test1 = Functions3.thirds(checker)
print("One third is %.2f" % test1)

test2 = Functions3.fourths(checker)
print("One fourth is %.2f" % test2)

test3 = input("What would you like to say? ")
Functions3.SayHi(test3)
```

This second file is going to use the functions that you defined in Listing 8.1. You need to import the file containing the functions. This file, also called a *module*, is a collection of code that generally serves a similar purpose. For beginners, this file usually includes functions, but as you become more advanced and learn additional programming concepts like object-oriented programming, you may use a module to store classes that you plan to use across multiple programs.

To import the module, you would use the `import` operation. Your module must be in the same directory as your program file. (Well, this is not entirely true; you can store it in a path that Python knows to search, but for now, keeping your program files in a single directory will make life easier for you.)

When you start building more robust files of functions, you might want to import only a single function from the module. To do this, you would add more information to the `import` statement. For example, if you only wanted the `thirds` function from the `Functions3` module, you would type:

```
Import thirds from Functions3
```

Now, it might not seem like you're not saving much time if you compare the work you would put into creating the separate module and program files. But this is a very simple example with only a few functions. Perhaps you'll decide to add another function, or you might find that more than one program needs one of the functions. This little investment of time up front will save you time down the road.

Another value of collecting a function into a single file becomes clear if you need to alter your information. Perhaps you have created a function that calculates sales tax for several different programs. But the sales tax rate changes from 7.5% to 7.75%. If you have a single function to calculate sales tax, you can change it just there as opposed to making the change in every program.

Testing the Program

When you finish writing program code with your structured format and your functions, you aren't completely done with the program. You must turn to the task of debugging the program, using the methods described in Hour 7, "Debugging Tools." You know that you need to eliminate as many bugs from the program as possible. You don't want the user of your program finding all kinds of mistakes that you made. Therefore, you must thoroughly test the program.

Knowing how to debug is only the first step in writing trouble-free programs. You already know what to do if bugs appear, but before you release a program for use, you need to ensure that you have put the program through thorough testing so that few, if any, bugs ever appear.

Here are the typical testing steps that programmers should follow before distributing a final version of a program to users:

1. Perform desk checking.

2. Perform a beta test.

3. Compare the results of the beta test against the old system's parallel test results.

Desk Checking

Most programmers go through a series of desk checks on their programs. *Desk checking* is the process of sitting in front of a computer and checking a program by using as many different data scenarios as possible to find weak spots and errors in the code. During desk checking, you should try extreme values, type bad input, and generally try your best to make the program fail. You should also try every option available in the program, using different combinations to see what happens in all situations.

Beta Testing

When desk checking is complete and you are as confident as you can be about the program's correctness, you should set up a group of users to try the program. This is known in the industry as the *beta testing* stage. The more beta testers (test users of the program) you find to test a program, the better the chance that errors will be found. Users often try things the programmer never thought of while writing the program.

Beta Testing Now Exists on a Grand Scale

More and more companies are openly inviting the public to help beta-test products. Microsoft, for example, is extremely open about distributing beta-test copies of its applications and operating systems long before the final release is available for sale. Most of these beta versions are available for download over the Internet. These beta-test products give reviewers and testers an early peek at the software, which also helps Microsoft because these testers can inform Microsoft about bugs they find.

As the beta audience grows, so does the time a company takes for the test. The problem is that today's software is highly complex, requiring as many as a few hundred programmers to produce a product as complicated as a new version of Windows. A large-scale beta test is about the only way that these companies can discover some of the bugs that must be fixed before such a product is released.

Parallel Testing

A user should never switch to a new program and abandon an old system right away. *Parallel testing* should be performed. For instance, if you write a payroll program to replace the manual payroll system for a dry cleaner, the dry cleaner shouldn't receive a copy of your program and then use only that. Instead, the dry cleaner should continue using its manual payroll system and use your program at the same time. Although this means that the payroll function takes a little longer each pay period, you can compare the results of the program with those of the manual system to see whether they match.

Only after several pay periods of well-matched parallel testing should the user feel confident enough to use the program without the manual backup.

During this testing period, programmers might have to make several changes to the program. Expect that changes will be necessary, and you won't feel disappointed or lose your programming confidence. Programmers rarely write a program correctly the first time. It usually takes many attempts to make programs correct. The thorough testing described in this section doesn't ensure a perfect program. Some errors might appear only after a program has been used for a while. The more testing you do, the less likely it is that errors will creep in later.

Profiling Code

A *profiler* is a program that monitors the execution of a program, looking for sluggish code that might be optimized for speed or size. Many of today's compilers are optimizing compilers that try to turn your code into the fastest possible machine code, but there is always room for improvement.

On average, 5% of a program takes 95% of the program's execution time. A profiler can help you improve the speed and efficiency of a program.

Advanced programming systems such as Visual C++ come with profiling tools that help you locate sluggish areas of a program. You cannot always speed up a program, but if parts of a program are slowing down the overall operation, you might be able to optimize the code to keep the program flowing smoothly. A profiler can also help you pinpoint when files get so large that faster disk drives and more memory might be beneficial to the operation of a program.

Getting Back to Programming

You're probably ready to get back into programming. That's good because it's time to do just that. You have now learned some important basics that many newcomers to programming never get. You know the importance of writing clear and concise code. You also know the importance of testing a program before you put the program into production, and you know how to debug any problems you might find.

The next lesson focuses on improving your programming skills by teaching you some fundamental programming topics such as data searching and sorting, as well as introducing some of Python's more advanced data types, such as lists and dictionaries.

Summary

The programming process requires more than sitting at the keyboard. Proper design is important, as are structured-programming techniques and proper testing. You and others can easily maintain a well-written program. Because of the changing world and the high maintenance requirements of programs, you should attempt to learn structured-programming techniques that help clarify programs. The three structured-programming constructs that you are now familiar with are sequence, decision, and looping. You also can save time and avoid repetition of code by creating functions.

The next hour explains some advanced programming concepts that you can apply to search for data as well as sort it. You'll then be ready to leave Python and move on to your next language, Java, as well as a key new topic: object-oriented programming.

Q&A

Q. How much testing is enough?

A. You can never test too much, but resources and the user's request for a program certainly bear on the decision to stop testing. If you know bugs exist in a program, you must remove them, and testing will help ensure that you've fixed all that you can fix.

Q. What tools are available to help me test my program?

A. Most of today's integrated debuggers are highly efficient at helping you spot and remove errors in your programs. You saw some of these in the previous hour, when you used Python's debugger to locate problems, examine values, and test programs.

Workshop

The quiz questions are provided for your further understanding.

Quiz

1. Why is the programming backlog still around?

2. Why do some programmers prefer to use and view pseudocode for logic design instead of flowcharts?

3. What is the opposite of spaghetti code?

4. What are the three structured-programming constructs?

5. Although it is not in Python, what statement do other programming languages use for branching?

6. Why can excessive branching be bad?

7. Write a function that takes an amount and calculates 6% sales tax on the amount and returns that value.

8. Which comes first: desk checking or beta testing?

9. What is the difference between parallel testing and beta testing?

10. What does a profiler do?

Answers

1. As computers are being used more and more, new programs need to be written, and older programs need to be updated.

2. Flowcharts can consume far too much space on paper for large systems and are cumbersome to draw.

3. The opposite of spaghetti code is clean, easily maintainable, well-structured code.

4. The three structured-programming constructs are sequence, decision, and looping.

5. The `goto` statement

6. Too much branching makes a program difficult to follow and maintain.

7. Your function might look slightly different, but as long as it gives the right answer, style is personal:

```
def function calculateTax(product):
    taxrate = .06
    tax = product * taxrate
    return (tax)
```

8. Desk checking must precede beta testing.

9. With parallel testing, the old system is used in conjunction with the new system, and the results of the two systems are compared.

10. A profiler analyzes a program for inefficient code.

HOUR 9
Programming Algorithms

In this hour, you will learn about programming algorithms that are common across all programming languages. An *algorithm* is a common procedure or methodology for performing a certain task. In mathematics, an algorithm provides a step-by-step method for solving a problem in a finite number of steps that can require some repetition. To keep things simple, in this hour you'll see algorithms in Python, but the concepts you'll learn here are important no matter which programming language you use.

You will learn how to use programs to count data values and accumulate totals. This technique has been touched on in earlier lessons, but this hour will formalize your understanding of the topic. The computer is a perfect tool for counting values such as the number of customers in a day, month, or year or the number of inventory items in a department's warehouse. A computer is capable of lightning-fast accumulations of totals. You can use a computer to easily determine the total amount of a weekly payroll or the total amount of your tax liability this year.

Computers are masterful at sorting and searching for data. When you sort data, you put it in alphabetical or numerical order. There are different methods for doing this, and this hour presents the most common one. There are also many ways to search a list of data for a specific value. You might give a computer a customer number, have it search a customer list, and then have it return the full name and account balance for that customer. Although computers are fast, it takes time to sift through thousands of data items, especially when searching through disk files (as the disk is much slower than memory). Therefore, it behooves you to gain some insight into some efficient means of performing a search.

After helping you master the sorting and searching techniques, this hour finishes by going a bit deeper with a topic you were introduced to in the last lesson: functions.

The highlights of this hour include the following:

▶ Counting with counter variables

▶ Storing data in array variables

▶ Totaling with accumulator variables

▶ Swapping the values of two variables

▶ Understanding ascending and descending sorts

- ▸ Using the bubble sort

- ▸ Searching for values in unsorted lists

- ▸ Using a binary search

- ▸ Using functions to divide the jobs in a program

- ▸ Nesting loops to improve a program's effectiveness

Counters and Accumulators

When you see a statement such as the following, what do you think?

```
number = number + 1
```

Your first impression might be that the statement isn't possible. After all, nothing can be equal to itself plus one. Take a second glance, however, and you will see that in a programming language such as Python, the equal sign acts like a left-pointing arrow. The assignment statement, in effect, says "Take whatever is on the right side of the equal sign, evaluate it, and put it in the variable to the left of the equal sign." Most other programming languages also use assignment statements that work like the Python assignment.

When Python reaches the statement just shown, it adds 1 to the contents in the variable named `number`. If `number` was equal to 7 to begin with, it is now equal to 8. After Python adds the 1 and gets 8, it then stores 8 in `number`, replacing the 7 that was originally there. The final result is one more than the initial value.

When you see a variable on both sides of an equal sign, and you are adding 1 to the variable, you are *incrementing* that variable's value. You might remember from earlier lessons that adding 1 to a variable is useful. Many programmers put such an assignment statement inside a loop to count items. The variable used is called a *counter*. Every time the loop repeats, 1 is added to the counter variable, incrementing it. When the loop finishes, the counter variable has the total of the loop.

Python (and other programming languages, such as C) have multiple ways to add 1 to a variable, and you've seen most of them already. Each of the following two statements adds 1 to the variable `count`:

```
count = count + 1;
```

```
count += 1;
```

As an added note, while you cannot use the following statement to increment a variable by 1 in Python, it does work in other languages, such as C and JavaScript:

```
count++;
```

For both choices that work with Python, they can add any number to your variable; you just need to change the 1 to the number you'd like to add. That includes integers or floating-point numbers. You can also add a variable in that spot as well, as the following line of code would add `newAmount` to `count`:

```
count += newAmount;
```

Subtracting 1 is just as easy. Again, the following two statements both subtract 1 from the variable `count`, and again you can subtract any number by replacing the 1 with that number:

```
count = count - 1;
```

```
count -= 1;
```

In languages other than Python, just as you can use `count++` to add 1, you can use `count--` to subtract 1 (but don't try this in Python, as it does support that operator).

TRY IT YOURSELF ▼

The program in Listing 9.1 uses a counter. The program lets the user keep guessing at a number until he or she guesses correctly. This program gives the user a hint about whether a guess is too low or too high, and it counts the number of guesses. The `tries` variable holds the count.

LISTING 9.1   A number-guessing game can use a counter variable

```
# Filename: guessinggame.py


# A program that generates a random
# number between 1 and 100 and then
# counts the number of guesses
# for the user to get it right



# The function to generate the random
# number is in the random module
import random


correctNum = random.randint(1,100)



# Initialize the number of guesses to 0
# Also set the guess being right tracker
```

```
# to N for the while loop


numGuesses = 0
guessRight = 'N'


print("It's time for the Python Guessing Game!")
print("How quick can you guess this number?")
print("It's between 1 and 100...")

# The loop will keep running until the guess is correct
while (guessRight == 'N'):

    # Get a guess and increment the number of guesses
    newGuess = int(input('What do you think the number is? '))
    numGuesses += 1

    # A series of if and elif statements comparing the guess
    # to the answer and will give a higher or lower hint

    if (newGuess > correctNum):
        print(newGuess, "is too large!")
        print("Try again!")
    elif (newGuess < correctNum):
        print(newGuess, "is too small!")
        print("Try again!")
    elif (newGuess == correctNum):
        print(newGuess, "is the right number!")
        print("Great job!")
        guessRight = 'Y'
print("It took only ", numGuesses, "guesses to get it right!")
```

Figure 9.1 shows a sample run of this program. Without the counter, the program would be unable to tell the user how many guesses have been tried.

```
It's time for the Python Guessing Game!
How quick can you guess this number?
It's between 1 and 100...
What do you think the number is? 65
65 is too small!
Try again!
What do you think the number is? 89
89 is too large!
Try again!
What do you think the number is? 77
77 is too small!
Try again!
What do you think the number is? 81
81 is too small!
Try again!
What do you think the number is? 85
85 is too large!
Try again!
What do you think the number is? 83
83 is too small!
Try again!
What do you think the number is? 84
84 is the right number!
Great job!
It took only  7 guesses to get it right!
```

FIGURE 9.1
The number-guessing game's counter keeps track of the number of tries.

Python Lists

Anytime you find yourself writing two or more sets of statements where the only differences are the variable names, you are probably not taking advantage of a better programming style. The program to check grades that you wrote in Hour 6, "Controlling Your Programs," was far more effective because you used lists for both the names of the students and their test scores.

TIP
_____
Another advantage to using lists for a set of similar variables is that you can take advantage of the powerful loop statements you learned in Hour 6. The goal of programming is to make your life simpler, not harder. Whenever you can put repetitive code into a loop, you save wear and tear on your fingers.
_____

Dictionaries

In Hour 6, you saw how to use lists to create a grading program. You created two lists—one with student names and another with the grades—and then printed the two, using the same index. This technique works well as long as you keep the two arrays aligned. Another way to handle this in Python is with a dictionary.

A *dictionary* is a collection of data with key/value pairs. It's easy to visualize if you consider an actual dictionary, which has words and then their definitions. The word is the key, and the definition is the value. If you were using Python to create a dictionary of the dictionary, it would look like this:

```
Webster = {"ant":"A small insect", "car":"a motor vehicle"}
```

A dictionary that defines only two words isn't the greatest, but you can make the dictionary as long as you want, and you can easily add additional entries. If you decided to add a third word to your Webster dictionary, you could easily do so, like this:

```
Webster["guitar"] = "a stringed musical instrument"
```

Now your dictionary has three elements. Unlike with strings or lists, you do not access an individual element by using a number; with a dictionary, you use the key. So if you want the definition of the third word, you don't use `Webster[2]`, as that generates an error message. You use `Webster["guitar"]`.

▼ TRY IT YOURSELF

Listing 9.2 shows a complete program for storing monthly sales totals. It creates a dictionary, asks for all the sales, and prints all the values. Without dictionaries, there isn't an easy way to duplicate this program, short of having 12 differently named sales variables and inputting them with 12 different statements.

LISTING 9.2   **This sales program stores data in a dictionary for each month**

```
# SalesTotals.py


# A program that initially creates a dictionary of months
# with 0 sales totals per month and then obtains the
# sales from the user, finally printing out values



# Dictionary created with the first six months and no sales
SalesMonths = {"Jan": 0, "Feb": 0, "Mar": 0, "Apr": 0, "May": 0, "Jun": 0}

# We forgot the second half of the year, so add them to the
dictionary
SalesMonths["Jul"] = 0
SalesMonths["Aug"] = 0
SalesMonths["Sep"] = 0
```

```
SalesMonths["Oct"] = 0
SalesMonths["Nov"] = 0
SalesMonths["Dec"] = 0


# Loop through all the months to get actual sales
for x in SalesMonths:
    Question = "What were the Sales in " + x + "? "
    SalesMonths[x] = float(input(Question))


# Print out the sales by month
print("\n\n")
for y in SalesMonths:
    print(y, SalesMonths[y])
```

Figure 9.2 shows the results of running Listing 9.2.

```
What were the Sales in Jan? 34
What were the Sales in Feb? 98
What were the Sales in Mar? 32
What were the Sales in Apr? 104
What were the Sales in May? 18
What were the Sales in Jun? 76
What were the Sales in Jul? 18
What were the Sales in Aug? 56
What were the Sales in Sep? 54
What were the Sales in Oct? 120
What were the Sales in Nov? 67
What were the Sales in Dec? 304


Jan 34.0
Feb 98.0
Mar 32.0
Apr 104.0
May 18.0
Jun 76.0
Jul 18.0
Aug 56.0
Sep 54.0
Oct 120.0
Nov 67.0
Dec 304.0
```

FIGURE 9.2
Looping through the dictionary prints the months and the sales.

The dictionary is initially created with the first six months of the year, and then a series of statements add the remaining six months. While the dictionary was initially created with 0 for each month's sales, you can loop through all the months and get the actual sales to update the value for each key.

Accumulators for Total

It's not terribly useful to just print the monthly sales total, so the program in Listing 9.3 adds the sales for the year as well as an average monthly sales total. You could take it even further and add quarterly totals or multi-year totals, but to do that, you'd need to specify the month and year in the keys as you cannot repeat keys in dictionaries. If you try to do so, you will just overwrite the previous entry.

LISTING 9.3   A sales-reporting and averaging program can use an accumulator for sales totals

```
# SalesTotals2.py

# A program that initially creates a dictionary of months
# with 0 sales totals per month and then obtains the
# sales from the user, finally printing out
# It then prints a total and an average


# Dictionary created with the first six months and no sales
SalesMonths = {"Jan": 0, "Feb": 0, "Mar": 0, "Apr": 0, "May": 0, "Jun": 0}

# We forgot the second half of the year, so add them to the dictionary
SalesMonths["Jul"] = 0
SalesMonths["Aug"] = 0
SalesMonths["Sep"] = 0
SalesMonths["Oct"] = 0
SalesMonths["Nov"] = 0
SalesMonths["Dec"] = 0

# Loop through all the months to get actual sales
for x in SalesMonths:
    Question = "What were the Sales in " + x + "? "
    SalesMonths[x] = float(input(Question))

# Print out the sales by month
print("\n\n")
for y in SalesMonths:
    print(y, SalesMonths[y])

# Calculate both total sales and average sales by month
TotYear = 0
Entries = 0
```

```
for y in SalesMonths:
    TotYear += SalesMonths[y]
    Entries += 1
print("Total year's sales were ", TotYear)
print("An average month's sales were ", (TotYear/Entries))
```

Figure 9.3 shows the results of running Listing 9.3.

```
What were the Sales in Jan? 34
What were the Sales in Feb? 98
What were the Sales in Mar? 32
What were the Sales in Apr? 104
What were the Sales in May? 18
What were the Sales in Jun? 76
What were the Sales in Jul? 18
What were the Sales in Aug? 56
What were the Sales in Sep? 54
What were the Sales in Oct? 120
What were the Sales in Nov? 67
What were the Sales in Dec? 304


Jan 34.0
Feb 98.0
Mar 32.0
Apr 104.0
May 18.0
Jun 76.0
Jul 18.0
Aug 56.0
Sep 54.0
Oct 120.0
Nov 67.0
Dec 304.0
Total year's sales were  981.0
An average month's sales were  81.75
```

FIGURE 9.3
You can use accumulator variables to calculate totals and averages.

The program in Listing 9.3 is almost the same as the one in Listing 9.2. The major difference is that Listing 9.3 totals all sales, prints that out, and calculates an average. This is a common method of development: adding functionality to a program that works. When you know a program works, you can add a little bit more and ensure that is still works. Users of a program may reach out and say, "this is great, but could it also…," and then you have to decide whether to put the time in to add the code needed to make it do more.

Swapping Values

The cornerstone of any sorting algorithm is data swapping. As you sort data, you have to rearrange it, swapping higher values for lower values. As Figure 9.4 shows, swapping values simply means replacing one variable's contents with another's and vice versa.

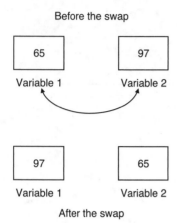

Before the swap

| 65 | | 97 |

Variable 1   Variable 2

| 97 | | 65 |

Variable 1   Variable 2

After the swap

FIGURE 9.4
Swapping the values of two variables.

Suppose you assigned two variables named `variable1` and `variable2` with the following statements:

```
variable1 = 65
variable2 = 97
```

How would you swap these variables? It's simple:

```
variable1 = variable2
variable2 = variable1
```

Can you see why these two assignment statements don't swap the values in the two variables? The first statement assigns `variable2` to `variable1`, which wipes out `variable1`'s original value. The second statement is then redundant because after the first statement, both variables already hold the same value.

An accurate approach to swapping variables is to use a third variable, often called a *temporary variable* because you don't use its value after you swap the original variables. Here is the code to perform the swapping accurately:

```
temp = variable1
variable1 = variable2
variable2 = temp
```

Sorting

The following list of numbers isn't sorted:

```
10
54
34
21
23
```

Here is the list sorted in *ascending order* (from lowest to highest):

```
10
21
23
34
54
```

Here is the list sorted in *descending order* (from highest to lowest):

```
54
34
23
21
10
```

You can also sort character string data, such as a list of names. Here is a list of five sorted names (unless otherwise specified, an ascending sort is always used):

```
Adams, Jim
Fowler, Lisa
Kingston, William
Stephenson, Mike
Williams, Pete
```

Using the Bubble Sort

There are several ways to sort lists of data. The most popular one for beginning programmers is to use the *bubble sort*. The bubble sort isn't the most efficient sorting algorithm. As a matter of fact, it is one of the slowest. However, the bubble sort, unlike other sorting algorithms (such as the heap sort and the quick sort) is easy to understand and to program.

NOTE
___
Lists in Python actually have a `sort()` function built right in! But how will you learn anything if you just use the built-in methods?
___

In Python, the data that you want to sort is typically stored in a list. Using the list subscripts, you can rearrange the array elements, swapping values until the list is sorted in the order you want.

In the bubble sort, the elements of an array are compared and swapped two at a time. Your program must perform several passes through the list before it is sorted. During each pass through the list, the bubble sort places the lowest value in the first element of the array. In effect, the smaller values "bubble" their way up the list—hence the name *bubble sort*.

After the first pass of the bubble sort (which is controlled by an outer loop in a nested `for` loop, as you will see in the following program), the lowest value, 10, is still at the top of the array (as it happened to be there already). In the second pass, 21 is placed right after the 10 and so on until no more swaps take place.

▼ TRY IT YOURSELF

The program in Listing 9.4 shows the bubble sort used on the five values shown earlier.

LISTING 9.4   You can sort a list of values with the bubble sort

```
# Filename bubblesort.py
# Uses the bubble sort algorithm to sort a
# set of values

values = [10, 54, 34, 21, 23]
temp = 0

# Outer loop
for x in range(len(values)):
    # Inner loop for comparisons
    for ctr in range(len(values)-1):
        if (values[ctr] > values [ctr+1]):
            temp = values[ctr]
            values[ctr] = values[ctr+1]
            values[ctr+1] = temp;

print("Here is the loop after sorting...");
print(values)
```

Here is the output from the program in Listing 9.4:

```
Here is the array after being sorted...
[10, 21, 23, 34, 54]
```

Analyzing the Bubble Sort

To give you a better understanding of the bubble sort routine used in this program, Figure 9.5 shows a flowchart of the bubble sort process. By using the flowchart and by following the program, you should be able to trace through the bubble sort and better understand how it works. At the heart of any sorting algorithm is a swapping routine, and you can see one in the body of the bubble sort's `for` loops.

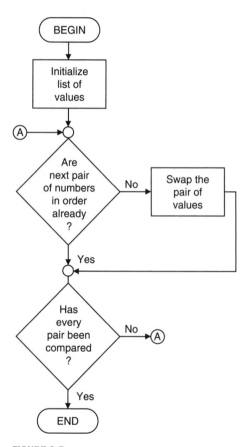

FIGURE 9.5
The flowchart of the bubble sort routine shows the swapping of values.

If you really want to see the bubble sort in action, you can add `print()` statements to your program to see a printout of the list before the sort begins and also see a printout after each step along the way. It can get a little tedious to see a printout after each step of the sort, but adding the print lines to Listing 9.4 would result in the following code:

```
# Filename bubblesort.py
# Uses the bubble sort algorithm to sort a
# set of values

values = [10, 54, 34, 21, 23]
temp = 0

# Outer loop
print("Here is the loop before sorting...")
print(values)

for x in range(len(values)):
    # Inner loop for comparisons
    for ctr in range(len(values)-1):
        if (values[ctr] > values [ctr+1]):
            temp = values[ctr]
            values[ctr] = values[ctr+1]
            values[ctr+1] = temp
        print("Here is the loop as the sort continues...")
        print(values)

print("Here is the loop after sorting...")
print(values)
```

Running the updated program would yield the following output:

```
Here is the loop before sorting...
[10, 54, 34, 21, 23]
Here is the loop as the sort continues...
[10, 54, 34, 21, 23]
Here is the loop as the sort continues...
[10, 34, 54, 21, 23]
Here is the loop as the sort continues...
[10, 34, 21, 54, 23]
Here is the loop as the sort continues...
[10, 34, 21, 23, 54]
Here is the loop as the sort continues...
[10, 34, 21, 23, 54]
Here is the loop as the sort continues...
[10, 21, 34, 23, 54]
Here is the loop as the sort continues...
[10, 21, 23, 34, 54]
```

```
Here is the loop as the sort continues...
[10, 21, 23, 34, 54]
Here is the loop as the sort continues...
[10, 21, 23, 34, 54]
Here is the loop as the sort continues...
[10, 21, 23, 34, 54]
Here is the loop as the sort continues...
[10, 21, 23, 34, 54]
Here is the loop as the sort continues...
[10, 21, 23, 34, 54]
Here is the loop as the sort continues...
[10, 21, 23, 34, 54]
Here is the loop as the sort continues...
[10, 21, 23, 34, 54]
Here is the loop as the sort continues...
[10, 21, 23, 34, 54]
Here is the loop as the sort continues...
[10, 21, 23, 34, 54]
Here is the loop as the sort continues...
[10, 21, 23, 34, 54]
Here is the loop as the sort continues...
[10, 21, 23, 34, 54]
Here is the loop as the sort continues...
[10, 21, 23, 34, 54]
Here is the loop as the sort continues...
[10, 21, 23, 34, 54]
Here is the loop after sorting...
[10, 21, 23, 34, 54]
```

TIP
_____

If you want a descending sort, you only have to change one statement in Listing 9.4's program—the first statement inside the `for` loops. Instead of swapping the values if the second item of the pair is lower, you can swap them if the second item of the pair is higher. The new line looks like this:

```
if (values[ctr] < values[ctr + 1])
```
_____

Searching Lists

There are many ways to search lists for a specific value. Suppose you have several parallel lists with inventory data. The first list, `partNo[]`, holds all your inventory item part numbers. The second list, `desc[]`, holds a description of each of those parts. The third list, `price[]`, contains the price of each corresponding part. You might keep all the inventory data in the cloud and then read that data into the parallel arrays when it is time to work with the data.

One use for an inventory program that uses parallel lists is a lookup routine. A user could type a part number, and the computer program would search the partNo[] list for a match. When it finds one (for example, at element subscript number 246), you could then print the 246th element in the desc[] and price[] arrays to show the user the description and price of the part number just entered.

There are several ways to search a list for values. The various searching methods each have own advantages. One of the easiest to program and understand, the *sequential search*, is also one of the least efficient. The search method you decide on depends on how much data you expect to search through and how skilled you are at understanding and writing advanced searching programs. The next few sections walk you through some introductory searching algorithms that you might use someday in the programs you write.

NOTE
Again, as with sorting, in Python, lists, sets, tuples, and dictionaries have built-in methods to make searching easier, but the point of this exercise is to get you to figure out how to write code to solve a problem.

Performing the Sequential Search

The sequential search technique is easy but inefficient. With it, you start at the beginning of the list and look at each value, in sequence, until you find a value in the list that matches the value for which you are searching. (You then can use the subscript of the matching element to look in corresponding parallel lists for related data.)

TIP
The list being searched doesn't have to be sorted for the sequential search to work. The fact that sequential searches work on unsorted lists makes them more useful than if they required sorted lists because you don't have to take the processing time (or programming time) to sort a list before each search.

Figure 9.6 shows a flowchart of the sequential search routine. As with most of the other flow-charts in this hour, only the new technique—in this case, the sequential search routine—is described, not the now-trivial task of filling the array with data through disk input/output (I/O) or user input. Study the flowchart and see if you can think of ways to improve the searching technique being used.

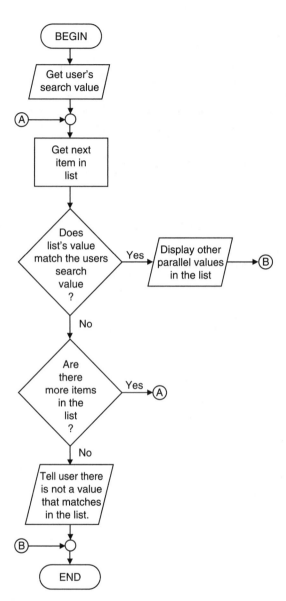

FIGURE 9.6
Flowcharting the sequential search technique.

▼ TRY IT YOURSELF

The program in Listing 9.5 shows the sequential search algorithm coded in Python. The inventory lists described earlier are used in the program. Each list has five items, which would surely be only a partial listing in a store, but it is enough to let you work through the search. After typing in the program, test several of the item numbers as well as some numbers not in the list. When you study the program, you should find that the sequential search is very easy to understand.

LISTING 9.5 **A sequential search can help an inventory application**

```python
# Filename: searchseq.py

# Sequential search for an item's description and price.

# This code would be part of a larger inventory program.

# This program assumes that the variable named TotalNumber
# contains the total number of items in the inventory,
# and therefore, in the lists as well.

TotalNumber = 5
partNo = [34, 87, 12, 99, 40]
desc = ["mouse", "printer", "monitor", "keyboard", "graphics card"]
price = [19.99, 49.50, 99.99, 35.00, 103.75]

# First, get the part number the user wants to look up
searchPt = int(input("What is the number of the part you want to see? "))


foundPart = 0 # a flag to know if the part is found

# Look through all inventory items
for i in range(TotalNumber):
    if (partNo[i] == searchPt):
        print("Part Number:",searchPt)
        print("Description:", desc[i])
        print("With a price of $", price[i])
```

```
          #Turn on the flag
          foundPart = 1;
          break;


#  Now check the found part flag to see whether we found the part
if (foundPart == 0):
     print("** Sorry, but that part number is not in the inventory.")
```

Performing the Binary Search

If your list is already sorted, you can use another technique that offers tremendous searching speed advantages over the sequential search shown in the previous section. This technique is known as the *binary search*. The binary search is more complex to understand and program than the sequential search, but, as with most other things in the programming world, it is worth the effort in many cases.

The binary search technique uses a divide-and-conquer approach for searching. One of the primary advantages of the binary search is that with every comparison you make, you can rule out one-half of the remaining array if a match isn't found. In other words, if you are searching for a value in a 100-element list, and the first comparison you make fails to match, you only have at most 50 elements left to search; with the sequential search, you would still have a possible 99 elements left to search. On the second search, assuming that there is no match, you rule out one-half of the remaining list, meaning that there are only 25 more items to search through.

The multiplicative advantages of a binary search will surprise you. If you have a friend write down a number from 1 to 1,000 and then use the binary search technique to make your guesses (your friend will only have to tell you if you are "too low" or "too high" with each guess), you can often zero in on the number in 5 to 15 tries. This is an amazing feat when there is a pool of 1,000 numbers to choose from!

The binary search technique is simple. Your first guess (or the computer's first try at matching a search value to one in the list) should be exactly in the middle of the sorted list. If you guess incorrectly, you only need to know if you were too high or too low. If you were too high, your next guess should split the lower half of the list. If you were too low, you should split the higher half of the list. Your new list (one-half the size of the original one) is now the list you split in the middle. Repeat the process until you guess the value.

Suppose your friend thinks of the number 390. Your first guess would be 500 (half of 1,000). When your friend says "too high," you would immediately know that your next guess should be between 1 and 499. Splitting that range takes you to your second guess, 250. "Too low," replies your friend, so you know the number is between 251 and 499. Splitting that gives you 375. "Too low" means the number is between 376 and 499. Your next guess might be 430, then 400, then 390—and you've guessed it. One out of 1,000 numbers, and it only took six guesses.

Listing 9.6 uses the binary search technique to find the correct inventory value. As you can see from the code, a binary search technique doesn't require a very long program. However, when you first learn the binary search, it takes some getting used to. Therefore, the flowchart in Figure 9.7 will help you understand the binary search technique a little better.

LISTING 9.6   A binary search can speed searching tremendously

```python
# Filename: searchbin.py

# Binary search for an item's description and price.
# (This assumes the arrays have been filled
# and SORTED in PartNum order elsewhere.)

#   This code would be part of a larger inventory program.
# ** This program assumes that the variable named TotalNumber
# contains the total number of items in the inventory,
# and therefore, in the arrays as well.

# for testing, here is the same parts as before, just in correct order
TotalNumber = 5
PartNo = [12, 34, 40, 87, 99]
Desc = ["monitor", "mouse", "keyboard", "printer", "graphics card"]
price = [99.99, 19.99, 35.00, 49.50, 103.75]

# First, get the part number the user wants to look up

searchPt = int(input('What is the number of the part you want to see? '))

first = 0 # Set the lower bound of your search
last = TotalNumber - 1 # The upperbound of the search
found = 0 # The flag that the part was found

while (first <= last):
    mid = int((first + last) / 2) # Set the middle and make it an int
    if (searchPt == PartNo[mid]):
        print("Part number", searchPt, "'s description is ")
        print(Desc[mid])
        print("With a price of $",price[mid])
        found = 1 # Turn the flag on
        break # Exit the while loop
    elif (searchPt < PartNo[mid]): # Check the lower half of the array
        last = mid - 1
    else:
        first = mid + 1 # Check the upper half of the array

if (found == 0): # The part was not in the array
    print("** Sorry, but that part number is not in the inventory.")
```

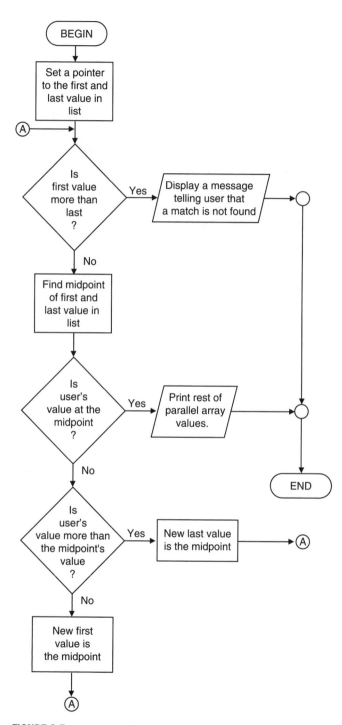

FIGURE 9.7
Flowcharting the binary search.

Taking Functions Further

User-created functions, introduced in Hour 6, deserve a bit more discussion. A function is like a detour; it is a side trip your program makes for a few statements, often to accomplish a specific task, and then the program gets back on the path it was executing and continues from there.

The function is a set of code that works as a unit, as a method works. Functions (also called *subroutines* in some programming languages) are available for all languages, and they aren't difficult to understand. The algorithms presented in this hour make perfect candidates for functions. A function turns your program into a collection of modules that you can integrate. Instead of being one long program, your program becomes lots of little sets (functions) of code.

Understanding the Need for Subroutines

Suppose you're writing a program that prints your name and address several times. Without using a function, you would write code similar to the snippet shown in Listing 9.7. The program repeats the same printing code over and over.

LISTING 9.7   A program outline that doesn't use functions can be hard to maintain

```
# Long program that prints name and address throughout
#   (The rest of the code is not shown.)

# # Program statements go here

print("Mark Cunningham")
print("1244 West Oak")
print("Canton, NH 63443")

#   More program statements go here

print("Mark Cunningham")
print("1244 West Oak")
print("Canton, NH 63443")

#   More program statements go here

print("Mark Cunningham")
print("1244 West Oak")
print("Canton, NH 63443")

#   More program statements go here

print("Mark Cunningham")
print("1244 West Oak")
print("Canton, NH 63443")

# Rest of program finishes up here
```

CAUTION

Not only is repeating the same code tedious, but by requiring more typing, it is extremely susceptible to errors. If you only have to type in the code once but can execute that code repeatedly whenever you want (as in a function), your chances of making typing errors decrease. Also, if your address ever changes, you only have to change it in one place (inside the subroutine) rather than everywhere it appears in the program.

If you put `print()` statements in a function, you can save yourself some typing. It also becomes easier to transfer the code to another program. All you need to do is write the function and then call it as often as you like.

Listing 9.8 is an improved version of the previous program. Notice that a statement begins the subroutine's name and address printing code. This is a label that you make up that names the subroutine's location.

LISTING 9.8   A program outline that uses functions is simple

```
# Function Example

def function printAddress():
"Here's where we print the address"
      print("Mark Cunningham")
      print("1244 West Oak")
      print("Canton, NH 63443")
      return
         }


# Long program that prints name and address throughout
# (The rest of the code is not shown.)


# Program statements go here

printAddress() # Runs the function

# More program statements go here

printAddress() # Runs the function

# More program statements go here


printAddress() # Runs the function

# More program statements go here
```

TIP

As mentioned in Hour 8, "Structured Techniques," you can put your commonly used functions in a separate `.py` file that you can then import into any other Python file that needs to use those functions.

▼ TRY IT YOURSELF

The purpose of creating a function is to be able to execute the same block of code more than once. Grouping a routine into a function makes a lot of sense; it helps organize your program. Listing 9.9 shows a complete program with three functions. The subroutines perform the following tasks:

1. Ask the user for a list of numbers.

2. Sort the numbers.

3. Print the numbers.

As you can see, the first part of the program is nothing more than a calling procedure that controls the execution of the functions. By breaking your program into functions as this program does, you can more easily zero in on code later if you want to change something. If you want to change to a different sorting method, you can quickly find the sorting routine without having to trace through a bunch of unrelated code.

LISTING 9.9   Using functions makes a program easier to maintain and understand

```python
# Filename: usefulFunctions.py


# Collection of functions that can be used
# in different programs that need to
# utilize data collection, sorting, and
# printing

# Get the values to sort
def askForData(values, size):
    for i in range(size):
        values.append(float(input("Enter a number: ")))
    return


# The sort function
def sortData(values,size):

    for x in range(size):
```

```
          for ctr in range(size - 1):
              if (values[ctr] > values[ctr+1]):
                  temp = values[ctr];
                  values[ctr] = values[ctr+1];
                  values[ctr+1] = temp;

def printData(values, size):
    for i in range(size):
        print(values[i])

# Filename functionProgram.py

# Uses the program functions to
# get a set of values and then sort them



import usefulFunctions

numSize = int(input("How many values do you want to enter? "))
numberSet = []

usefulFunctions.askForData(numberSet, numSize)

print("Before sorting...")
usefulFunctions.printData(numberSet, numSize)

usefulFunctions.sortData(numberSet, numSize)

print("After sorting...")
usefulFunctions.printData(numberSet, numSize)
```

TIP

By asking users how many numbers they want to enter, the program has far more value than a program that can only sort a set number of values. Printing the numbers before and after the sort shows the value of functions, as you've called the function twice in the program but had to write the code only once.

Nested Loops

As with almost all other statements, you can nest two or more loops inside one another. Several listings in this hour, including Listing 9.9, have done just that. As a programmer, you must make sure you understand the concept of nested loops. Anytime your program needs to repeat a loop more than once, use a *nested loop*. Think of the inside loop as looping "faster" than the outside loop. The inside loop iterates faster because the counter variable of the inside loop goes through all its iterations before the outside loop's first iteration has completed. The outside loop doesn't repeat until its block of code is complete. When the outside loop finally does iterate a second time, the inside loop starts all over again.

So, if you have an outer loop that is set to run 5 times and an inner loop that is set to run 10 times, the inner loop executes a total of 50 times. The outside loop iterates 5 times, and the inside loop executes 10 times for each iteration of the outer loop.

Summary

The techniques you learned in this hour will be useful throughout your programming career. Sorting, searching, and functions are needed for useful data processing. The computer, thanks to your programs, can do these mundane tasks while you concentrate on more important things.

The next hour gives you a break from algorithms and shows you how to write some programs that use graphics. Programming can be fun, and graphics are quite possibly the most fun part of programming.

Q&A

Q. How do functions improve a program's accuracy?

A. A program is easier to write and maintain when you group routine code into functions. The functions help you focus on specific parts of the program that you need to change or fix if bugs exist in the code. When your program is composed of small routines, in functions, you make your code more modular, which helps ensure that code in one part of the program doesn't affect code in another part of the program.

Workshop

The quiz questions are provided for your further understanding.

Quiz

1. What is an accumulator?

2. True or false: The following statement is an accumulator statement:

   ```
   num = num - 1
   ```

3. What is the difference between the terms *ascending sort* and *descending sort*?

4. Why is a third variable needed when you want to swap the values of two variables?

5. Which sort is the easiest to write and understand?

6. True or false: A counter statement is a special kind of accumulator statement.

7. What is the simplest kind of search technique?

8. Which is more efficient: the binary search or the sequential search?

9. Write a function that doubles a number, adds 2, and returns the new value.

10. True or false: Using functions prevents you from typing the same code over and over throughout a program.

Answers

1. An accumulator is a variable whose value is updated.

2. False. Although the statement might actually be using an accumulator variable, the statement happens to be decreasing the value stored there, whereas accumulators are usually added to.

3. An ascending sort puts lists in order from low to high, and a descending sort puts lists in order from high to low.

4. The third variable is needed to hold one of the values temporarily.

5. The bubble sort is one of the simplest sorts to write and understand.

6. True

7. A sequential search is the simplest type of search.

8. The binary search is far more efficient than the sequential search.

9. Your answer might be slightly different but this is one possible answer:

```
def changenumber(x):
        var y = x * 2
        z = y + 2
        return (z)
```

10. True

HOUR 10
Programming with Java

The Java language is a shapeshifter that has been used for three dramatically different purposes in its 25-year history.

First, it was a simple language perfectly suited to running on embedded devices such as appliances and as small programs embedded on web pages.

Next, it grew into a sophisticated general-purpose language that ran on web servers, powering websites, relational databases, and other Internet servers behind the scenes.

Finally, it has become a mobile language for creating apps, small programs that run on phones and tablets using the Android operating system. There are a staggering number of devices in the world running Java programs—more than 3 billion—and many of them are the phones we carry with us all day long.

NOTE
One of the most popular games in the world over the past few years, Minecraft, was written in Java!

For this introductory hour, it will be most instructive to go back to Java's roots and see how it got started as a killer way to add some interactivity to the web.

The world of web pages gained an unexpected boost in capabilities when the Java language was introduced in 1995. Originally designed to be used for devices such as digital TV set-top boxes, Java became the first widely available language used to make web pages dynamic with animation, games, and other constantly updated content. Java almost single-handedly rescued us from static web pages and turned the web into an interactive medium where users can interact with changing web pages.

Although today there are many other tools for making the web more interactive, including HTML5 and JavaScript, Java can still be used to create web pages that run like standalone computer programs. Despite its capabilities, Java is simple to learn. The inventors of Java used C and C++ as a model for their language. Java is no longer a small language, but it is an extremely robust one for creating programs that work without modification on many kinds of computers, phones, tablets, and other devices.

The highlights of this hour include the following:

▶ Seeing what Java is all about

▶ Running Java programs that travel with web pages

▶ Understanding the need for small Java programs

▶ Comparing Java to other languages

▶ Compiling Java programs

▶ Extending the built-in Java classes for your Java programs

Introducing Java

Colorful web browsers brought the Internet to the world by taking it out of the exclusive hands of scientific, military, and educational researchers. The new web browsers made the Internet accessible to everybody, with simple navigational tools and an appealing graphical nature. Soon, millions of users all over the world were jumping from one website to another in a global medium of text, images, and hyperlinks.

Browsers filled the job requirements better than anyone could have imagined but grew stale due to the static nature of web pages. Despite the colorful and cross-linked pages that browsers made available to the world, the pages did not have enough action in them to keep users occupied. Browser technology was too static to make websites truly come alive.

NOTE

Think about this: As PCs became faster, became more graphical, and began supporting multimedia, viewing only pictures and text, which was at first unique online, became dull quickly. Users needed more interaction to keep their attention when online.

Users wanted more from the Internet than just a distributed set of interconnected graphical screens. Despite the web's hypertext nature, those hypertext links simply take you from one page to another, without doing any work for you except eliminating the need to type long web page addresses. Users want real computing power coming at them from the websites they visit. For example, instead of reading cooking recipe, you might want to see the food being cooked by an expert or take an introductory, graphical tutorial on the steps required to make that food.

Java, developed by Sun Microsystems in the mid-1990s and managed today by Oracle (by its acquisition of Sun in 2010), changed the way that websites operate. Java is a programming language with language features similar to those of C++. Fortunately, Java also contains many language features that are similar to those of Python, such as the `for` loop, the `if` statement, and the `while` loop.

Java's Overnight Success

Upon its launch in 1995, Java was designed to be a better C++ than C++. Both C++ and Java are efficient programming languages that you can use to write almost any computer application. Java's initial emphasis, though, was online, Internet programming. Java was a small and efficient language, with safeguards in place to add security to online programs that C++ simply couldn't handle.

Today, Java works in many environments; some programmers develop large, complex applications in Java, and those applications have nothing to do with the Internet. Java's similarity to the already popular C++ language helped ensure rapid acceptance and usage in the programming world.

Instead of using web browsers to view data, with Java capabilities, browsers now can seamlessly download programs written in Java and execute those programs on the end user's computer as opposed to the remote server serving up the web page. When you view a Java-enabled web page, you see the usual graphical page, and you are also able to interact with Java programs that run on your own computer, brought to your computer via the web's connection.

Originally, you could write four kinds of Java programs, although one version is not so common anymore:

- ▶ *Java applets* are small programs that travel with web page code and execute on the web user's computer. Java applets were deprecated in the 2017 release of Java 9 and removed from Java SE 11, which was released in 2018.

NOTE

In the world of technology, *deprecate* means to no longer support. This term is occasionally used in programming to refer to a statement or function that was common in earlier releases of a language but is no longer the best choice in a later version (often because a new method of completing the task has been created, or the old way posed security risks), so the former method is deprecated.

- ▶ *Java applications* are complete standalone programs that don't require a web browser to execute.

- ▶ *Java servlets* are programs that run on a web server and are delivered to users as web pages.

- ▶ *Java apps* are small programs that run on smartphones and other mobile devices that run the Android operating system.

The first Java programs appeared as Java applets. The original goal of Java was to place executable code on web pages so that users could interact with websites in more compelling and attention-getting ways. As Java became more popular, programmers began using Java to write standalone programs that executed without the need for web browsers. For example, if you want to write a rental property management application that runs independently of an Internet connection, you can use Java to develop the application.

Java Provides Executable Content

NOTE

As mentioned earlier, Java applets are not really created any more, but it is still instructive to understand how they used to work in order to understand how Java has evolved as a programming language.

When working with Java, you'll often hear and read about *executable content*. Executable content is what Java is really all about. A web page contains executable content via web commands in the form of a Java applet. Any web page's content is executable on the target user's computer. Figure 10.1 provides an overview of a web document with two embedded Java applets. The language behind web pages is called *HTML*, and you'll learn more about it in Hour 13, "HTML5 and CSS3."

FIGURE 10.1
HTML serves up Java's executable content.

When the user enters the URL that displays the page shown in Figure 10.1 (or when the user clicks hypertext links to navigate to the page), the user's web-browsing software loads the HTML code, formats the page's text according to the HTML commands, displays any graphics images that appear on the page, and loads the executable content (as applets). The executable content executes either immediately or upon the occurrence of a predetermined event, such as a mouse click on the web page.

The best method of running Java applets is not always obvious to the user. When an applet is providing animation, the look of that animation is smooth because the animation program runs on the user's computer. Because of the applet, the speed of the animation is not dependent on the download time or on Internet traffic.

Before Java-enabled web pages, the user did have some interaction with the remote site. However, that interaction was severely limited. Web page animation was controlled by the user's animation software. If a computer system had no software that could display animation, that feature of the web page was unavailable to that system's user. If the user wanted to interact with the remote site in a question-and-answer session, such as order taking, the user often had to fill in the form completely before error checking could be done to any of the user's responses. The user would have to trigger any and all interactions with the remote site; the response would then be limited by the remote site's speed and the current traffic flow on the Internet.

NOTE

The first way that web pages took user input was through simple forms that were transmitted using the *CGI* (*Common Gateway Interface*). When you go to a website's Contact Us page and use the form to provide your name, email address, and a comment and then click a Send button to submit it, there's a program collecting and transmitting that information with the CGI. These programs are not usually Java applets. But some of them might be servlets, the programs mentioned earlier that are run by web servers.

Seamless Execution

Surely you have traveled to a website, downloaded software, and then logged off to execute that software. Java applets do this without requiring that you ever leave your browser. When you travel to a remote site, the Java applet runs without you doing anything at all. In addition, the software applet automatically downloads itself to your PC, runs when you trigger its execution, and then goes away when you leave the website, without taking up permanent disk space. Think of the possibilities for software developers; users can test-drive your software without running an installation program and without needing to remove the software when the demonstration concludes.

Multi-Platform Executable Content

Now that you know how Java-enabled websites appear to the user, think about the requirements of such executable content. When you write a Java-based web page, you want the code to work on the user's computer no matter what kind of computer the user operates.

Most language compilers, such as Visual C++, turn programs into machine-dependent executable programs, but Java development tools don't go quite that far. All Java compilers translate your Java code into a special machine-independent module. The Java compiler first compiles the code into an in-between stage called *bytecode*. Your Java-enabled web-browsing software then translates this compiled bytecode into instructions that your computer executes.

No computer can directly read bytecode, but each computer's Java-enabled browser can. In other words, given a Java applet's bytecode, a PC can run the applet using a web browser, and an Android tablet can run that very same bytecode by using its own Java-enabled browser. All modern browsers can run Java applets with an enhancement offered by Oracle called the Java plug-in, including Google Chrome, Microsoft Edge, Mozilla Firefox, and Apple Safari. The Java plug-in is a computer-within-a-computer called the Java Virtual Machine (JVM) that interprets the machine-dependent bytecode and translates that bytecode into machine-specific instructions that a particular computer can understand (see Figure 10.2).

Running Java on a Virtual Machine

Figure 10.2 shows the Java compilation/translation scenario. You use the Java language to produce bytecode for a *virtual machine*, not for a specific machine, because the bytecode is machine independent. The JVM is not a particular kind of computer but is an imaginary computer. Each computer must have a virtual machine interpreter to run Java code. The interpreter translates the compiled bytecode into specific instructions for that computer. Therefore, the Java compiler doesn't have to compile for any one computer; it just has to compile bytecode for the virtual machine. The bytecode is sent to the web page that is to contain the applet, and when the user requests that web page, the user's web browser reads the bytecode and automatically interprets the bytecode into code that is readable by the user's computer. The user is unaware that all this took place; the web page is displayed, and the executing applet is seen, along with the rest of the web page's content.

FIGURE 10.2
Your Java session produces compiled bytecode that a computer's JVM translates to run the program.

The web browser automatically runs the Java applet. Some applets run automatically, and some run in response to a user event such as a mouse click. It's important that you realize that the user doesn't necessarily know or care that a small program is running. To the user, the Java-based web page simply does more than one without Java. The page usually responds much more quickly—as quickly as the user's computer can translate the Java bytecode into executable content. All traces of the program go away when the applet ends or when the user leaves the web page.

All Java programs are compiled into bytecode and run by a JVM on a user's computer. If you use Java to design a program that must be downloaded and installed by a user, that computer must have a virtual machine. Oracle has a website where people can see if they have one installed. Visit www.java.com in a web browser and look for a "Do I Have Java?" link.

Java Usage Summary

As a newcomer to Java technology, you might appreciate a summary of the process you go through when viewing a Java-enabled web page with a Java-aware web browser. Here are the steps that occur:

1. In a web browser, you enter the URL of a Java-enabled website.

2. The serving computer sends the web page, in HTML format, to your web browser.

3. The HTML-based document's commands inform your web browser of the web page's Java-based executable content.

4. Your web browser downloads graphics images from the server if any graphics appear on the web page.

5. Depending on how the Java applet is to be triggered (either automatically or by a user's event), the server also sends the bytecode to your computer when the time is right.

6. Your browser's Java plug-in interprets the bytecode and executes the Java-executable content.

7. When you leave the web page, the executable content goes away. (Some web browsers keep the Java code in memory for a while, in case you return to the page.)

The previous steps are based on the user's perspective, but this is also a good time to explain what you, the Java programmer, go through to create web pages with Java applets. Here are the general steps you follow:

1. Start your Java programming environment.

2. Write the Java applet.

3. Create the HTML web page that will contain the Java applet. Use appropriate HTML commands to indicate the applet and its parameters.

4. Compile the Java applet. Your Java development environment may offer a way to place the applet in its appropriate location for the HTML web page that will contain the applet.

5. If the compiler finds errors, fix them and recompile the file.

6. Test and debug the applet.

7. Store the applet and HTML on your web server, where they await a user's request.

Start with Standalone Java

Although up to this point you've learned about Java applets rather than using Java for standalone applications, you won't be learning Java from the applet perspective going forward. With Java applets deprecated, you'll find that it only makes sense to learn Java by mastering the standalone Java language. You will also use Java as the basis for learning object-oriented programming.

The Java language wasn't originally intended to be a competitor to C++ and the other languages people use to write non-web, standalone applications, but Java has surpassed its authors' hopes and dreams and become a major competitor in the programming language field.

Developers quickly learned that Java is a great language. Standalone Java applications run from a program window and not from a web browser, as Java applets used to do. A Java application looks and acts just like any application written in any traditional programming language.

When Is Java Not Java?

Although JavaScript and Java have similar names and a few of their commands and operators overlap, JavaScript is little like Java. Even though both work inside the HTML of web pages, add interactivity to web pages, and share some language elements, JavaScript is deployed differently than Java and generally serves different purposes.

JavaScript began as a small language used for causing buttons and other web page elements to move and change in response to mouse clicks and keypresses. JavaScript also enables you to create menus and other interactive web page features. It later was put to use creating Asynchronous JavaScript and XML (AJAX) applications that function like static web pages but pull data dynamically in response to user input. But you cannot write JavaScript applications that stand by themselves outside the web pages encompassing them. Java is a more powerful, complex language that can be used on full-blown standalone applications or applets.

Java's Interface

Java's interface elements—items such as check boxes and command buttons—can take on different appearances to match different computer platforms or can look the same on all of them. This is referred to as the program's *look and feel*. Programs can look the same on Macs as they do on

Windows computers. When other languages are used (such as C++), interface elements typically take on the parent computer's operating system style. If you really want your Java programs to achieve the specific look of a particular operating system, such as Microsoft Windows 10, you can designate a look and feel for your program that takes on the operating system's style.

Over time, Java has become even more portable across different kinds of hardware. With each major release (13 so far), the Java language grows, adding a richer set of supporting libraries so you code less and get more done faster. Using these libraries, programmers can more easily maintain Java software because less coding means less work when a change must be made to a program. Java includes support for a fantastic library called JavaFX that lets you place windows, dialog boxes, and other graphical user interface elements in a program without much effort. Of course, you could ignore JavaFX and do it all the hard way and not get any sleep. But by taking advantage of JavaFX, you'll put together interactive code faster.

Just look at some of the standard features in Java that aren't available in some other languages:

- ▶ **Drag and drop:** Enables users to move items from one screen location or program to another by dragging those items with the mouse.

- ▶ **Sound:** Adds sound effects to spice up your programs.

- ▶ **Network support:** Allows access to other computers on a user's network after proper security clearance is obtained from the user.

- ▶ **Collections:** Stores data in advanced data structure repositories such as linked lists.

- ▶ **2D and 3D graphics:** Dazzles the audience with eye-catching creations.

- ▶ **Database API:** Supports Java Database Connectivity (JDBC), a heavy-duty database *application programming interface* (API) that enables your code to access, report, and retrieve from a data source such as a company database.

- ▶ **Timers:** Enables you to drop into your programs time-keeping routines that produce timed input responses, clocks, calendars, and other time-related operations.

Security Issues

Security should always be your concern when writing programs run over the Internet. In practice, Java-enabled applets can be prone to security problems if the proper precautions aren't in place. After all, when you visit a Java-enabled web page, you aren't always sure if an applet is running or what exactly an applet is trying to do to your computer's disk or memory.

Fortunately, Java was designed to be a network-based programming language. Therefore, security is inherent in the language, both for the developer and for the Internet user. The following are some of the default security-related protections built into the Java language:

▶ A Java applet is not allowed to venture where it doesn't belong in the user's memory areas.

▶ A Java applet cannot create, read, rename, copy, or write files on the user's file system.

▶ A Java applet cannot connect to additional machines on the user's network.

▶ A Java applet cannot call system routines on the user's system.

CAUTION

You can locally load and run a Java applet from your own browser by loading an applet from your own disk drive or network. In the case of a locally loaded applet, the applet generally has permission to read and write to the local file system. In addition, some applet viewers do let the user specify a list of files that a web applet can access.

As you can see, Java developers do understand the need for security, and the most obvious security footholds are barred from an applet's access. As more people write Java applets, additional security concerns are sure to enter the picture.

Java changes as technology and computers change. Modern Java compilers support a number of modern security methods, such as *digital signatures* (for signing documents online), *public* and *private keys* (for encryption of data to hide it from others), and *site certificates* (whereby the web browser checks to ensure the software is valid and certified to be safe).

Java as a Game-Development Language

Java is the once and future king of fun little games. In the 1990s, thousands of games were created as Java applets and presented on web pages. As other game development alternatives, such as Flash, arose, Java faded as a game programmer's favorite. But then Android phones came along, and now millions of Java games are running on those phones and other mobile devices as apps. Every game you play on an Android device was written with Java.

Java Language Specifics

Java is not a difficult language to learn. However, becoming proficient requires time as you need to learn how to exploit all the Java code offered by Oracle and other providers that has been made available so you don't have to reinvent the wheel in your own programs. Java includes several prebuilt procedures that are often used to perform standard operations such as I/O, connecting to web servers, and accessing databases. Java is an *OOP* (*object-oriented programming*) language and is similar to C++ in many ways. Both languages have common keywords, comments, and built-in functions. Java's OOP nature means that you can extend language objects that others write to complete applications faster.

TIP

Given Java's C++ roots, once you learn Java, you will already know a lot about C++. However, Java's developers did try to make Java better than C++. For example, unlike C++ (or C) but similarly to JavaScript, Java supports the string data type. Java also leaves out some features of C++ that are difficult to learn and error prone to use, such as pointers.

Java Example

Listing 10.1 shows a very simple Java program so that you can familiarize yourself with the format of the language. This program bears little resemblance to Python programs, but you'll soon see that your knowledge of that language will speed your mastery of Java.

LISTING 10.1   Your first Java program may look cryptic

```
// A simple Java applet

import java.applet.*;      // required support files
import java.awt.*;

// Main class
public class Simple extends Applet {

    public void init() {
        resize(320, 240); // applet's window size
    }

    public void paint(Graphics g) {
        // change subsequent text color to red
        g.setColor(Color.red);
        // write a simple message in the window
        g.drawString("Free the bound periodicals!", 75, 100);
    }
}
```

When embedded inside a web page, Listing 10.1 is displays the message "Free the bound periodicals!" in red on the screen's browser, 75 pixels from the right edge and 100 pixels from the top of the screen. The screen in this case would be whichever Java-enabled web browser is used to view the page with the HTML code that contains this applet.

Before going into the specifics of Listing 10.1, take a moment to consider these points:

▶ A comment, which as you know is an explanatory remark for programmers, begins with two forward slashes (//).

▶ All Java programs are case-sensitive. Therefore, if you initially name a variable intSum, you shouldn't refer to that variable later as INTSUM because Java will not recognize them as the same.

▶ Java is a free-form language. You can indent and include lots of whitespace to make your programs easier to read and maintain (or exclude it, if you like making things harder for yourself later).

▶ A semicolon generally follows each complete executable line. No semicolons follow comments or braces, however. Also, a class's or procedure's definition line (the first line in a class or procedure) doesn't end with a semicolon because these statements define classes and procedures but don't execute or produce output.

▶ A pair of braces encloses a group of lines that Java treats as a single block of code. Generally, a block can appear anywhere that a single statement can appear. The braces also designate start and stop points for procedures.

These Java coding principles apply to small as well as large standalone Java programs.

Gain a Deeper Understanding of the Code

Some of the details of Listing 10.1 should be easy to understand. In the listing, comments help divide the sections of the applet from one another as well as document some lines in the code.

The import commands in Listing 10.1 appear in almost every Java program that you'll write. You've already used import in your Python programs to load additional code and functions. The import command is also somewhat analogous to the C and C++ #include preprocessor directive, but import is a Java command and not a language directive. Another difference is that import does not import code (despite its name). Instead, it makes it easier to refer to existing classes from special class packages provided by the Java compiler. Remember that with OOP, a class defines an object. A *package* is a collection of classes that are logically grouped together. For example, graphics routines often appear in a package. You can refer to the graphics objects from the class as long as you import that package.

The import command can use these two formats:

```
import specificPackage.specificClass;

import specificPackage.*;
```

When you know the name of a class that you want to use, you can specify that name inside the import command. *specificPackage* is the name of the class package from which you want to import the class named *specificClass*. For example, if you want to import a class package file named nu.xom.Builder, you use this:

```
import nu.xom.Builder;
```

With second format of import shown above, you use the * wildcard character to specify that you want to import *all* classes from a class package. Listing 10.1 uses this import format for its imported classes. The java.applet class package is a class you need to use when the applet is to be embedded in a web page. Therefore, you'll always import java.applet and all its classes at the top of every applet that you write. The java.awt class package contains many graphics routines that enable you to send output to a web page's applet window. Instead of printing text onscreen, your applet must *draw the text* pixel by pixel. Listing 10.1 contains a drawString() function that is a class procedure defined in the java.awt class package.

If you don't use import, you must always refer to every class by its full names, including the package and the class name.

The following line from Listing 10.1 defines a class named Simple:

```
public class Simple extends Applet {
```

The opening brace in this public statement begins the body of the applet's Simple class; the class doesn't terminate until the closing brace. A statement such as this public statement must appear in your applet because your applet is actually an entirely new class, from the predefined Applet class, that you are extending. In this example, the applet is extending the generic class called Applet (defined in the java.applet class package) by naming the copy Simple; the code in the body of Simple is the added functionality for this newly extended class. Without the added code, Simple would be no different from the built-in Applet class, and the applet would appear in the web page but could do nothing. The new code is what makes the applet perform.

The next few lines in Listing 10.1 define a new method called init(). (*Methods* act much like functions except that you apply the methods to objects such as the screen window object.) The listing is actually redefining a method that already exists. When the subclassed Applet became Simple, a method named init() came with the Applet class, but it does nothing except prepare the applet to run. init() is a method that's applied to the Simple class. Every Java applet programmer *must* redefine init(), and almost every applet includes the resize() function in the body of init(), as shown here:

```
public void init() {
    resize(320, 240); // applet's window size
}
```

The resize() method simply informs your class of your applet's window size in the target web page. You also can insert any other code inside init() that you want executed after the initial loading of the applet. resize() requires two arguments: an *x* coordinate and a *y* coordinate. Enter the coordinates in pixels. In Listing 10.1, the resize() function is defining the Java applet's window size (the window will appear inside the web page on the user's machine) as 320 pixels wide by 240 pixels high.

The `paint()` method should appear in every applet that you create, and it should follow `init()`. Your applet executes `paint()` every time your applet window needs to be redrawn. If the user hides the applet's window with another window and then unhides it later, the hidden portion must reappear, and it is `paint()` that determines what happens every time the window is redrawn. As long as you've supplied a `paint()` method—and you must for anything to be displayed—you can be assured that your applet window will reappear properly with the text, colors, and anything else `paint()` puts on the window.

In Listing 10.1, the `paint()` method looks like this:

```
public void paint(Graphics g) {
    // change subsequent text color to red
    g.setColor(Color.red);
    // write a simple message in the window
    g.drawString("Free the bound periodicals!", 75, 100);
}
```

NOTE

Unlike `init()`, `paint()` requires an argument inside its parentheses. The argument is a value that the `paint()` method operates on. Although `Graphics g` may seem like a strange argument, the argument represents your web page's graphical applet window. Whatever `paint()` does to the value named g happens to your applet's window.

The `setColor()` method, therefore, sets the color for all text that will subsequently appear on the output window, g, until another `setColor()` appears. Although the window's background remains gray (you can change the background color if you want), text that appears will be red. After the applet sets the text color to red, four red words appear in the applet's window due to this line:

```
g.drawString("Free the bound periodicals!", 75, 100);
```

`drawString()` is a commonly used Java method that sends text strings to the applet's window. `drawString()` respects the color set by `setColor()`, so the text "Free the bound periodicals!" appears in red. Notice the g before the method name. You could, if you opened several different windows with an applet, send text to different windows by prefacing `drawString()` with each window's designated context name, such as g used here. The two arguments that end the `drawString()` method indicate how wide and high, in pixels, the text is to appear.

You now know all there is to know about Listing 10.1's applet. If you're still somewhat confused, don't panic because the next few hours cover the language in more detail. Java statements can be tricky due to the object and class situations brought on by OOP.

Get Ready to Begin

The best way to get into Java programming quickly is to install an integrated development environment (IDE) that has been designed for Java programmers. There are several excellent IDEs for Java, some that can be downloaded over the Internet at no cost and others that are commercial products. One of the best is NetBeans, a free IDE offered by Oracle that began many years ago under the name Forte for Java. NetBeans is available from the website www.netbeans.org.

If you've not yet installed NetBeans for Java, see Appendix B, "Using the NetBeans Integrated Development Environment" (available for download after registering this book at informit.com/register), and follow the installation instructions. You will then be ready to write your first Java program in the next hour.

Summary

In this lesson you have gotten an introduction to the Java language with a primer on applets, the simplest type of Java programs. Java adds a jolt to web pages by sending these small interactive programs along with web pages. You have also seen an overview of the language. Unlike with more traditional programming languages, such as C++, a Java program is sometimes part of something else, such as a web page. The program travels with the web page to a user's machine and executes using the user's own computing power.

You may not understand much of the Java language yet, but you can understand a simple Java program better now that you've finished this lesson. An applet is actually a subclass—an inherited version of a predefined class—that comes with the Java compiler. You can add functionality to the Java `Applet` class to make a program your own.

Q&A

Q. Do I embed my Java program code directly inside the HTML code on my web page?

A. No. HTML is only for formatting a web page's appearance and for placing the applet in the correct location. Your compiled applet, in bytecode, travels along with a web page to the destination computer. HTML always appears and downloads in source code format, whereas a Java program always downloads in bytecode format. Therefore, the two files must travel to the user's computer separately.

Q. Can a user stop my Java program from executing?

A. Certain web-based security features can keep Java applets that arrive with a web page from executing on the user's machine. Although the Java language includes built-in security controls to keep Java authors from invading a user's machine from the Internet, the user can still keep an applet from executing by setting certain browser options.

Workshop

The quiz questions are provided for your further understanding.

Quiz

1. True or false: The most popular use of Java today is for creating Java applets.

2. What is the name of the language that is behind web page formatting?

3. What is bytecode?

4. Why is the concept of a Java Virtual Machine (JVM) important?

5. How does the Java language provide security support for an end user who views Java-enabled web pages?

6. What is the purpose of the `import` command?

7. How do you send text to the screen in a Java applet?

8. Why is the `paint()` method important?

9. How do you indicate a comment in Java programs?

Answers

1. False. The support for applet development has been deprecated from Java.

2. HTML is the language that formats web pages.

3. Bytecode is the language into which Java compiles Java code.

4. By emulating a virtual machine, any computer in the world can run any compiled Java program.

5. Java handles security in many ways. For example, Java must receive proper security clearance from the user before accessing a network; cannot access memory space that it has no right to; and cannot create, read, rename, copy, or write files on the end user's computer. In addition, Java applets cannot call internal system routines on the end user's system.

6. The `import` command brings object libraries into a Java program.

7. The `drawString()` function writes characters to the screen.

8. The `paint()` method determines what happens when a window is redrawn.

9. Java comments begin with `//` or are enclosed inside a `/*` and `*/` pair.

HOUR 11
Java's Details

In this hour, you will gain a deeper understanding of the Java programming language. Java has its roots in C and C++. Once you become familiar with Java, you will then be familiar with much of C and C++. Java has overtaken C++ to become the most widely used programming language in the world.

Java is simpler to learn than C++ because much of Java programming involves knowing which internal prebuilt Java procedures to run. As you saw in the previous hour's overview, when you want to print a message in color, you don't have to do much more than find the name of the prebuilt procedure that first sets the color, find the name of the procedure that prints in an output window, and then use those procedures in your program.

The highlights of this hour include the following:

- ▶ Seeing how Java treats literals
- ▶ Declaring variables
- ▶ Understanding operators
- ▶ Controlling programs with `if` statements
- ▶ Validating user input
- ▶ Looping with the `for` and `while` statements

Defining Java Data

Python supports numeric and string data types. Most languages, including Java, further break down data into several different types. Data can be either *literals*, constant values that do not change such as your first name or date of birth, and *variables*, which, as you know already from Python, are named storage locations for data that can change.

Java Literals

A literal is just a number, character, or string of characters. Several kinds of Java literals exist. Java supports *integer* (whole numbers without decimal places) and *floating-point* (numbers with decimal place) literals. Here are some valid integer literals:

```
23 -53819 0
```

Here are some examples of floating-point literals:

```
90544.5432211 -.0000324 -2.354 67.1
```

With integer literals you can use the underscore (_) character to make them more readable:

```
7_500_000 8_650_300_000
```

Thanks to the _, just you can see at a glance that the first number is 7.5 million without needing to count the zeroes. The Java compiler ignores the underscores.

Java also supports two *Boolean* literals: `true` and `false`. You'll use Boolean literals to test or set Boolean values to `true` or `false` to determine if certain events are to occur.

A character literal is a single character. You must enclose character literals inside single quotation marks. The following are character literals:

```
'J'    '@'    '4'    'p'
```

A character literal doesn't have to be alphabetic. You cannot compute with a number inside a character literal. Therefore, `'4'` is a character literal, but 4 is an integer literal. If you need to represent several characters as a single literal, use a string literal as described at the end of this section. Programmers work with literals all the time, such as when printing a corporation's name on a report.

Java supports special character literals called *escape sequences*. Due to the nature of some character literals, you cannot always represent a character inside single quotation marks. For example, a tab character can appear on a screen to move the cursor forward a few characters to the next tab stop. But to store a tab character in a variable, you cannot assign the tab key directly to a variable; you must use an escape sequence to represent the tab character. These escape characters do consume more than one position inside the single quotes, such as `'\n'`, but they only take one character's storage location, as do all character literals. Table 11.1 lists some Java escape sequence characters.

TABLE 11.1 Java's escape sequence characters represent nontypable characters

Escape Sequence	Represents
`'\f'`	Form feed
`'\n'`	Newline (linefeed followed by a carriage return)
`'\t'`	Tab (horizontal)
`'\007'`	Ring the PC's speaker
`'\''`	Single quotation mark
`'\"'`	Quotation mark

NOTE

Remember that Java came from C and C++. C and C++ support the same data types as Java (except for strings) as well as the same escape sequences. As you learn more about Java's operators and control statements throughout the rest of this hour, virtually all you learn is applicable in C and C++ as well.

You can use an escape character to move the cursor down a line with the newline escape sequence, or you could use one to place a single quotation mark on a window. You could not represent a single quote by placing it inside two single quotes like this: `' ' '`.

Specify string literals by enclosing them in quotation marks. All the following items are string literals:

```
"This is a string."    "12345"    ""    "q"
```

TIP

You can place an escape sequence character inside a string. Therefore, the following string literal contains starting and ending quotation marks due to the two escape sequences that represent the quote marks: `"\"Java\""`.

Java Variables

As in Python, you're in charge of naming Java variables. You must inform Java that you need to use a variable by declaring that variable before you use it. Unlike in Python, when you declare a variable in Java, you tell Java the name and data type of that variable. Java then reserves storage for that variable throughout the variable's lifetime. A variable's life may be for the entire program (as is the case with *global* variables) or may exist only for a few lines of code (as is the case with *local* variables), depending on how and where you declare the variable. Once you declare a variable, Java protects that variable's data type; you cannot, for example, store a string in an integer variable.

Integer Variables

Table 11.2 lists the four kinds of integer variables Java supports. The integer variable you use depends on what you're going to store in that variable. For example, if you're going to store a child's age in a variable, you could do so in a `byte` variable. If you are going to store intergalactic distances, you need to use a `long` integer.

TABLE 11.2   Java variable sizes determine which integer variable you use

Data Type	Storage Needed	Data Range
byte	1 byte	–127 to 128
short	2 bytes	–32,767 to 32,768
int	4 bytes	–2,147,483,647 to 2,147,483,648
long	8 bytes	–9.2233 times 10 to the 18th power to 9.2233 times 10 to the 18th power

A byte of memory represents a single character of storage. Therefore, you can store approximately 16 million characters, or byte integers, in 16 million bytes of free memory.

Generally, you find variable declarations near the beginning of Java programs and procedures. To declare a variable, tell Java the kind of variable you require by specifying one of the data types on the first column of Table 11.2. The following statement declares an integer variable named numKeys:

```
int numKeys;    //    defines a 4-byte integer variable
```

Remember to follow each variable declaration (like any other Java statement) with a semicolon. The following statements define four variables, one for each type of Java integer:

```
byte a;
short b;
int c;
long d;
```

You can define several variables of the same data type on one line, like this:

```
int x, y, z;    //    defines 3 integer variables
```

CAUTION

Java declares variables but does not initialize variables for you. Therefore, don't assume that zero or blanks are in numeric and string variables. Be sure to initialize each variable with a value before you use that variable inside a calculation.

Use the assignment operator (=) to assign values to your variables. You can assign a variable an initial value at the same time you define the variable. The following statements declare four variables and initialize three of them:

```
byte f = 32;
int c, d = 7639; // defines but does not initialize c
long highCount = 0;
```

Floating-Point Variables

Table 11.3 lists the two kinds of floating-point variables that Java supports. You use the larger floating-point variable, double, to represent extremely large or small values with a high degree of accuracy. Generally, only scientific and mathematically related programs need the double data type. For most floating-point calculations, float works just fine.

TABLE 11.3   Java supports two floating-point variable data types

Data Type	Storage Needed	Decimal Accuracy
float	4 bytes	6 decimal places
double	8 bytes	14 decimal places

The following statements declare and initialize floating-point variables that can hold decimal numbers:

```
float w = -234.4332F;
float x = 76545.39F;
double y = -0.29384848458, z = 9283.11223344;
```

The first two values are followed by an uppercase F, which indicates that they are float values instead of double. Java's default for decimal numbers is double.

Boolean Variables

Use the boolean keyword to declare Boolean variables. A Boolean variable can hold only true or false. The following statements declare and initialize three Boolean variables:

```
boolean hasPrinted = false;
boolean gotAnswer = false, keyPressed = true;
```

These conditional values specify whether or not an event took place.

Character Variables

Declare character variables with the `char` keyword, as the following statements do:

```
char firstInitial;
char lastInitial = 'Z';
```

You may assign any of the character literals you learned about earlier this hour, including escape sequences, to character variables. The following statements store the letter A in one variable and a tab character in another variable:

```
c1 = 'A';
tabChar = '\t';
```

String Variables

Java does not actually support string variables, and neither do C or C++, but Java includes a built-in class that defines string data as variables so you can declare string variables just as you can the other data types. Use the `String` keyword (notice the uppercase *S*; most programmers use an initial uppercase letter for names of classes) to declare string variables. You cannot directly change a string variable after you declare and initialize it, but you can use built-in functions to change string variables.

The following statements declare three strings:

```
String s; // no initialization
String langName = "Java"; // an initialized string
String warning = "Don't press Enter yet!"; // initialized
```

Arrays

Java supports arrays, which are lists of zero or more variables of the same data type. Like sets and lists in Python, all array subscripts begin at 0, so a 10-element array named `ara` utilizes array elements `ara[0]` through `ara[9]`. Of course, you don't have to name arrays `ara`; you can assign any name you wish to an array.

To define an array, use the `new` command. The following statements define three arrays:

```
int countList[] = new int[100]; // declare an array of 100 elements
double temps[] = new double[30]; // declare 30 double elements
char initials[] = new char[1000]; // declare 1,000 characters
```

Although these declarations require more typing than do non-array variables, once you've declared arrays, you can use the array elements just as you use other variables. For example, the following statements work with individual array elements:

```
countList[0] = 10;
countList[50] = 394;
temps[2] = 34334.9298;
initials[1] = 'a';
initials[2] = initials[1];
```

Operators

Java supports several mathematical and conditional operators. You don't have to be a math expert to understand them, but Java's operators are somewhat more involved than Python's due to Java's heavier reliance on operators. (C and C++ also rely heavily on operators.)

The Primary Math Operators

Table 11.4 contains Java's primary math operators.

TABLE 11.4 Java supports fundamental math operators

Operator	Name	Example
+	Addition	`4 + count`
–	Subtraction	`gross - net`
*	Multiplication	`pay * taxRate`
/	Division	`bonus / factor`
%	Modulus	`bonus % factor`

You can use parentheses to group calculations together. Java normally computes division and multiplication in a formula before addition and subtraction, but by using parentheses as shown here, you can ensure that addition is computed first so an average can result:

```
average = (sales1 + sales2 + sales3 + sales4) / 4;
```

The modulus operator returns the remainder when you divide one integer into another. The assignment operator evaluates from right to left so you can combine multiple assignments, as in this statement:

```
a = b = c = d = e = 0;    // Stores 0 in all five variables
```

Increment and Decrement Operators

As you learned in Hour 9, "Programming Algorithms," programs often keep track of running totals or count down or up to a value such as a total score. To add 1 to or subtract 1 from a variable, you can use Java's increment (++) and decrement (--) operators, as follows:

```
runningTotal++;  // adds 1 to variable
countdown--;     // subtracts 1 from variable
```

You can place increment and decrement operators inside expressions, as in this example:

```
answer = aVar++ * 4;
```

You can place increment and decrement operators on either side of a variable. If you place them on the left, it's called *prefix* notation, and Java computes the increment or decrement before other operators. If you place them on the right, it's called *postfix* notation, and Java computes the increment and decrement after other operators.

Assuming that x contains 5 before the next statement, `answer` receives the value 12:

```
answer = ++x * 2;    // evaluate prefix first
```

The next statement performs a different calculation, however, due to the postfix notation. Java does not update x until after x is evaluated in the rest of the expression:

```
answer = x++ * 2;    // evaluate postfix last
```

In this expression, `answer` contains 10 because the multiplication occurs before x increments. As with the prefix version, x always ends up with 6 before the statement completes. The choice of prefix or postfix depends on how you formulate the expression. If, for example, you used the same variable more than once on the right side of the equal sign, you should use postfix notation if you increment the variable so the expression is accurate. In other words, the following assignment statement uses a postfix increment because `age` is incremented after it's used for the assignment:

```
ageFactor = age++ * .45 + age;    // uses postfix
```

This statement uses the value of `age` twice in the calculation and then, after assigning the answer to `ageFactor`, increments the value in `age`. If a prefix increment were used, `age` would first be incremented before being used in the expression.

Arithmetic Assignments

Often, you will update or change the value of a variable based on that variable's existing value. For example, suppose you are keeping track of a 10-question polling result. Every time the user answers a polling questionnaire, you'll add 10 to a running total. Any time you want to modify the value of a variable, while using that variable's current value in the expression, put the variable on both sides of the assignment operator. The following statement adds 10 to the variable named `totalAnswers`:

```
totalAnswers = totalAnswers + 10;    // adds 10
```

This example shows how to divide the variable `aVar` by 2:

```
aVar = aVar / 2.0;
```

Updating of variables occurs so frequently that the Java language borrowed common C and C++ operators called *arithmetic assignment* operators. Table 11.5 explains these.

TABLE 11.5   Java's arithmetic operators shortcut the updating of variables

Operator	Example	Description
+=	n += 2	Adds to a variable
-=	netPay -= 10.0	Subtracts from a variable
*=	pay *= .7	Multiplies a variable's contents
/=	bonus /= scale	Divides a variable's contents
%=	num %= 1	Computes the remainder based on a variable's current contents

The following statements use the arithmetic assignments shown in Table 11.5 to produce the same results described before the table:

```
totalAnswers += 10; // same as totalAnswers = totalAnswers + 10;
aVar /= 2.0; // same as aVar = aVar / 2.0;
```

Comparison Operators

Table 11.6 describes Java's conditional operators. These operators do not perform mathematical operations but return Boolean `true` and `false` results that indicate how one data value relates to another. You should have little trouble understanding these operators, as they are similar to Python's comparison operators.

TABLE 11.6   Java's comparison operators compare how data values relate to one another

Operator	Example	Description
==	sales == max	Tests for equality
!=	profit != goal	Tests for inequality
<	n < m	Tests for less than
>	amt > 0	Tests for greater than
<=	top <= bottom	Tests for less than or equal to
>=	age >= 21	Tests for greater than or equal to

CAUTION

Don't confuse the equality operator (==), with the assignment operator (=). Python, Java, C, and C++ use = for assignment and == to test for equality.

The Conditional Operator

The *conditional operator* is the only Java operator that requires three values. The conditional operator actually combines *if-then-else* logic into a simple, clear operation. The conditional operator returns one of two values, depending on the result of a comparison operator.

Here is the general format of the conditional operator:

```
(comparison) ? true result : false result;
```

Often, you'll assign a conditional to a variable as in the following statement:

```
minVal = (a < b) ? a: b;    //  stores the lesser of a or b
```

If the comparison of (a < b) results in true, a is assigned to minVal. Otherwise, if (a < b) is false, the conditional assigns b to minVal. Although you'll learn about Java's if statement later this hour, Java's if statement is close enough to Python's if statement that you can understand much of it now. As a comparison, and to help strengthen your understanding of the conditional operator, here is the identical logic using if-else statements:

```
if (a < b)
   minVal = a;
else
   minVal = b;
```

Use a conditional when you must make a fairly simple calculation based on the result of a comparison, such as (a < b) here. In most instances, a multi-statement if-else is easier to maintain than a conditional statement that tries to do too much.

Programming Control

Now that you know how to define Java data and work with Java's operators, you need to know how to manipulate that data through program control. Java programmers group statements together in *blocks* of code. A block of code is one or more statements enclosed within a pair of braces, such as this:

```
{
   count++;
   System.out.println("The count is now higher");
}
```

Blocks can contain other blocks, so you can *nest* one block inside another. The indention of a block's body helps show where the block begins and ends, which is especially helpful in long programs.

Learn the Format

As you learn programming languages, you'll see how statements are formatted or put together. A general notation is often used to show you how to code a programming language statement.

Italicized words are placeholders that you fill in with your own values. The non-italicized words, such as `if`, are required. If any part of the format appears inside square brackets, with the exception of array brackets, that part of the statement is optional.

The following format shows that `if` is required, but the `else` portion is optional. You fill in the italicized placeholder code with other programming statements:

```
if (condition) {
    block of one or more Java statements;
} else {
    block of one or more Java statements;
}
```

The `if` and `if-else` Statements

Here is the general format of the `if` statement:

```
if (condition) {
    block of one or more Java statements;
}
```

CAUTION

Never put a semicolon at the end of a condition's parentheses! A semicolon goes only at the end of an executable statement. The condition does not terminate the `if` statement but only introduces the `if`. If you placed a semicolon after the condition, then a *null statement* would execute, meaning nothing would happen no matter how the condition tested, and the block would always execute.

Consider the following `if` statement:

```
if (age >= 21) {
    g.drawString("You have authorization for the payment", 25, 50);
    makePmt(pmt);
}
// rest of program goes here
```

The two statements in the body of the `if` execute only if `age` contains a value of 21 or more. If `age` is less than 21, the block of code does *not* execute. Whether or not the block executes does not keep the subsequent statements in the program from continuing.

A common use of `if` is for *input verification*. When you ask the user for a value, you should check the value to make sure the user entered a reasonable answer. For example, the following code asks the user for his or her age. If the user enters zero or a negative value, the program's `if` statement displays an error message and prompts the user again:

```
getAge(age); // calls a procedure to get the user's age
if (age <= 0) {
    // the following lines output to the user's screen
    System.out.println("You entered a bad age value.");
    System.out.println("Try again please.");
    getAge(age);
}
// code goes here to process the age
```

The `if-else` adds an `else` block to the `if` statement. Here is the format of the `if-else` statement:

```
if (condition) {
  block of one or more Java statements;
} else {
  block of one or more Java statements;
}
```

If the condition evaluates to `true`, the first block of Java statements executes. If, however, the condition evaluates to `false`, the second block of Java statements executes.

The section of Java code in Listing 11.1 computes a payroll amount based on the following general rules:

▶ If the employee works 40 or fewer hours, the employee gets paid an hourly rate times the number of hours worked.

▶ If the employee works from 40 to 50 hours, the employee gets paid one-and-one-half times the hourly pay for all hours over 40.

▶ If the employee works more than 50 hours, the employee gets paid twice the hourly rate for hours over 50.

LISTING 11.1   Using `if-else` **to compute an employee's overtime**

```
//   assume all variables are declared and initialized
//   to 0 in earlier code

//   check for double-time first
if  (hours > 50) {
    doubleTime = 2.0 * payRate * (hours - 50);
    // 1.5 pay for middle 10 hours
    halftime = 1.5 * payRate * 10.0;
```

```
} else {
    // no double because no hours over 50
    doubleTime = 0.0;
}


// check for time-and-a-half
if ((hours > 40) && (hours <= 50)) {
    halftime = 1.5 * payRate * (hours - 40);
}


// compute regular pay for everybody
if (hours <= 40) {
    regPay = hours * payRate;
} else {
    regPay = 40 * payRate;
}


// add the parts to get total gross pay
totalPay = regPay + halftime + doubleTime;
```

NOTE

You'll notice a new operator in Listing 11.1: the *and* operator (`&&`). `&&` combines two conditions, and both conditions must be true for the entire `if` to be true. Therefore, `if ((hours > 40) && (hours <= 50))` means the hours must be over 40 and less than or equal to 50 for the `if` to be true.

NOTE

When initially learning to program, beginners often use floating-point or decimal values for money values (like the ones in the previous listing), but Java has a much better solution: `BigDecimal`. You have much more precision in financial calculations when you use the `BigDecimal` class, so use it any time you have money variables. For more details about `BigDecimal`, visit https://docs.oracle.com/javase/1.5.0/docs/api/java/math/BigDecimal.html.

The while Loop

Java supports several kinds of loops. The `while` loop continues as long as a condition is true. Here is the format of the `while` loop:

```
while (condition) {
    block of one or more Java statements;
}
```

While the *condition* remains true, the block repeats, but as soon as the *condition* becomes false, the loop body stops executing. It's incumbent upon you to modify the *condition* inside the loop's body, or the loop will never stop.

In some cases, the body of the while loop will never execute. If the *condition* is false upon entering the loop, Java skips the loop's body and continues with the rest of the program. Earlier, you saw how an if statement can inform a user if the user enters invalid data. With looping, you can take the user's input validation a step further: You can keep asking the user for an answer until the user enters a value that falls within your program's expected range.

The following code uses a while loop to keep asking the user for an age value until the user enters a value greater than zero:

```
getAge(age); // calls a procedure to get the user's age
while (age <= 0) {
    // user didn't enter proper age
    System.out.println("\nYou entered a bad age value.");
    System.out.println("Try again please.");
    getAge(age);
}
System.out.println("\nThank you");
// when execution gets here, age contains a positive value
```

Here is an example of the output:

```
How old are you? -16
<beep>

You entered a bad age value.
Try again please.
How old are you? 0
<beep>

You entered a bad age value.
Try again please.
How old are you? 22

Thank you
```

The for Loop

The simplest for loop in Java works a little differently than Python's for loop. Here is the general format of the Java for loop:

```
for (startExpression; testExpression; countExpression) {
    block of one or more Java statements;
}
```

Java evaluates the *startExpression* before the loop begins. Typically, the *startExpression* is an assignment statement (such as `ctr = 1;`), but the *startExpression* can be any legal expression you specify. Java evaluates the *startExpression* only once, at the top of the loop, just before the loop begins.

CAUTION

Although semicolons appear twice in the `for`'s parenthetical control statement, you should never put a semicolon after the `for`'s closing parenthesis, or the `for` loop will never repeat its body of code.

The `for` statement tests its condition at the top of the loop. Here's the way the test works:

▸ If the *testExpression* is `true` when the loop begins, the body of the loop executes.

▸ If the *testExpression* is `false` when the loop begins, the body of the loop never executes.

A counting example can help you see how the `for` loop operates. Consider the following `for` loop:

```
for (int ctr = 1; ctr <= 13; ctr++) {
      System.out.print(ctr);
      System.out.print(" ");
}
```

When the code runs, here is what the user sees:

```
1 2 3 4 5 6 7 8 9 10 11 12 13
```

You don't have to increment the *countExpression*. You can increment or decrement the variable by any value each time the loop executes. The following code prints all even numbers below 20:

```
System.out.println("Even numbers below 20:");
for (int num = 2; num <= 20; num+= 2) { // adds 2 each loop iteration
      System.out.println(num);
}
```

NOTE

Java's `for` statement also has another form—one designed to easily loop through arrays or collections—and it's a little closer to the Python `for` loop. If you have an array of integers defined, such as `scores`, the `for` statement:

```
for (int indiv : scores) {
        block of code to execute
}
```

loops through all the items in the score array and executes the code inside the block. It's a cleaner-looking block of code than a typical `for` loop, so you should use it when possible.

From Details to High Level

Throughout this hour, you've been studying the details of the Java language. If you've made it through without too many scars, you will be surprised at how much you also know of C and C++ when you look at a program written in one of those two languages.

It was important to focus on the language specifics in this hour. In the next hour you will learn about two other areas of Java programming:

- ▸ Input and output (I/O)

- ▸ Object-oriented programming (OOP) concepts

Fortunately, I/O is rather simple in Java because the built-in library routines that come with Java enable you to get the user's input and display output relatively easily. As you learn about Java I/O in the next hour, you'll also learn about how Java supports OOP.

Summary

The goal of this hour was to teach you about Java operators and the language's fundamental commands. You now understand how to control Java programs and how to form mathematical expressions in Java. You saw that knowledge of Python helps you master Java more quickly due to the similarities between the programming languages.

When you finish the next hour, you will be able to put everything together and begin using NetBeans to enter and test the programs you write.

Q&A

Q. Why should I use escape characters?

A. Escape characters were more important before the advent of Windows-type environments due to the row and column textual nature of older computer screens, but you can still use escape characters in modern-day Java (and C and C++) programs to represent characters that you cannot type directly from your keyboard, such as a carriage return character.

Q. Which should I use: the conditional operator or the `if` statement?

A. Although you saw both the conditional operator and an equivalent `if` statement for comparison in this hour, the two are for different purposes. The `if` statement can be much more complex than the conditional statement because you can use `else` and blocks to execute many statements, depending on the complexity of the problem you're coding. Use the conditional for short, one-statement conditional bodies that produce results that you'll assign to other variables. Most of the time, a multiline `if-else` statement is easier to maintain than a complex conditional statement.

Workshop

The quiz questions are provided for your further understanding.

Quiz

1. True or false: You can change a Java literal just as you can change the value of a variable.

2. How would you store a quotation mark in a character variable named `aQuote`?

3. How many integer data types does Java support?

4. What is the lowest subscript in a Java array?

5. How many different values can a Boolean variable hold?

6. Describe what the modulus operator does.

7. Rewrite the following code in Java using only one variable and one operator:

   ```
   sum = sum * 18;
   ```

8. What is in the value of `y` when the following code completes?

   ```
   int x, y;
   x = 4;
   y = ++x + 3 * 2;
   ```

9. What is wrong with the following `for` loop?

```
for   (int num = 1; num > 20; num++); {
        System.out.println("Hello!");
}
```

10. True or false: You must increment the `for` loop's variable by 1 each time through the loop.

Answers

1. False. You cannot change a literal.

2. Store the escape character for the quotation mark.

3. Java supports four integer data types: `byte`, `short`, `int`, and `long`.

4. The first subscript in a Java array is `0`.

5. A Boolean variable can hold one of two possible values.

6. The modulus operator returns the integer remainder of a division between two integers.

7. `sum*=18;`

8. `11`

9. The semicolon at the end of the `for` statement causes the loop to execute without ever doing anything but looping. When the loop finishes, the `System.out.println()` executes one time.

10. False. You can increment, decrement, or change the loop variable by whatever value you want.

HOUR 12
Java Has Class

In this hour, you will learn all about Java classes after performing some hands-on programming with the NetBeans integrated development environment (IDE). This, perhaps, is one of the heaviest hours in this 24-hour tutorial due to the nature of object-oriented programming (OOP).

Most Java programming revolves around an object's class data and methods. Java contains all kinds of rules and conventions for specifying class data and methods. In this hour, you'll learn how methods perform their work, and you'll see how to set up data that responds to those methods.

The highlights of this hour include the following:

- ▶ Working inside the NetBeans IDE
- ▶ Displaying Java output in windows
- ▶ Using classes to define objects
- ▶ Understanding how methods behave
- ▶ Passing and returning arguments
- ▶ Overloading methods to ease programming duties

Using NetBeans to Run a Java Program

You probably don't want to wait any longer to begin coding in Java. You've now got enough of the language's background to begin with some hands-on work.

Listing 12.1 contains a Java source program that asks for two numbers and displays the sum of them. The Java source code might seem rather long for such a simple calculation; after all, a pocket calculator could do this in four button presses. The apparent wordiness of the code is because some overhead is required for Java applications, and the OOP mechanisms, such as private data members, add some code, as you'll see throughout the last half of this hour. Fortunately, the wordiness does not increase in direct proportion to an application's requirements.

LISTING 12.1   **This simple java program adds two numbers together**

```
public class Calculator {

    /**
     * @param args the command line arguments
     */
    public static void main (String args[]) {
    int intSum;                     // holds the sum

     // compute sum
     intSum = 14 + 35;

     // show user the sum
     System.out.println("The total is " + intSum);

      System.exit(0); // stops the execution
   }
}
```

To create the program in Listing 12.1, just follow these steps:

1. Start NetBeans. A startup dialog appears for a few moments, and the IDE opens with a start page displayed in the main editing window, as shown in Figure 12.1. Java programs you create with NetBeans belong to projects, so you must create one. Click the New Project button, shown in Figure 12.1.

2. In the New Project dialog, select Java in the Categories pane and Java Application in the Projects pane; then click Next.

3. In the Project Name field, enter FirstProject (or anything else you like). Deselect the Create Main Class box and make a note of the value in the Project Location text field. This is the place on your disk where NetBeans saves all the Java programs you put in this project.

4. Click Finish. NetBeans creates the project and adds it to the Projects pane, which is on the left-hand side, right below the New Project button.

5. With a project open, you're ready to begin creating a Java program. Click New File, the button adjacent to New Project. The New File dialog opens.

FIGURE 12.1
Creating a new project in NetBeans. *(Credit: © 2017-2019 The Apache Software Foundation)*

6. Choose Java from the Categories pane and Java Main Class from File Types; then click Next. You are telling NetBeans that you want to create a standalone Java application. All Java programs use `main` as the starting point of the program's execution. `main` is the name of a method, or routine, and some small Java programs contain only a `main` method. NetBeans actually builds part of the `main` procedure for you so that you don't have to type the entire program in Listing 12.1.

7. In the Class Name field, enter `Calculator`. This will be the name of the program.

8. Click Finish. NetBeans builds the outline of your program, shown in Listing 12.2.

LISTING 12.2   NetBeans builds an outline of your code so you have less to type

```
/*
 * To change this template, choose Tools | Templates
 * and open the template in the editor.
 */

/**
```

```
 *
 * @author Greg Perry
 */
public class Calculator {

 /**
  * @param args the command line arguments
  */
 public static void main(String[] args) {
     // TODO code application logic here
 }
}
```

NetBeans adds several comments and uses the same syntax as C uses, which is still supported by the Java language. The compiler considers all text between an opening /* and a closing */ pair of characters, even if the words span multiple lines, to be a comment. NetBeans adds several comments to your code that begin with asterisks just to help separate the comments from executable program code. You can also use the newer-style comments that begin with //. The advantage of the old style is that in multiple lines of comments, only the first one has to begin with //.

Commented items that begin with an ampersand (@) are special commented lines supplied by NetBeans that you should replace with something other than the default values, such as your name (for example, @author). Of course, because they're inside comments, you can put anything you want there. But as you learned in Hour 3, "Designing a Program," maintenance is vital when a group of programmers are working together, and each programmer should put his or her name in the source code along with a version number of the code to show what was worked on. For now, you can remove these comment lines preceded by the ampersand by selecting and deleting them as you would do in a word processor.

The class name chosen for a Java program determines its filename. So, because this class is called Calculator, the filename is Calculator.java. All Java source code ends in the .java filename extension.

Within the file, NetBeans creates a method, the regular main method. The main method has the words public static void before the name to define how this method is to be viewed. These keywords basically tell the compiler that main is a public method that can be seen from the rest of the files in the project, if the project has additional files and the main method returns no values.

Values, called *arguments*, are placed inside main's parentheses in order to be passed to main from other places. When your programs have multiple methods, those methods can transfer values back and forth through this argument list. main's argument list is there in case you want to send values from the operating system to the program when the program first starts. In most cases you won't do this, but a string array exists in the main method just in case.

Java created this program shell for you so that your only job is to fill in the source code with the rest of Listing 12.1's code, compile the program, and see the results. To finish the program, follow these steps:

1. Delete the comment `// TODO code application logic here` and at that same spot, type `main`'s body of code, shown in Listing 12.3.

LISTING 12.3   Type this to complete the `main` procedure that NetBeans began for you

```java
public static void main(String args[]) {
    int intSum;              // holds the sum

    // compute sum
    intSum = 14 + 35;

    // show user the sum
    System.out.println("The total is " + intSum);

    System.exit(0);         // stops the execution
}
```

2. Your program should now look like the one in Listing 12.4. Although you may have changed, added, or deleted some comments, your non-comment code should exactly match that of the listing.

LISTING 12.4   The completed version of the calculator program

```java
/**
 *
 * @author Greg Perry
 */
public class Calculator {

    /**
     * @param args the command line arguments
     */
    public static void main(String args[]) {
        int intSum;       // holds the sum

        // compute sum
        intSum = 14 + 35;

        // show user the sum
        System.out.println("The total is " + intSum);

        System.exit(0); // stops the execution
    }
}
```

3. You can now run the program. NetBeans compiles the program automatically if there are no errors. To run it, press Shift+F6 or choose the menu command Run, Run File. If you don't see the Output window, click the Output tab at the bottom of the editing window where you entered the program's source code. The output window shows the following program result:

```
The total is 49
```

Going GUI

You've successfully run your first Java program, but the output is text based and does not take advantage of a graphical environment very well. Listing 12.5 contains the same program as the previous one except for two added lines that take advantage of Swing (the precursor of JavaFX). Like JavaFX, Swing was a Java library that enables you to add message boxes, get input from input boxes, and add windowlike features to your program, among many other capabilities.

Create a new Java program following the same steps undertaken with `Calculator` but make `SwingCalculator` the class name when you're asked for it in the New File dialog.

LISTING 12.5   Move away from text mode and into windowed features

```java
import javax.swing.*;

/**
 *
 * @author Greg Perry
 */
public class SwingCalculator {

    /**
     * @param args the command line arguments
     */
    public static void main(String[] args) {
        int intSum;      // holds the sum

        // compute sum
        intSum = 14 + 35;

        // show user the sum
        JOptionPane.showMessageDialog(null, "The total is " + intSum);

        System.exit(0); // stops the execution

    }
}
```

When you execute your program, the message box shown in Figure 12.2 appears. This is better and more modern than outputting straight text, isn't it? Click the message box's OK button to close the message box window when you're done.

Figure 12.2
In this program, Swing powers a Java program's graphical user interface (GUI).

The Java libraries, such as Swing and JavaFX, are full of objects you can bring into your own code and use. Part of the fun in getting to know Java is figuring out what the language can do for you through the use of these object-oriented library routines. Need to add a command button or another feature to your program? Look for an object library that supplies that feature and just plug the object into your program! This is one of the beauties of Java and OOP.

NOTE

The Swing object library can be used by this program because of the `import` command that imports, or brings into your program, all the windowlike objects from the library named `javax. swing`. One of the many features of this library is the `JOptionPane` program, which enables you to send output to a windowed message box instead of as text in a window, as you did in the previous section using `System.out.println`. `System` is actually an object, your computer, and `out` is a subobject, or a *derived* object, that represents a text window.

Java and OOP

Java is an *OOP (object-oriented programming)* language, and just about everything you do in it involves working with an object of some kind. An object is a place where more than one variable resides, with methods that do things to (and with) those variables. Objects give their variables special treatment, such as protecting the variables' details from the rest of the code, but still, an object is a place where two or more variables often appear together in a group.

Consider this object declaration:

```
public class Employee {
    protected String firstName[15] = new String;
    protected String lastName[15] = new String;
    protected float salary;
    protected int age;
    // rest of object's declaration follows
}
```

Although several variables are declared here, two as arrays, they are collected together into the class called Employee. Just as the integer data type is not a variable but defines data, neither is Employee a variable; it is a class that declares what subsequent variables will look like. The class simply defines the format of an object that you generate from that class, just as the integer data type defines the format of a variable that you generate from the integer data type. The protected keyword tells Java that those members are not accessible from outside the class; that is, only code that you subsequently place inside the class can use the protected data.

Figure 12.3 shows how the Employee object's data values appear in memory. Variables inside objects are called *members*, but they're really just variables. After the variable members are defined in the object, the rest of the declaration often contains procedures called *methods*, which are routines that act on the object's data.

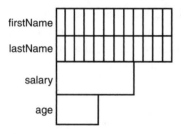

Figure 12.3
Objects can contain lots of variables, and their data types don't have to match.

Overview of Classes

All Java programs are actually objects themselves. An entire Java program is an object. There is a special top-level object called java.lang.Object. Your program is a derivation from that object. When you *derive* one object from another, or inherit an object from another, the derived object takes on all the properties of its parent object, the higher-level object.

Here is the line that derived from this special Java application object in this lesson's earlier programs:

```
public class Calculator extends java.lang.Object {
```

In other words, you created a Java application, an object, from the java.lang.Object object. More specifically, you created a new class by inheriting from the java.lang.Object class. You extended a new object from an existing one that represented a generic Java application.

Why Inherit?

You inherit to eliminate redundant coding. When you inherit from a class, your derived class (sometimes called the *subclass*) inherits all methods and data values from the parent class. Therefore, with the simple extends keyword, your new class that you inherit from a parent class gains all the parent's power, behaviors, and data.

When you define methods and data members in the inherited class, that class becomes stronger than its parent class because the inherited class now has extended abilities.

An object is more than a variable. An object is an active variable that, with its data and methods, not only has characteristics from the data values but also can perform operations on that data with its member code. As you pursue your programming career and learn more about objects, you will learn how languages such as Java specifically activate objects so that you can use those objects in other programs you write. You can reuse an object from a program that you previously wrote simply by copying the object's class definition to your new program.

Unlike with the built-in data types, such as int, if you perform a math operation on one of your objects, you have to teach Java how to do the math by writing a method that performs the work. Once you supply the code, however, calculating with the objects is basically as easy to do as calculating with the built-in types.

Listing 12.6 demonstrates a class with data values (often called *data members* or just *members*) and methods (procedures inside the class).

LISTING 12.6   A class can have both data members and procedure methods

```
// The Box Class

class Box {       // a new class, so there is no
     // extension or inheritance from another class
    float area; // a class data member
    int colorCode; // a class data member

    void calcArea(float width, float length) {
      // computes a value from data passed to the object
      area = width * length;
    }

    void setColor(int colorValue) {
       // sets a color for the object
       colorCode = colorValue;
    }
}
```

`Box` is a class with four members: Two of `Box`'s members are data members (`area` and `colorCode`), and two are methods (`calcArea()` and `setColor()`). `Box` is not an object, just a definition of the object (the class). You can, however, instantiate objects from the `Box` class, meaning you can define object variables.

NOTE

`Box` is not a fully working, complete class. You would need to add additional members to effectively define a full class with ample data and methods.

Java does not normally know what a `Box` is. Only after you declare the `Box` class, as in Listing 12.6, can you then define (instantiate) an object like this:

```
Box hatHolder;     // create variable for a new object
```

The new variable named `hatHolder` is an object variable. Can you see that, loosely speaking, an object is a lot like a variable? You first have to tell Java about the object's type by defining the object's class, and you then have to define one or more objects, just as you can define one or more variables. Unlike a variable, however, the `hatHolder` objects contain more than a single data type; `hatHolder` is a combination `int` and `float` value, along with two methods that manipulate those data values.

If you want to execute one of the object's methods, you only need to use the dot operator. Suppose you wanted to calculate the area of the `hatHolder` object. The following statement executes `hatHolder`'s `calcArea()` method:

```
hatHolder.calcArea(4.3, 10.244);    // executes the calcArea method
```

In the previous hour, you learned how to use the `new` keyword to declare an array. `new` also defines objects. Here is how you would instantiate a `Box` object using `new`:

```
Box hatHolder = new Box();    // instantiates a new Box object
```

Always use the parentheses when you use `new` with object instantiation. You can instantiate two `Box` objects as follows:

```
Box slot1 = new Box();
Box slot2 = new Box();
```

You now can calculate the area for the second `Box` object:

```
slot2.calcArea(1.0, 5.0); // sets the second object's area
```

You can specify the color for the first box as follows:

```
slot1.setColor(4); // sets the first object's color
```

Do You Understand OOP?

The nature of objects and OOP sneaks up on you. Relax if you don't feel as though you're mastering objects as quickly as you learned the non-OOP parts of the Java language, such as `for` loops. This is your first book of programming! Complete books much thicker than this one are devoted to the explanation of OOP concepts.

OOP requires a special kind of thinking that does not always come quickly. Throughout this hour, you'll familiarize yourself with OOP. When you're ready to return to OOP with Java or another OOP-based language such as C++, this introduction will pay dividends.

Methods Do the Work in Classes

Although you've seen methods in action, and although you know a little about what methods are all about, this section explains methods in a little more detail and fills in a few more pieces of the method puzzle.

A Method's Execution

Methods perform work. Methods operate on class data by using the controlling statements you learned about in the previous hour and also by utilizing variables to hold data. A method's argument list inside the method's parentheses may contain values, or the list may be empty. If arguments exist, the code that calls the method must initialize those values and send the expected arguments and types.

TIP

Think of an argument as a variable that's passed from one statement to a method. Arguments act like variables.

Figure 12.4 shows how the code in one method calls another method and sends that called method two arguments. Java sends a copy of the argument but does not really send the argument variables themselves. Therefore, if the called method changes an argument in any way, the change is not noticed when the calling code regains control.

NOTE

Java is known as a *call-by-value* language because a called method can never change the calling method's argument data. The called method can use and modify the arguments within the called method's statements, but when control returns to the calling code, the variables sent as arguments to the methods are unmodified in the calling method.

Figure 12.4's receiving method takes two values, computes with them, prints their newly computed values, and then returns control to the calling class.

Here is the output from Figure 12.4's code:

```
In method...
a=456.000
b=4608.294930876

In calling class...
a=10.0
b=20.0
```

Figure 12.4
The calling code sends two expected arguments to the called code.

As you can see, the called method receives two values and changes those values, but the changes last only inside the method. The calling class code's variables are not, and cannot be, changed by the method.

The method arguments in Figure 12.4 are named x and y, even though the calling program names those variables a and b. The received names might or might not match those in the calling code because only values are passed and not variables. The biggest concern you must have when passing data to methods is to get the number of arguments and data types correct. The method is expecting a float followed by a double, as you can see from this method's declaration line:

```
void myMethod(float x, double y)
```

The calling code must provide two variables that match this pattern. The first definition line of a called method must always declare the arguments and their data types.

The passing of data between code and methods is not strictly one way. A method can return a value to the calling code. Although you can send zero, one, or multiple arguments to a method, a method can return only one value. Figure 12.5 illustrates the return nature of methods.

```
Calling program                          Called method

// Beginning of
// calling program
   float a = 10.0;                                      10.0
   float doub;
// Send a value and                       float doubleIt(float a)
// capture the returned value             {
   doub = doubleIt (a);                       float aBy2;
                                              aBy2 = a * 2.0;
                                              return aBy2;
                                          }
                                                  20.0
// Here, a is unchanged and doub
// received the returned value
   System.out.println ("/nln calling code...);
   System.out.println ("a=" + a);
   System. out. println ( "doub=" +doub);
// Code continues
```

Figure 12.5
A called method can return only a single value.

Here is the output from Figure 12.5's program:

```
In calling class...
a=10.0
b=20.0
```

The `doubleIt()` method is a two-way method in that the calling code passes an argument, and the method also returns a value to the calling code. The called method does not change any value and returns the doubled value back to the calling code. The calling code captures the return value in the variable named `doub`.

If a method requires no arguments, leave the argument list empty.

Summary

You now know the basics of OOP. You should have a better idea what classes, methods, and data are all about. The `new` operator creates the class objects that your program can use. The object is much more than just a variable that holds data; objects contain methods, so objects are more active than variables.

The next hour takes a quick tour of Java-based web applets. You'll see exactly how to embed a Java program inside a web page and how to set up the program to run when the user loads the page inside a web browser.

Q&A

Q. NetBeans has many options. How can I learn more about it?

A. NetBeans certainly is a comprehensive package with which you can develop many different kinds of Java programs. The online help system is complete, and Oracle's www.netbeans. org website contains information about the IDE and all aspects of the Java language, from the programmer's perspective as well as the user's.

Q. If I wanted to pass arguments to `main()` **from my operating system, how would I do that?**

A. Suppose you wrote a Java program that calculated the sales commission for any salesperson in your company. You could pass the salesperson's employee number to `main()`, and the program would then calculate the appropriate commission after looking up that salesperson's sales data in the company files. Several ways exist to pass such an employee number. One way on Windows would be to place the program in your Start menu, right-click on the compiled program's filename, select Properties, and type the number to the right of the filename. All arguments passed to the program appear to the right of the filename when you execute the file in such a way. Of course, changing the program's properties is a tedious way to execute the program for all salespeople for whom you want to calculate commission. These command-line arguments actually were more important in the pre-Windows DOS operating system, where typing filenames to execute programs was more common. In such an application today, you would make your program more usable by forgoing the command-line arguments in favor of prompting the user for the salesperson's employee number inside the program after the program starts.

Workshop

The quiz questions are provided for your further understanding.

Quiz

1. What alternative to using `//` can you use for commenting code in Java?

2. What are arguments?

3. Where does the argument list reside in the `main()` procedure?

4. What do Swing and JavaFX add to Java programs?

5. What command brings Java object libraries into Java programs?

6. How does a class differ from an object?

7. True or false: All Java programs derive from a single Java object named `java.lang.Object`.

8. What takes place when you instantiate an object?

9. What happens when you extend one object from another?

10. True or false: If an argument list requires no arguments, you should keep the argument list empty.

Answers

1. You can enclose comments in `/*` and `*/`.

2. Arguments are values passed between a calling procedure and a called procedure.

3. The `main()` argument list is there so that users can pass arguments from the operating system environment to the program.

4. Swing and JavaFX add windowed controls to a program.

5. The `import` command brings Java object libraries into programs.

6. A class defines the way objects look and behave.

7. True

8. The program builds an object based on the class definition.

9. The extended object inherits the data and methods from the parent object.

10. True. You should keep the argument list empty if the argument list requires no arguments. (However, you do place `void` inside empty argument lists in C and C++.)

HOUR 13
HTML5 and CSS3

Hypertext Markup Language (HTML) is the code behind web pages. Using HTML, you place text, graphics, JavaScript, Java and other active content, and hyperlinks throughout web pages to give those pages the look you desire. Unlike traditional programming languages (but like JavaScript), HTML is interpreted as a web page loads. A web page, formatted with HTML code, goes across the Internet to any user who requests it. That user's browser interprets the HTML elements to format the page properly.

This lesson introduces you to the world of HTML coding. You will learn how HTML formats text, graphics, and other web page elements. HTML is a fairly simple language because, instead of issuing commands to process data as you do with procedural languages such as C++, most HTML includes simple formatting instructions to adjust the appearance of the web page.

The highlights of this hour include the following:

- ▶ Understanding how HTML formats web pages
- ▶ Recognizing HTML tags
- ▶ Working with HTML text
- ▶ Placing graphics on a web page
- ▶ Introducing CSS
- ▶ Generating web page hyperlinks

HTML Programming

A web page might contain text, graphics, icons and text containing links (also known as *hyperlinks* or *hot spots*), Java applets, JavaScript code, and multimedia content. One of the goals of web page designers is to make web pages appear uniform, no matter what kind of computer the user uses (or, more accurately, which *platform* the user uses, which might be a PC, a tablet, or a phone, running one of a number of operating systems). Although the same web page still looks different on different computers and different browser versions, a steady progression is being made to a truly universal browser standard that will show all web pages uniformly (see the sidebar "W3C Attempts to Standardize HTML"). *HTML is a machine-independent language that web developers use to design web pages.* A page's HTML listing is a set of text elements that, when viewed with a web browser, produces a web page that conforms to the look the author intended.

TIP
_____

No matter what programming language you decide to master next, whether it is advanced Java, C++, or another, you should learn the fundamentals of HTML. HTML and JavaScript (which you will cover in the next few lessons) in concert can be used to accomplish some fairly impressive tasks. The Internet plays a huge role in computers today, and you'll almost certainly be connecting your programming efforts to the web in some way. HTML is the primary web page language. All the other web page languages use HTML in some way. Fortunately, HTML is primarily a formatting and hyperlinking language that is rather simple to master, and will even be easier once you understand the way JavaScript works.

_____

Simple HTML markup produces visually appealing web pages, but many times beginners don't use HTML to produce a web page today; instead, they rely on website-creation tools that allow them to choose basic templates and then make simple changes to the look and feel. These sites translate the page created in this way into HTML elements. Microsoft Word and other word processors can often save documents (with formatted text as well as embedded tables, graphics, and multimedia) as HTML pages that Word translates to HTML code.

TIP
_____

You can use website-creation tools and Word to generate code for you, but you'll never learn without doing, and frankly the code that is automatically generated is often sloppy and poorly executed. You are far better off in the long run learning to write your own HTML from scratch.

_____

W3C Attempts to Standardize HTML

The *World Wide Web Consortium*, known as *W3C*, is a standards committee supported and staffed by the computer industry. The goal of W3C is to define standards for HTML and HTML-based languages and web browsers.

Although web browsers and HTML language systems don't have to follow the W3C's suggestions for HTML coding, those that do help to ensure that their websites have a better chance of being seen properly in all web browsers. The W3C makes many coding suggestions and also defines new HTML elements that browser makers can adopt to make HTML coding easier and to make web pages richer with content. The most recent update is HTML5.

You can visit the W3C's website at www.w3.org and learn more about the consortium.

Following an HTML Example

Figure 13.1 shows a web page that looks rather simple and is free of clutter.

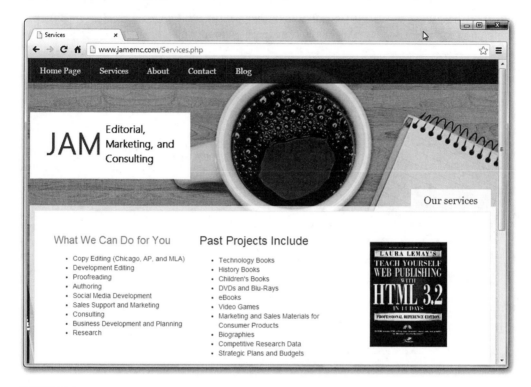

FIGURE 13.1
A web page created using HTML code.

Figure 13.2 contains some of the HTML markup that produced the web page shown in Figure 13.1.

Take a moment to compare Figure 13.2's HTML markup to Figure 13.1's web page. The full HTML code required to display Figure 13.1 is even longer than what you see in Figure 13.2. The HTML code that you do see is rather advanced, so the excerpt of this HTML listing looks a little forbidding. Nevertheless, as you keep comparing the HTML code to the web page, you'll begin to see some ways that the HTML language formatted and placed text on parts of the web page.

Be warned that Figure 13.2 contains virtually no whitespace and alignment that would make the page easier to maintain. Often, web pages generated with website creation programs are rather compact; web pages that an HTML programmer designs from scratch are more likely to be easy to read. Before this hour is over, you will see simpler HTML code written by a programmer that demonstrates more readability. You'll inevitably find both kinds of HTML-based pages because many of the web pages you use today are generated by web page design programs instead of coded by hand in HTML. Actually, many web page programmers use a web page designing program to produce the initial HTML code, and then they modify the generated HTML code, often cleaning up the code's spacing to make the code more maintainable.

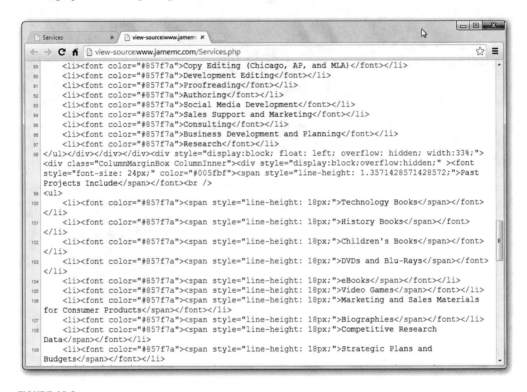

FIGURE 13.2
Part of the HTML markup that produced the web page in Figure 13.1.

You will notice that the HTML code snippet shown in Figure 13.2 uses lowercase for the tags (the HTML elements between angled brackets, < and >) and attributes (the words that specify how some of the tags look and behave, such as color). At one time, the W3C recommended all uppercase in tags and attributes. Most web pages use lowercase, or a mixture of both lowercase and uppercase HTML tags and attributes. Although the browser ignores case and doesn't care which you use, for all new web development, it's now strongly recommended to take the all-lowercase approach.

Displaying a Web Page

When you navigate to view a web page, the remote server sends to your browser only the HTML text, and the browser responds to the markup by formatting text appropriately and placing links and graphics images where the HTML code dictates they should appear. Your browser first receives the full HTML page and then receives whatever graphics images and multimedia content are needed to complete the page.

Browsers provide a Stop button that you can click, or you can press Esc, to keep from receiving graphics and multimedia images for those times when you don't want to wait on them but want to read the text that has already been sent to your browser. In place of the images and multimedia content, most browsers display an icon that shows where the image would appear if you had let the image load to your computer.

Command Tags

The terms within angled brackets (< and >) are called *tag references* (or *tag commands*). Tag commands are central to the HTML program. Many commands contain a beginning and ending tag (a forward slash, /, always precedes an ending tag). A nonbracketed text item is a *literal* (a value that does not change), such as a title that is to appear on the web page. The tags primarily determine the placement of figures, the content of text, and links to other websites. For example, <title> marks the beginning of a title and </title> marks the end. In versions prior to HTML5, the presentation of content was also accomplished with HTML tags, but many of those tags have been *deprecated* (that is, they are no longer supported in code compliant with HTML5), and those functions have been moved to Cascading Style Sheets (CSS), which is touched upon later in the hour.

Many of the tags in Figure 13.2 are formatting tag codes that specify font style and size instructions for the web browser.

Tags don't contain formatted text; they offer formatting instructions that your web browser is to follow. For example, when your web browser sees the <center> tag, your web browser knows to center the text that runs up to the subsequent </center> ending tag as the following HTML code would do:

```
<center>Fran's Place</center>
```

The HTML code completely determines how text appears. Therefore, except for keeping your HTML code readable, no advantage exists for adding spacing. HTML ignores extra spaces that come before your web page's text. The following code produces the same centered title as the previous code, even though the text now has some extra spaces at the beginning:

```
<center>
     Fran's Place
</center>
```

You can document HTML code with the following comment tag:

```
<!-- This is an HTML comment -->
```

Everything between <!-- and --> is treated as an HTML comment, even if the comment spans multiple lines. As you have seen in other sections of this book, comments are for the benefit of the people reading the code and are ignored when the HTML is interpreted by the browser; the information between those character sets does not display on the page.

A Simpler Example

Many websites are a good deal simpler than the one previously shown. You don't need to get bogged down in advanced HTML commands when you first begin studying HTML because even simple HTML commands can produce quite attractive and complete web pages. For example, consider how simple Listing 13.1's HTML code appears. You should have little trouble following the HTML commands even if HTML is new to you. If you do find yourself unsure, don't worry. This is actually a code listing from later in the hour, and its particulars will be covered in more detail.

LISTING 13.1   **Simple HTML commands can produce attractive web pages**

```
<!DOCTYPE html>
<html>
    <head>
      <title>Using styles</title>
<style>
    body
    {
        background-color:pink;
    }
    h1
    {
        color:orange;
        text-align:center;
    }
    img.imgBlue { border: 12px solid; color: blue; padding:5px;}
    p.ex1 {color:red; font-family:Georgia; font-size:20px;}
    p.ex2 {color:blue;font-family:Courier; font-size: 24px;}
    p.ex3 {color:green;font-size:8px;}
</style>
    </head>
    <body>
<h1>Let's try CSS with our HTML</h1>
<p class="ex1">Text using the ex1 attributes.</p>
<p class="ex2">Text using the ex2 attributes<br>
```

```
This is a second line still using ex2 as it isn't turned off yet.</p>
<p class="ex3">Hard to read, but this is the third style, ex3.</p>
<img src="img1.gif" class=imgBlue>
    </body>
</html>
```

This example code combines HTML and CSS and will be analyzed and run later in the hour. However, nothing about this quick example should be too intimidating.

Transferring a packet of HTML code, such as that in Listing 13.1, is much less time-consuming than transferring a graphics image of the web page. Your web browser reads the HTML commands and then formats the text or graphics images according to their instructions.

As stated earlier, several powerful web design tools and sites exist to help you create web pages using modern graphical cut-and-paste methods; but you also can create a fancy web page simply by using a text editor and knowing HTML. Often, programmers use graphical tools to lay out a web page and then use a text editor to hone the HTML source code to finalize the page.

A Quick HTML Primer

All web pages require some fundamental HTML code. Listing 13.2 shows the minimal HTML code needed to display a web page.

LISTING 13.2   The general format for all HTML web pages

```
<!DOCTYPE html>
<html>
  <!-- This is a comment -->
  <head>
    <title>The window's title bar text goes here</title>
  </head>
  <body>
    <!-- The bulk of the web page text, graphics, and HTML
         code goes here -->
  </body>
</html>
```

All listings start with the `<!DOCTYPE html>` tag. This tag serves as a declaration to tell your browser what version of HTML is being used to author the web page. The angled bracket commands are the HTML command tags that format the page's data and tell the browser how to display the page. Many HTML tags appear in pairs, such as `<body>` and `</body>`. The closing tag, indicated with a slash (/), tells the browser where the tag command ends. However, some tags are singular; that is, they do not need a closing tag.

Notice that the first tag in all web pages should be `<html>`, indicating the beginning of the HTML code. The end tag is `</html>`, indicating that the web page is finished.

The heading section, enclosed with `<head>` and `</head>`, contains title bar information using the `<title>` and `</title>` tags and other preliminary web page data, such as *metatags*, advanced HTML code that programmers can place inside web pages to get noticed by search engines. As you will see in the next three lessons, you often define JavaScript functions in the heading section of your HTML pages. If you don't use JavaScript, the title bar is the only text that appears in the heading section.

The body section, enclosed with `<body>` and `</body>`, includes the bulk of the web page content. The user is most interested in the data between these two tags.

HTML Text Formatting

To make text appear on the browser's screen, simply type the text inside the HTML code. Your web page body could include lines of text like this:

```
<body>
This text will appear
on whatever web browser screen
opens this HTML code.
</body>
```

Web browsers do not automatically format text. These three lines of text all appear on one line inside the browser, like this:

```
This text will appear on whatever web browser screen opens this HTML code.
```

If you want to add line breaks, you must include the `<br/>` tag (no ending `<br>` tag is needed). `<br/>` tells the web browser to break the line at that point and move to the next line. The following `<body>` section displays three lines of text:

```
<body>
This text will appear<br/>
on whatever Web browser screen<br/>
opens this HTML code.
</body>
```

Again, the text breaks onto three lines only because of the <br> tags and not because the lines happen to end there.

You can add italic, boldface, and underline to your text. The following HTML code contains such formatting:

```
This line contains <u>two underlined</u> words.
This line contains <i>two italicized</i> words.
This line contains <b>two boldfaced</b> words.
```

CAUTION

Generally, web page designers refrain from using underlining on web pages because most hyperlinks appear as underlined text. If you include underlined text that does not serve as a link to another web page, users may waste time trying to click on those underlined words to see what happens.

TRY IT YOURSELF ▼

The <h> tag controls the size of headlines that you use as titles on your page. You can use <h1> (the most important) through <h6> (the least important) to display headlines. Figure 13.3 shows the web page created by the HTML code in Listing 13.3.

LISTING 13.3   Examples of the <h> tag show how to change headline text size

```
<!DOCTYPE html>
<html>
    <head>
        <title>Headline sizes</title>
    </head>
    <body>
        <!-- An automatic line break
            occurs after each headline -->
        <h1>Number 1 headline </h1>
        <h2>Number 2 headline </h2>
        <h3>Number 3 headline </h3>
        <h4>Number 4 headline </h4>
        <h5>Number 5 headline </h5>
        <h6>Number 6 headline </h6>
    </body>
</html>
```

FIGURE 13.3
HTML supports up to six headline sizes.

Using CSS to Control How Your Text Looks

Versions of HTML before 5 used to use a `<font>` tag as an additional method to control the size of text. HTML5 has eliminated this, and you now need to use CSS to accomplish the same goal. CSS3 is the latest version of CSS—and there will not be a CSS4, just more features added to CSS3—and it can be used to control the appearance of your text on HTML web pages. This information can be included directly on your HTML page, or you can create a separate file with the information. This is an excellent method for reusing your favorite type styles, in terms of color, font size, font type, and more. The use of CSS3 with HTML5 enables web developers to use HTML to focus on the content of the document rather than the presentation of that content, which can now be better controlled across a variety of formats with CSS.

There is a lot to CSS in terms of what you can do with your web page. This lesson can only touch on some very basic points, as the goal of the book is to get you back into programming, but you should know of the presence and goals of CSS3, particularly with the release of HTML5, which has deprecated (phased out) some of the previous font, table, color, and size tags and attributes of previous versions based on the idea that these functions will be better executed with CSS. Obviously, the browser support of those tags from previous versions cannot simply end; there are literally millions of web pages out there written in earlier versions of HTML, and they still need to be viewable. But you should design web pages with an eye to the future and not the past, so if you'd like to learn more about HTML5 and CSS3, please pick up *Sams Teach Yourself HTML and CSS in 24 Hours*, 9th edition.

While you will eventually want to consider creating your own files with your style information, the example shown in Listing 13.4 puts the style information directly into your HTML document. The information should be placed in the header section of the file and needs to be surrounded by the `<style>` and `</style>` tags.

LISTING 13.4 Examples of setting your own styles using CSS to control font color, size, and typeface

```
<!DOCTYPE html>
<html>
  <head>
    <title>Using styles</title>
<style>
  body
  {
     background-color:pink;
  }
   h1
   {
     color:orange;
     text-align:center;
   }
   p.ex1 {color:red; font-family:Georgia; font-size:20px;}
   p.ex2 {color:blue;font-family:Courier; font-size: 24px;}
   p.ex3 {color:green;font-size:8px;}
</style>
  </head>
  <body>
  <h1>Let's try CSS with our HTML</h1>

  <p class="ex1">Text using the ex1 attributes.</p>
```

```
<p class="ex2">Text using the ex2 attributes<br>

This is a second line still using ex2 as it isn't turned off yet.</p>

<p class="ex3">Hard to read, but this is the third style, ex3.</p>
</body>
</html>
```

There's no way the image you see in Figure 13.4 would be considered good design by anyone. (You should really be thankful the printed book is black and white.) However, it's an excellent example of the way you can alter the attributes of headings, paragraphs, and the web page's background. In fact, as the example demonstrates, you can come up with multiple styles and designs for paragraphs. You just need to set a specific name for the class of paragraph and then call it within the body of your HTML text. The best way to figure out what styles work for you is to experiment. When you find combinations that work for you, you can create a file with that information as a .css file that you can then call in any HTML file you want to use your new style combinations.

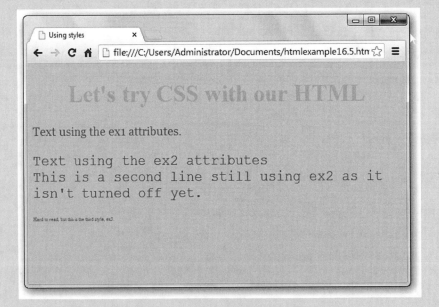

FIGURE 13.4
You have the ability to change a number of text attributes. Text size grows as you increase the font size.

NOTE

While you can specify colors in CSS by using their names, as shown in this simple example, you have far more flexibility when you use RGB notation. This involves passing three integers between 0 and 255—for example, `rgb(255,0,255)`. The first value is red, the second green, and the third blue. Black would be achieved by setting all three to `0`, and white results from setting them all to `255`. In between black and white, these three values can result in more than 16 million color combinations—far more than you can get just by using color names.

Including Graphics in a Website with HTML

The `<img>` tag places an image on a web pages when you use the `src=` attribute with the tag. After you designate an image's location and filename, the image appears. Displaying graphics is simple, and the `<img>` tag is all you need for many of your web page graphics.

Here is a simple web page command that displays an image on the screen:

```
<img src="images/myphoto.jpg">
```

The image appears wherever this `<img/>` tag appears inside the HTML code. It's up to you to ensure that the image is formatted as a type of file that browsers can display. The common image formats are GIF, JPEG, and PNG, and most graphics programs produce images in these three formats.

Older versions of HTML allowed you to place a border around a graphic, in effect adding a framed image to your web page. However, HTML5 has phased out the `<border>` attribute, but CSS3 can help you out again. For example, by adding the following line to the style section of the head:

```
img.imgBlue { border: 12px solid; color: blue; padding:5px;}
```

you can put a solid blue border around the image if you add the class info to your image placement like this:

```
<img src="img1.gif" class=imgBlue>
```

Again, experimentation is the best way to learn about what is possible with CSS, but if you plan to make compelling sites, CSS can be just as powerful a tool for you as the programs you can write with JavaScript (which will be covered in the next three lessons).

Using Hyperlinks

An *anchor* tag, indicated by `<a>` and `</a>`, creates a hyperlink to another page location. The browser that displays your web page creates an underlined link at the point of your HTML's `<a>` tag.

The following lines send the user to the Pearson Education website when the user clicks the hyperlink:

```
<a href="http://www.pearsoned.com">
Click for great learning
</a>
```

Everything between the `<a>` tag and the closing `</a>` tag comprises the anchor, and the `href` attribute forces the hyperlink. The four words `Click for great learning` will be underlined on the screen, and the user can click anywhere in that text to access the corresponding website.

You can even specify graphics and multiline text as hyperlinks. When the user clicks the hyperlink, the browser accesses the linked web page. The user can click the browser's Back button to access the current page.

The HTML statement that follows shows you how to use an image as a hyperlink:

```
<a href="http://www.informit.com">
   <img src="images/Flag.gif">
</a>
```

Remember that everything you place between the initial `<a href>` tag and attribute and the `</a>` ending tag is a hyperlink, whether you place graphics, text, or both there. When the web page that includes this statement appears, the user's mouse pointer will change to a hand when the user points to the image on the screen that is named `Flag.gif`. If the user then clicks the image, the browser opens the page located at www.informit.com.

Summary

At this point, you have a preliminary understanding of how to use HTML and CSS to code and format web pages. When you understand the general nature of HTML code, creating and formatting web pages is a rather simple matter. When you want to add tables, frames, and other advanced elements to your page, you need to master more advanced command tags, but you should have little trouble doing so as long as you gradually build on the knowledge you have already acquired. Using only the tags discussed in this lesson, you can create nice-looking, although simple, web pages that contain text, graphics, and links to other sites.

Q&A

Q. Why do some HTML tags require both opening and ending tags while others do not use ending tags?

A. A command tag requires a beginning tag and an ending tag when you are about to format a specific element on the web page. For example, when italicizing text, you must begin the italics with the `<i>` tag, and the italicized text follows. Without the ending tag, `</i>`, all text on the rest of the web page would be italicized. Command tags such as line breaks, `<br/>`, do not format specific text or graphics and can stand alone because they cause a single action (a line break in the case of `<br/>`).

Q. Do I need web page designer software to practice learning HTML and CSS?

A. You do not—any text editor will do. Start Notepad and enter your HTML and CSS commands. Save your text with any of the following filename extensions: .htm, .html, .HTM, or .HTML (the case doesn't matter). If you don't specify an extension, Notepad saves a file as a text file with the .TXT extension. Web pages should always use one of the extensions just listed. You can then start your web browser, such as Google Chrome or Edge, and select File, Open and locate the file you just created. When you click OK, your HTML-based web page appears. If you did not code something properly, you do not get an error, but the page does not look right.

Workshop

The quiz questions are provided for your further understanding.

Quiz

1. Why is a working knowledge of HTML so important for all programmers today?

2. For what does CSS stand?

3. What is a command tag?

4. How do you code an HTML comment?

5. What do the `<title>` and `</title>` command tags control?

6. How do you increase the size of headline text?

7. How do you increase the size of regular web page text?

8. What does the `<a>` stand for?

9. True or false: You can turn both graphics and text into hyperlinks on a web page.

10. Why is it generally a bad practice to underline text on a web page?

Answers

1. HTML is used by Java programmers, as well as programmers of other languages, and the web is integrated into many programming environments today.

2. CSS stands for Cascading Style Sheets.

3. A command tag is an HTML command.

4. An HTML command begins with `<!--` and ends with `-->`.

5. These tags define the title that appears inside the web page window's title bar.

6. Use the `<hn>` tag to increase headline text, replacing n with a number between 1 and 6. The `<h1>` tag is for the largest head, and each subsequent number makes a smaller-sized head.

7. Use CSS to define the type, size, and weight of your text font.

8. The anchor tag

9. True

10. Unless the underlined text is a link to another element, underlines imply that a link exists when it doesn't.

HOUR 14
JavaScript

Most of the techniques related to Python and Java that you've already learned can be applied in other programming languages. You might wonder why you should learn another language. Isn't one enough? Different languages have different strengths, so in different situations, it makes sense to pick the language that will best enable you to perform the specific task you are looking to accomplish. For example, JavaScript is a programming language that enables you to improve websites by letting you customize the look and feel of your site's presentation, increasing interaction with your website users, and validating any data they enter. You may think JavaScript is specifically for web masters and site designers, but it's a simple language, and learning its basics can help you reinforce basic programming concepts.

Another advantage to JavaScript is that most programming languages need you to install an interpreter or compiler on your computer in order to execute your code, as you saw with Python. With JavaScript (and HTML), you only need a text editor. You type in your code, save it with an .html extension (or you can use .htm), and then open the saved file with your web browser.

Despite its name, JavaScript is not tied to the Java programming language (which is covered in Part III, "Java and Object-Oriented Programming," of this book). In fact, the name has caused some confusion as computer fans thought that JavaScript was either an extension to or spin-off of Java, but it got the name because Java was a hot new language at the time, and some thought the connection of the scripting language to the web development language would benefit the adoption and growth of JavaScript. Misleading name aside, the more you learn JavaScript, the more you can make any websites you create stand out.

The highlights of this hour include the following:

▶ Entering a first JavaScript program

▶ Input and output with JavaScript, including mouse events

▶ Variables in JavaScript

▶ Recursion and conditionals in JavaScript

Getting Started with JavaScript

You can write JavaScript code in either a text editor or a word processor. If you choose the latter, you must make sure to save your files as text only. Save a program with an `.html` extension and then when you double-click on the file, it should automatically open with your default web browser.

NOTE
_____

This lesson provides a quick overview of JavaScript, but the main points of it—comments, input, output, variables, operators, conditionals, and recursion—are similar to what you've already learned about Python and Java, just with minor syntactical differences. As mentioned earlier, the programming concepts covered in earlier hours will give you a leg up on learning other languages.

_____

Using Comments in JavaScript

Just as you learned in earlier hours, when you studied Python and Java, the best programs have comments to make clear what is going on. JavaScript has both single-line and multi-line comments. As in Java, in JavaScript comments either start with a slash and asterisk (/*) or two consecutive slashes (//). The double-slash comment is known as a *single-line comment*. JavaScript ignores all text to the right of the two slashes. On the next line of code, JavaScript starts paying attention to the code again. When JavaScript encounters a comment that begins with the slash and asterisk, it treats everything that follows as a comment until it sees a closing asterisk and slash (*/). This type of comment can appear on a single line:

```
/* Next, the code calculates the area of the circle. */
```

Or it can go on for several lines:

```
/* This section is used to enter a contact
The user can enter a name, physical address,
up to 5 email addresses, home, work, and cell
phone numbers, and any additional comments
to help remember how they know the person. */
```

Entering Your First JavaScript Program

It's time to jump in and write a JavaScript program. The program will be simple—particularly compared to the programs you've already written in Python. The goal here is to get you used to using to seeing how JavaScript and HTML work hand-in-hand.

Type the code shown in Listing 14.1 into your text editor.

LISTING 14.1   Type your first program into a text editor

```
<!DOCTYPE html>
<html>
<head>
<script>

/* This is the function that gets
called when the user clicks the
button on the main page */

function displayAnswer()
{
document.write("Just 24 1-hour lessons!");
}
</script>
</head>
<body>



<h1>My First Program</h1>
<p id="demo">How long will it take for me to learn to program?</p>

<button type="button" onclick="displayAnswer()">How many hours?</button>

</body>
</html>
```

Save the program as text only and give it a name with an .htm ending (for example, Hour14Program1.htm). After you save the program, either double-click the file's icon in your explorer or open the file in your web browser. You should see the web page shown in Figure 14.1 to start and then, when you click the button, you should see the page shown in Figure 14.2.

NOTE

The page you load into your web browser should have an .htm extension (.html works as well). Eventually, you will want to separate your JavaScript code into its own files, using .js files. For now, you can embed all your code into .htm files.

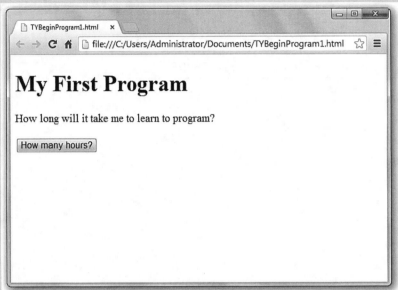

FIGURE 14.1
With fewer than two dozen lines of code, you've created a simple web page,
complete with a button for a visitor to click.

FIGURE 14.2
Once you click the button on your web page, you get a new page with more information.
Awesome interactivity, right?

If your program contains an error, the page does not look like the ones in Figures 14.1 and 14.2, and you need to work through your version line-by-line to see where the error might be, using some of the techniques discussed in Hour 7, "Debugging Tools."

TIP

In addition to checking for errors, it is also a smart idea to check your created pages in different browsers when possible to see the subtle difference in presentation from browser to browser.

Printing to the Screen with JavaScript

JavaScript has several ways to output to the screen. One of the easiest ways to print words on a website is to enclose them in quotation marks after a `document.write` statement. The following four statements embedded in an HTML document print names on the screen:

```
<script>
document.write("Sally Brown<br>");
document.write("John Wilson");
</script>
```

These statements produce the following output:

```
Sally Brown
John Wilson
```

NOTE

In JavaScript, using `document.write` is not always the best way to output text to a page. In fact, it has several limitations. But right now, you're learning good generalized programming techniques, and it's more about simple output than optimized output.

With any JavaScript statements, you need to bracket them with the `<script>` and `</script>` tags. You may also be wondering about the `<br>` tag at the end of the Sally Brown name. This signals to the browser to jump down to the next line and insert a line break. Without it, your output would look like this:

```
Sally BrownJohn Wilson
```

The quotation marks are not printed; they mark the string to be printed. But what if you want to print quotation marks? JavaScript has an easy solution. If you enclose your string to be printed in single quote marks, you can then include the double quotation marks as something to print. For example, if you added the line:

```
document.write('"what if I wanted to print quotation marks?"');
```

the output would be:

```
"what if I wanted to print quotation marks?"
```

Variables in JavaScript

Much like programs in Python (and all other programming languages), JavaScript programs store data in *variables*. The data might be a number, character, or string of characters.

Your programs can have as many variables as you need. As with Python, you should use descriptive names for your JavaScript variables when possible. However, you shouldn't give a variable the same name as a JavaScript command or function, or you will create an error. Variables can hold numbers or character strings. You can use the optional command `var` to define a variable and the assignment operator (=) to assign a value to the newly created variable. Here are two sample variable statements:

```
sales = 956.34
```

```
var rate = .28
```

TIP

The `var` keyword is optional and requires more typing. However, many other programming languages require that you use a keyword to first declare a variable, so it's good programming practice to use the optional `var` keyword.

Instead of using `document.write`, you can use the `alert` method to print values stored in variables. Just as in Python, you can print the variable names without quotes around them. If you have a variable with the area of a circle in it, the following two statements print the area and half area:

```
alert("The area of a circle with a radius of 3 is " + area);
```

```
alert("The area of a half circle is " + area/2);
```

Getting Keyboard Data with `prompt`

To make your JavaScript programs more valuable and your websites more interesting, you need to get information from users.

The `prompt` method is the opposite of alert. The `prompt` method receives values from the keyboard. You can then assign the values typed by the user to variables. When a program reaches a `prompt` call, it creates a dialog box that stays until the user types a value and clicks the OK button. Here is a prompt:

```
prompt("What is your favorite color?");
```

When program execution reaches this statement, the computer displays a dialog box with the message typed in the quotation marks. The dialog box is a signal to the user that something is being asked, and a response is desired. The clearer you make the statement you send to `prompt`, the easier it will be for the user to enter the correct information. If you created a program with the following `prompt` statement, it would produce the dialog box shown in Figure 14.3:

```
var radius = prompt("What is the radius of the circle? ");
```

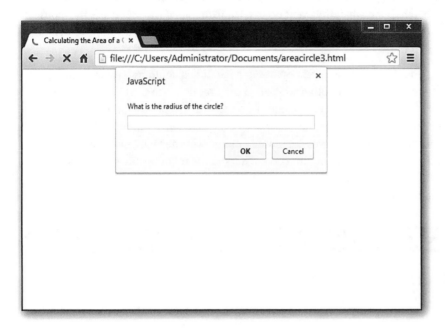

FIGURE 14.3
The program does not advance until the user enters a value and then presses Enter or clicks OK.

When the user enters a value for the radius and clicks OK, the program proceeds.

Inputting Strings

Unlike in many other programming languages, a variable in JavaScript can hold either a number or a string. A user can enter any type of variable, numeric or string, through a `prompt` dialog box. For example, this line waits for the user to enter a string value:

```
var fname = prompt("What is your first name");
```

When the user types the name in response to the question, the name is put into the `fname` variable.

CAUTION

If the user only presses OK without entering a value in response to the `prompt`, JavaScript puts a value called *null* into the variable. A null value is a zero for numeric variables or an empty string for string variables. An empty string—a string variable with nothing in it—is literally zero characters long.

Capturing Mouse Events

JavaScript does not just interact with the keyboard entries from users. In addition, it can understand when the user either clicks the mouse on a specific button or passes into a particular region. These types of actions are called *events*; an event can trigger an action if you have written code for something to happen when the event occurs. For example, if the user clicks the mouse over a button on a web page form, the button's `onClick` event is triggered if you have written code for it.

A rollover effect can apply to buttons or text on a web page. If text contains a rollover, the text can change color or can change in another way when the user points to the text. Often, such rollover effects are used for menu selection. Figure 14.4 shows a web page with JavaScript-enabled text before the user moves the mouse pointer over one of the text items. Figure 14.5 shows how the `Store` text changes when the user moves the mouse pointer over the text. This rollover effect is possible because the JavaScript that contains code to handle the rollover comes to the user's computer inside the HTML web page. The code must run on the user's computer to respond immediately to the mouse movement.

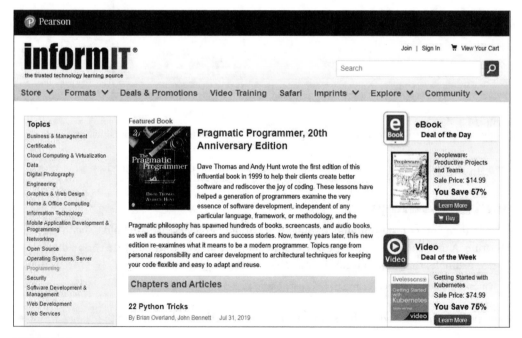

FIGURE 14.4
A web page with JavaScript looks like any other web page until the user activates a JavaScript scriptlet.

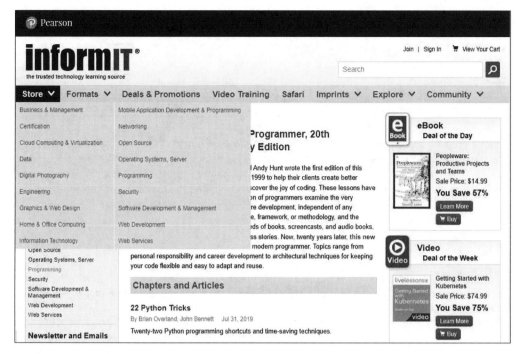

FIGURE 14.5
When the mouse pointer moves over text with a rollover effect, the JavaScript code changes the text's appearance.

TRY IT YOURSELF ▼

Listing 14.2 contains code that produces a command button's rollover effect. (You will not be able to reproduce this actual effect because you won't have graphics to use for the before and after rollover effects.) Not all the code will be clear even after you complete this hour; JavaScript can't be taught or learned in one short hour, but this example helps you grasp the fundamentals of how JavaScript activates such command buttons.

LISTING 14.2   A JavaScript script that performs a button change when the user points to the button

```
<! DOCTYPE html>
<html>
<head>
        <title>Image Test</title>
</head>
```

```
<body>
<img src="img1.gif" alt="img1"onmouseover="this.src='img2.gif';"
onmouseout="this.src='img1.gif';" />
</body>
</html>
```

This code probably looks a bit complicated, but when you type it in and load the page, it generates some cool results. To see how it works, make sure you have two image files, named `img1.gif` and `img2.gif`, in the same directory as the code. It doesn't matter what they are, but similar sizes are best. The first image, `img1.gif`, will be displayed when you load the web page. When you move your mouse cursor over the image, it will change to `img2.gif`, and when you move the mouse cursor off the image, you again see the original image.

NOTE

You can do a lot with input and output in JavaScript, but this hour covers just programming basics. If you want to learn more, please pick up a tutorial devoted to the language; users of your websites will thank you if you do!

Understanding Arrays

Just as words and sentences are collections of single letters, strings are collections of characters, including words, spaces, letters, and any other special characters you choose to type or add by using ASCII functions. When you assign a string to a variable, like this:

```
var hometown = "Salt Lake City, Utah"
```

JavaScript considers this an array of characters and lets you access either the whole name or individual elements of that name. If you call the `alert` method and send `hometown` to it:

```
alert(hometown);
```

as you can probably guess, your output is a dialog box displaying:

```
Salt Lake City, Utah
```

What is probably not obvious is what would happen if you called the `alert` method and sent `hometown[3]` to it, as in this example:

```
alert(hometown[3]);
```

If you did this, you would get a single letter in the dialog box:

```
t
```

You may have figured out that the number in brackets refers to a specific letter or character in the string. (Good job if you did!) But you might wonder why it doesn't output the letter 1? After all, it is the third character in the name of the city. Recall that many programming languages start their counting with 0 instead of 1. So the S is hometown[0], the a is hometown[1], and the t is hometown[3]. You might be wondering what character corresponds to hometown[4]. It is the space, and the L is hometown[5]. When figuring arrays, JavaScript counts every character, including spaces. In this hometown variable, spaces are the 4, 9, and 15 spots in the array, and the comma is the 14 spot. This may seem confusing, but understanding arrays is important for almost every programming language. (It is important for some more than others. C, for example, does not have a string data type, so to work with strings in C, you need to create an array of characters.) For now, just know that every single character in a string corresponds to a specific number and that if you're counting characters, start with 0 and include all spaces, characters, letters, and numbers.

Comparing Data with `if`

JavaScript provides the ability for a program to make a choice and to perform one action or another, depending on a condition. A JavaScript decision statement has two possibilities. To decide which path to take in a JavaScript program, you must use the `if` statement. The following `if` statement prints only if the value stored in `age` is less than 21:

```
if (age < 21)
    document.write("You cannot order alcohol");
```

As you saw with Python, you can test a series of relational statements. Whereas Python uses the `if...elif...elif...else` statements, JavaScript uses `if...else if...else if...else`.

NOTE

JavaScript allows for multiple `if...else if...else if...else` layers, but there is another way to handle several possible conditions or values to a single variable: by using the `switch` statement, which is not available in Python.

Looping Statements

Looping statements are another important feature of any programming language. JavaScript supplies three statements that control loops: `for`, `while`, and `do...while`.

Using the `for` Statement

The `for` statement is broken into three parts enclosed in parentheses to the right of the `for`:

```
for (i = 1; i <= 10; i++)
{
    document.write(i+"<br>");
}
```

Generally, the first part sets up a counter variable, and the second tests the counter variable using a relational operator. In this `for` statement, the variable `i` is set to `1`, and `1` is clearly less than `10`. Because the statement is true, the block of code inside the braces prints below the `for` statement. In this case, there's only a single line of code in the block, but it prints the current value of `i`, which is `1`.

When the block finishes executing, the third part of the `for` statement, the increment operator, runs. The increment operator (++) adds 1 to the variable, increasing `i` from `1` to `2`. Now the `for` statement returns to the second part of the parenthetical section and again tests the relational statement there. `2` is still less than `10`, so once again the block of code executes, printing the current value of `i`, which is `2`. When the block is complete, the third portion of the `for` loop kicks in again, incrementing `i` by 1 to `3`, and testing and looping continue until `i` is not less than or equal to `10`, at which point the loop terminates, and the program proceeds to the next section of code.

NOTE

You don't have to increase your test variable by 1. You can use a different operator (+=) to increase the value by any number. The statement `i += 2` increases the counter by 2, and if you changed `i++` to `i += 2` in the earlier example, you would print only the odd numbers.

Using the `while` and `do...while` Loops

The `while` loop supplies a way to control loops through a relational test. Such a relational test uses the same relational operators used with `if` statements. (Refer to Table 6.1 in Hour 6, "Controlling Your Programs," for a complete list of relational operators.)

Let's return to the teacher-grading Python program from Hour 6. Listing 14.3 shows the same program but with JavaScript's take on a `while` loop. Notice that the `while` continues looping while a certain condition is true. The condition is the teacher's answer in response to having more tests to enter.

LISTING 14.3   You can control the grade program with a `while` loop

```
<! DOCTYPE html>
<html>
<head>
        <title>Grading Papers</title>
</head>
<body>

        <script>

        // Filename gradingpapers.html
        // program loops until the teacher does
        // not have any additional students

        var names = new Array();
        var grades = new Array();
        var ans = 'Y';
        i = 0;
        total = 0;
        while (ans == 'Y')
        {
                names[i] = prompt("Enter student name:");
                grades[i] = prompt("What was their test grade?");
                total += parseFloat(grades[i]);
                ans = prompt("Do you have another grade? (Y/N)");
                i++;
        }
        for (j = 0; j < i; j++)
        {
                document.write(names[j]+" got a "+grades[j]+"!<br>");
        }
        average = total / j;
        document.write("<p>The class average was "+average);
        </script>
</body>
</html>
```

This program keeps looping until the teacher indicates that there are no more grades to enter. Notice that the `while` is followed by a relational test, the result of which (`true` or `false`) determines whether the loop repeats again or quits. So if the conditional statement is `false` the first time, the block of code does not run at all. This program guarantees that the code will run one time because the `ans` variable is set to `'Y'` to trigger the first pass through the loop. This is where a `do...while` loop can be more efficient. The only difference between a `while` loop and a `do...while` loop is the placement of the test expression. In Listing 14.3, the condition is tested, and then the code runs. A do...while loop runs at least once before the condition is tested. The following snippet is the while from the previous program rewritten as a do...while loop:

```
do
{
          names[i] = prompt("Enter student name:");
          grades[i] = prompt("What was their test grade?");
          total += parseFloat(grades[i]);
          ans = prompt("Do you have another grade? (Y/N)");
          i++;
} while (ans == 'Y');
```

This code would make more sense for your grading program; you would not have to set ans equal to 'Y' before the loop, and you'd run the code at least one time, which should almost always happen (unless every single student was sick on a particular day. Senior skip day, anyone?).

One added bonus to this program is the addition of a total variable, which gets the value of all grades and then is divided by the number of students who took the test in order to get an average grade. The program calculates this extra piece of information to add some additional programming value.

TIP

When using a while or do...while loop, make sure that somewhere in the block of code, you are altering the variable you are testing in the relational statement. Otherwise, you might get caught in an infinite loop where the program never ends.

Summary

This hour covers a lot of ground in some ways, but in others it serves as a bit of a review of what you learned in earlier hours, but now with JavaScript's spin on these programming basics. You saw that it's easy to enter and test JavaScript programs—as long as you have a browser to do so. JavaScript also has specific methods to handle mouse events, and this hour covers two of them. The next hour examines some additional ways you can use JavaScript to improve a website.

Q&A

Q. What is the difference between an alert dialog box and a prompt dialog box?

A. An alert dialog shares information with the website visitor, while a prompt dialog asks the user to enter specific information.

Workshop

The quiz questions are provided for your further understanding.

Quiz

1. True or false: Java and JavaScript are related to each other.

2. What filename extension should you use when you create a JavaScript program?

3. True or false: There's no problem writing your programs in your typical word-processing program.

4. Tweak the program in Listing 14.1 so the dialog box asks, "Who wrote this program?" and so the answer the user gets upon clicking the button is your name.

5. How do you print words in the output window?

6. True or false: You use the same code to jump down a line in both `document.write` and `alert` methods.

7. What do the `onmouseover` and `onmouseout` events do?

8. What is the difference between a `while` loop and a `do...while` loop?

Answers

1. False. JavaScript and Java only share a name; JavaScript is a scripting language that was developed at the same time Java was hot, and it was named as it was to take advantage of Java's popularity.

2. If your code is going to stay in an HTML document, you can use `.html` or `.htm`, but when you create separate JavaScript files, use `.js`.

3. False. The default method of saving files in word processors adds formatting codes that generate errors when you try to run your program. You can use a word processor, but you must always remember to save your files as plain text.

4. Here is one possible solution:

```
<!DOCTYPE html>
<html>
<head>
<script>

/* This is the function that gets
called when the user clicks the
button on the main page */
```

```
function displayProgrammer()
{
document.write("Dean Miller did!");
}
</script>
</head>
<body>


<h1>My First Program</h1>
<p id="demo">Who wrote this program?</p>

<button type="button" onclick="displayProgrammer()">And the answer is...
</button>

</body>
</html>
```

5. Use `document.write` to display words in an output window. If you want to create a dialog box with the displayed words, use the `alert` method.

6. False. For `document.write,` you use the `<br>` code, which would not work in an alert (as it would print `<br>` to the screen). If you want to jump down a line, use the escape character `"\n".` (Don't feel bad if you got this wrong; we haven't covered it yet.)

7. The `onmouseover` event triggers some code when the user's mouse pointer passes into a specific object (such as an image, a banner, or a block of text). The `onmouseout` event triggers some code when the user's mouse pointer leaves that object.

8. A `do...while` loop executes at least once before the conditional is tested, whereas a `while` op might never execute if the conditional is `false`.

HOUR 15
Having Fun with JavaScript

Now is the time to sit back and have some fun with JavaScript. Sure, programming is fun in itself, and you already know how easy and enjoyable writing programs can be. Nevertheless, unlike with Python, with JavaScript you can easily do more than write data-processing programs for business and engineering. You can also use JavaScript to jazz up your websites.

The material presented in this hour gives you a framework for adding pizzazz to your programs. You will get an idea of how game programmers do their jobs. You will learn some fundamental concepts that you need in order to write programs that capture a user's attention.

The highlights of this hour include the following:

- ▶ Rotating images on a page
- ▶ Adding interactivity to your web photos
- ▶ Using the `onmouseover()` event
- ▶ Adding a ticker to your website

Rotating Images on a Page

Static pages can be boring pages. If your business is trying to attract customers or if you're showing off your favorite photos of your children, your garden, or your dog, a single photo is nice, but a series of photos can be even better. You can use your knowledge of arrays and other programming constructs to create a photo rotation for a page.

TRY IT YOURSELF

For this project, you need a series of photos that you want to display. While not necessary, putting them all in the same folder as your code will make things easier. The sample program shown in Listing 15.1 uses six photos, named `alice.jpg`, `john.jpg`, `maggie.jpg`, `nieces.jpg`, `family1.jpg`, and `familyhike.jpg`. You would change those names in the code to the names of the photos you want to use.

▼ **LISTING 15.1**   Adding a photo rotator to your web page is easy with JavaScript

```html
<!DOCTYPE html>
<html>
<head>

        <title>Family Photos!</title>
        <script>

        // First, create an array of images to rotate
        var famPhotos = new Array();
        famPhotos[0] = new Image();
        famPhotos[0].src = "alice.jpg";
        famPhotos[1] = new Image();
        famPhotos[1].src = "john.jpg";
        famPhotos[2] = new Image();
        famPhotos[2].src = "maggie.jpg";
        famPhotos[3] = new Image();
        famPhotos[3].src = "nieces.jpg";
        famPhotos[4] = new Image();
        famPhotos[4].src = "familyhike.jpg";
        famPhotos[5] = new Image();
        famPhotos[5].src = "family1.jpg";

        var i=0;
        function rotator() {
                document.getElementById("image1").src = famPhotos[i].src;
                i++;
                if (i==famPhotos.length) {
                        i = 0;
                }
                setTimeout(function() { rotator(); }, 2000);
        }

        </script>
</head>
```

```
<body onload = "rotator('image1', famPhotos);" >
<h1>FAMILY PHOTO TIME</h1>
Our family had a great summer! Here's some photos of what we did...
<div id="img"> <img id="image1" height="600px" width="400px"
      border="5" style="border-color:white;" /></div>
</body>
</html>
```

Figure 15.1 shows the page that results when you run this program. (Obviously, you will not see the same photo, unless your wife and children are dead ringers for mine!)

FIGURE 15.1
With JavaScript, you can enhance the graphical elements of your website.

By setting up an array of images in the header, you can easily go back and add more pictures or delete some pictures as needed. When you declare an array, you first let JavaScript know an element is an image with the `Image()` function, and then you can set the `.src` for each element in the array to a `.jpg` image. If your `.jpg` photos are in the same directory as the `.html` file, you don't need to type in the entire file directory path. You can also use a web address there for your filenames. Adding an additional photo is as simple as adding two additional lines: a subsequent new `image()` call, and then a file location setting.

When your array is set, it's time to create a function to rotate the images in the array. Despite being less than 10 lines of code, the rotator function probably looks a bit intimidating. It shouldn't. The method `document.getElementbyId` is used to set `image1` to the first element in your array of photos, `famPhotos[0]`. It gets this element because before you defined the function, you set `i` to 0. However, after it sets `image1` to `famPhotos[0]`, it increments the variable `i` by 1. This means the next time the function is called, it will set `image1` to the second element in your array of photos, `famPhotos[1]`. This method keeps setting the image to a new element in your array of photos until it reaches the last element. That's when the handy `if` statement jumps in. If `i` is incremented to 1 past the last element of the array, the `if` statement automatically resets `i` to 0, and you can loop through the images in the photo array again from the beginning.

In the last line of code, `setTimeout()` is a handy JavaScript function that keeps calling your rotator function (and therefore places new photos on the page) but waits a set amount of time. The last number, currently set to 2,000, is the delay and is equal to milliseconds. So 2,000 is a 2-second delay. Feel free to experiment with this number to create different transition delays. Be careful not to use a number that is too small; I got a bit of a headache watching my photos rotate every 200 milliseconds.

That's it for the function. All that's left is to call the function in the body of the HTML document. The function is called within the body definition by way of the `onload` event. This ensures that the code function runs as soon as everything is loaded on the page. Within the body, you use a little HTML to set a heading for the page and a little text before `image1` is placed. (HTML is covered in greater detail in Hour 13, "HTML5 and CSS3.") The information that follows `image1` on that line sets the width and height of the image as well as the size and color of the image's border. You can also experiment with these numbers (and colors) to get different effects.

NOTE

By default, all images have the same aspect ratio, so if you mix portrait and landscape pictures, some photos will be stretched to fit the box. Your photos will look best if you choose a set of photos that are either all portrait or all landscape.

Adding Interactivity to Your Web Photos

Another way to add value to your web page is to make your graphics and photos interactive. The best web pages are not static but give the user a chance to interact. Thinking back to our small store example from earlier hours, it would be nice to create a page with photos of products in inventory. Obviously, you could also add product information—such as a description and price—next to or under the photos, but you could make the page cleaner by showing only photos and having information pop up when a user clicks on a photo. JavaScript can make this type of interactivity possible, thanks to the `onclick()` method. Within each photo placement line, you can add the `onclick()` method, which runs a chunk of JavaScript code when the user clicks a specific photo.

Listing 15.2 is a simple example that demonstrates how to use the `onclick()` method with different photos. Three functions are defined in the header section for the three photos placed in the HTML section of the code. To run this code, you need to place photos in the same folder as your code. The ones in this example are named `product1.jpg`, `product2.jpg`, and `product3.jpg`. If you want to use differently named photos, just change the names in the listing to match your choices.

LISTING 15.2   Adding interactivity to your web photos

```
<!DOCTYPE html>
<html>
<head>
        <title>Product Information</title>
        <script>
        function Product1Info() {
        alert("Summer product! On sale until Labor Day for $9.99.");
        }
        function Product2Info() {
        alert("One of our bestsellers! A bargain at $19.50.");
        }
        function Product3Info() {
        alert("Everyone could use one of these at $1.99!");
        }

        </script>
</head>
```

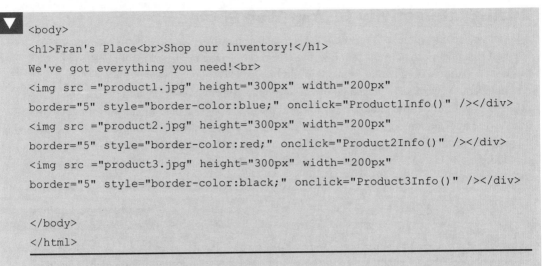

```
<body>
<h1>Fran's Place<br>Shop our inventory!</h1>
We've got everything you need!<br>
<img src ="product1.jpg" height="300px" width="200px"
border="5" style="border-color:blue;" onclick="Product1Info()" /></div>
<img src ="product2.jpg" height="300px" width="200px"
border="5" style="border-color:red;" onclick="Product2Info()" /></div>
<img src ="product3.jpg" height="300px" width="200px"
border="5" style="border-color:black;" onclick="Product3Info()" /></div>

</body>
</html>
```

Figure 15.2 shows the results of running the code in Listing 15.2 (although your three photos will differ).

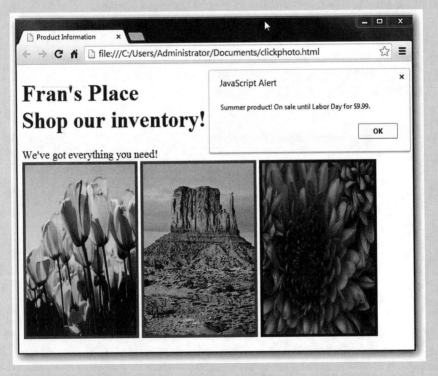

FIGURE 15.2
You can run code that presents as much information as you want when the web user clicks an image.
(Credits: Creative Mani/Shutterstock; Brian Jannsen/Alamy Stock Photo)

Like the last example, this program mixes HTML and JavaScript. If you want to add real power and pizzazz to your web pages, you need to become familiar with them both, particularly the exciting combination of HTML5 and CSS3, the topics of Hour 13. The `onclick()` method used in this example is useful with any object—not just images, as demonstrated here. You can also build a function of JavaScript code to run if users click buttons, banners, or blocks of text.

TIP

Each of the three photos placed on the page in Figure 15.2 has a border of a different color (red, blue, and black). Normally, using consistently colored borders would make for a more elegant web design, but this example shows you the variety of color you can add to a page.

The code presented here is also as simple as can be—a single line of information presented to the screen in an `alert()` method. Sometimes a simple line of information is all you need. However, if you want to present more information or build a more complex function that executes upon a mouse click, you can do that as well.

Capturing the Position of the Mouse

Giving your website visitors additional information when they click a photo or some other object on your page is a nice way to add complexity to your website. However, you can give additional data without even requiring a click from the user. As discussed in Hour 14, "JavaScript," JavaScript has a built-in method that captures the position of the mouse and can trigger some code if the user moves the mouse pointer over a specific photo or other object.

TRY IT YOURSELF

In this hour you have already seen an example in which the user can get additional information about a product by clicking a product image. Now say that you want to have the name and price appear in an alert box on the page if the user moved the mouse pointer onto a product photo. Listing 15.3 should be easy to follow given what you just did in Listing 15.2.

LISTING 15.3 **Adding different interactivity to your web photos with the** `onmouseover()` **event**

```
<!DOCTYPE html>
<html>
<head>
        <title>Product Information</title>
        <script>
```

▼

```
        function Product1Info() {
        alert("Summer product! On sale until Labor Day for $9.99.");
        }
        function Product2Info() {
        alert("One of our bestsellers! A bargain at $19.50.");
        }
        function Product3Info() {
        alert("Everyone could use one of these at $1.99!");
        }


        </script>
</head>
<body>
<h1>Fran's Place<br>Shop our inventory!</h1>
We've got everything you need!<br>
<img src ="product1.jpg" height="300px" width="200px"
border="5" style="border-color:blue;" onmouseover="Product1Info()" />
</div>
<img src ="product2.jpg" height="300px" width="200px"
border="5" style="border-color:red;" onmouseover="Product2Info()" /></div>
<img src ="product3.jpg" height="300px" width="200px"
border="5" style="border-color:black;" onmouseover="Product3Info()" />
</div>

</body>
</html>
```

The code is virtually identical to the code in Listing 15.2. The only difference is that the
`onclick()` methods in each of the three photo placements have been replaced with
`onmouseover()` methods. Now users don't need to click in order to get the information;
they just need to hover the mouse over the page.

TIP
_____

If you want the text to disappear when the mouse pointer leaves the image or object, there is a
second method, `onmouseout()`, that you can use to trigger different code when the mouse is no
longer in the specific area. Often these two methods are used in concert to achieve a specific "on
and off" effect.

The alert box in this example can be a little clunky because visitors cannot do more on the page until the box is dismissed. As an additional project, you could try to alter the code in the functions to place text on the page instead of in an alert box.

Adding a Repeating News Ticker to Your Website

Another cool feature you could add to your website is one of those news-style tickers that repeats information over and over. If you're a small business, perhaps you could use such a ticker to display your shop's hours or address and phone numbers. If you are building a family website, you might add a reminder to your children to do their chores and homework, hoping that repetition will eventually sink in. (Take it from me: It won't.)

Let's return to Fran's Place, the little store from previous hours and the two most recent examples. Instead of building a fresh example like the ones you've seen so far, in this case you'll add ticker code to the preceding example. After all, when you start to build your programs and websites, it's unlikely that they'll do just one job; they will accomplish multiple goals and purposes. The example shown in Listing 15.4 still has the three product photos that generate alert boxes when a user hovers over a photo, but the page now also has a box below the photos that shows a few rotating messages.

LISTING 15.4   **The website for the small store is starting to be more robust**

```
<html>
<head>
<title>Welcome to Fran's Place</title>

<script>

// Set the scrolling message, and you can add as many pieces
// as you want
var scrollMsg = "We are open Daily from 9AM to 10PM...";
scrollMsg += "We've got the largest variety of products";
scrollMsg += " in the tri-state area...";
scrollMsg += "Our prices will not be beat!...";
```

▼
```
//Our three product information functions
function Product1Info() {
        alert("Summer product! On sale until Labor Day for $9.99.");
        }
        function Product2Info() {
        alert("One of our bestsellers! A bargain at $19.50.");
        }
        function Product3Info() {
        alert("Everyone could use one of these at $1.99!");
        }


//The scrolling function
var beginPos = 0;
function scrollingMsg() {
document.msgForm.scrollingMsgBox.value =
scrollMsg.substring(beginPos,scrollMsg.length)+scrollMsg.
substring(0,beginPos);
beginPos = beginPos + 1;
if (beginPos > scrollMsg.length) {
beginPos = 0
}
window.setTimeout("scrollingMsg()",90)
}


</script>

</head>
<body BGCOLOR="WHITE" onload="scrollingMsg()">
<h1>Fran's Place<br>Shop our inventory!</h1>
We've got everything you need!<br>

<img src ="product1.jpg" height="300px" width="200px"
border="5" style="border-color:blue;" onmouseover="Product1Info()" />
</div>
<img src ="product2.jpg" height="300px" width="200px"
border="5" style="border-color:red;" onmouseover="Product2Info()" /></div>
```

```
<img src ="product3.jpg" height="300px" width="200px"
border="5" style="border-color:black;" onmouseover="Product3Info()" />
</div>
<form name="msgForm">
<input type="text" name="scrollingMsgBox" size="88">
</form>


<p> </p>
<p><b>Thanks for Shopping at Fran's Place</b>.</p>
</body>
</html>
```

Figure 15.3 shows the results of running the code in Listing 15.4.

FIGURE 15.3
By adding several different interactive features, you can create a website that people will want to visit repeatedly. *(Credits: Creative Mani/Shutterstock; Brian Jannsen/Alamy Stock Photo)*

Much of this code has now been present for the past three examples, but there is some new code to discuss here. Within the header, a string variable named `scrollMsg` is created, and any and all information you want to appear on your ticker is added to the string using the string concatenation operation (+=). Remember that by using this operator, you can add the string listed on the right side of the operator to the end of the string indicated on the left side of the operator. So you can use the concatenation operator to build a string of significant size. A larger scroll of information will keep visitors interested longer. The value to putting the string up in the header is that you can easily find it to change the information as needed, such as a new special of the week or extended hours around the holidays.

The function `scrollingMsg` follows and takes the completed `scrollMsg` string and prints it to the created text box, starting with the first character in the string; this happens because the `beginPos` counter is set to 0 before the function is called. When the string is printed, the `beginPos` counter is incremented by 1 and then, after a short delay, the function is called again. This time the string is printed in the text box starting from the second character in the string, and the counter is incremented again. Continually printing the string, advanced by a single character, creates a scrolling, animated effect. The function would print the message only once if it weren't for the `if` statement that follows the incrementing of the `beginPos` counter. Each time the function runs, this `if` statement checks whether the counter is higher than the length of the string. If it is, there's no more string to print. So the counter is set back to 0, and the rotation begins again, giving the illusion of a never-ending repeating ticker.

The `setTimeout()` method you used in the photo rotator is used here to scroll the message. Again, the number at the end of the `setTimeout()` call sets the delay between the function calls, and it therefore sets the speed of the scroll. Again, feel free to experiment with this number to set a pace you feel is right.

Summary

People most often use JavaScript to add fun interactivity to their websites. While many people use existing web-creation tools to add bells, whistles, and widgets to their sites, there is something extremely satisfying about creating the effects yourself. Much of what you learned about Python in the first nine hours can be applied to JavaScript (with some minor syntax changes) to create interactivity and other effects.

The examples presented in this lesson just scratch the surface of what's possible. You can also use JavaScript to add animation, sound, video, and much more. This book cannot cover it all, but there are numerous other options out there, including *Sams Teach Yourself JavaScript in 24 Hours* from Sams Publishing.

The next hour covers a few more advanced topics as a JavaScript sendoff before turning to SQL, Visual Studio, and other topics.

Q&A

Q. If one or two of these interactive techniques are good, more would be better, right?

A. Be careful not to overdo interactivity and pizzazz on your website. Too much of it can be distracting and may detract from the look and feel of a professional site. If your site has multiple pages, consider using one or two effects per page and spread them out. Another idea would be to change the interactivity on your page monthly so that it constantly feels fresh and updated. Old content, even if it is interactive, may alienate your visitors. If you don't seem to care enough about your site to update it, why should they care enough to visit it?

Q. Will these types of effects work if my website visitors view it using a mobile device, like a phone or tablet?

A. Mobile devices have created an additional level of complexity in web development (and more work for web developers!). For now, continue to develop web pages the way you are doing, but as you get more proficient, you should start to consider developing mobile sites as well. When you do, go simple. Some of the best effects on full-page websites do not look good on smaller screens, if they work at all.

Workshop

The quiz questions are provided for your further understanding.

Quiz

1. What is the advantage of putting image files in the same folder as your JavaScript code?

2. Where do you place a function in the HTML body code if you want it to run as soon as the page loads?

3. What method can you use to repeatedly call a function after a preset delay?

4. What measure of time is used for the delay in the method from question 3?

5. True or false: When you're working with images, you can only set them up to be interactively clickable.

6. What method would be used to trigger code if a pointer leaves a specific object?

7. True or false: You cannot select the color of the banner around an image.

8. True or false: You can rotate through a maximum of 10 images on a website.

9. What is the difference between `onclick()` and `onmouseover()`?

10. How do you add a string to the end of another string?

Answers

1. You don't have to type the entire file path to your image files if they are in the same file as your program file.

2. Within the `<body>` declaration, you can add a function with the `onload()` method, and it will run as soon as the page loads.

3. The `setTimeout()` method

4. Milliseconds

5. False. You can also set images to be interactive when the mouse pointer hovers over them.

6. `onmouseout`

7. False. You can change the color of the borders around images.

8. False. There is no limit to the number of images you can rotate through on a website.

9. `onmouseover()` triggers code when the mouse pointer hovers over a specific object. You must click the object in order to trigger the code if you use the `onclick()` method.

10. You use the string concatenation method (+=). For example, if you have the string `name = "Bobby"`, and you want to add the last name `"Smith"` to the string name, you would write:

    `name += " Smith"`

    Notice the space before the name `Smith` in this string. If you didn't add that, `name` would equal `"BobbySmith"`.

HOUR 16
JavaScript and AJAX

As you've seen with the JavaScript examples so far in this book, JavaScript is a client-side programming language that allows you to display and interact with information in a web browser. AJAX, on the other hand, is a set of technologies (one of which is JavaScript) that allows you to move beyond the client-side boundaries of a web browser and work with files on a web server or with responses from server-side programs.

This hour introduces you to the basics of working with AJAX, including the following highlights:

▶ How AJAX enables JavaScript to communicate with server-side programs and files

▶ Using the XMLHttpRequest object's properties and methods

▶ Creating your own AJAX library

▶ Using AJAX to read data from an XML file

▶ Using AJAX to communicate with a server-side program

Introducing AJAX

Traditionally, one of the major limitations of JavaScript was that it couldn't communicate with a web server because it is a client-side technology—that is, it stays within the browser. For example, you could create a game in JavaScript, but keeping a list of high scores stored on a server would require submitting a page to a server-side form, which JavaScript could not do (because, as you've learned, it wasn't meant to do that).

Speaking purely about user interactions, one of the limitations of web pages in general used to be that getting data from the user to the server or from the server to the user generally required a new page to be loaded and displayed. But today, you likely run across websites every day that enable you to interact with content without loading a new page every time you click or submit a button.

AJAX (Asynchronous JavaScript and XML) is the answer to both these problems. AJAX refers to JavaScript's capability to use a built-in object, XMLHttpRequest, to communicate with a web server without submitting a form or loading a page. This object is supported by Internet Explorer, Firefox, Chrome, and all other modern browsers.

Although the term *AJAX* was coined in 2005, `XMLHttpRequest` has been supported by browsers for years; it was developed by Microsoft and first appeared in Internet Explorer 5. Nonetheless, in the past few years, using AJAX has become a popular way of developing applications because browsers that support it have become more common. Another name for this technique is *remote scripting*.

NOTE
_____

The term *AJAX* first appeared in an online article by Jesse James Garrett of Adaptive Path on February 18, 2005.
_____

The JavaScript Client (Front End)

JavaScript has traditionally had one way of communicating with a server: by submitting a form. Remote scripting allows for much more versatile communication with the server. The *A* in AJAX stands for *asynchronous*, which means that the browser (and the user) aren't left hanging while waiting for the server to respond. Here's how a typical AJAX request works:

1. The script creates an `XMLHttpRequest` object and sends it to the web server. The script can continue after sending the request.

2. The server responds by sending the contents of a file or the output of a server-side program.

3. When the response arrives from the server, a JavaScript function is triggered to act on the data.

4. Because the goal is a more responsive user interface, the script usually displays the data from the server by using the DOM (Document Object Model), eliminating the need for a page refresh.

In practice, this happens quickly, but even with a slow server, it can still work. Also, because the requests are asynchronous, more than one request can be in progress at a time.

The Server-Side Script (Back End)

The part of an application that resides on the web server is commonly referred to as the *back end*. The simplest back end is a static file on the server, such as an XML or text file that holds data; JavaScript can request such a file with `XMLHttpRequest` and then read and act on its contents. More commonly, the back end is a server-side program running in a language such as PHP, Perl, or Ruby, and these server-side programs output results in XML or JSON (JavaScript Object Notation) format.

JavaScript can send data to a server-side program by using GET or POST methods—the same methods used in an HTML form. In a GET request, the data is encoded in the URL that loads the program. In a POST request, it is sent separately and can contain more data.

XML

The *X* in AJAX stands for *XML* (Extensible Markup Language), the universal markup language on which the latest versions of HTML are built. A server-side file or program can send data in XML format, and JavaScript can act on the data by using its methods for working with XML.

Keep in mind that using XML is just one way to send data, and it's not always the easiest. The server could just as easily send plain text, which the script could display, or HTML, which the script could insert into the page by using the innerHTML property. Some programmers have even used server-side scripts to return data in JavaScript format, which can be easily executed using the eval function.

NOTE

JSON formalizes the idea of encoding data in JavaScript, and this a very popular method for transferring data. See www.json.org for details and code examples in many languages.

Popular Examples of AJAX

Whereas HTML and JavaScript are typically used to build web pages and sites, AJAX techniques often result in *web applications*—web-based services that perform work for the user. Here are a few well-known examples of AJAX:

▶ Google's Gmail mail client (http://mail.google.com) uses AJAX to make a fast-responding email application. You can delete messages and perform other tasks without waiting for a new page to load.

▶ Amazon.com uses AJAX for some functions. For example, if you click on one of the Yes/No voting buttons for a product comment, it sends your vote to the server, and a message appears next to the button thanking you—all without loading a page.

▶ Facebook (www.facebook.com) and other sites that allow you to "like" something are probably the most prevalent examples of AJAX in our daily lives. Every single time you click to "like" something, either on Facebook or elsewhere, you are using AJAX to communicate that click to a server-side script somewhere, which then seamlessly updates the "like" count—without reloading the page.

These are just a few examples. Subtle bits of remote scripting appear all over the web, and you might not even notice them—although you might be annoyed a little bit less often about having to wait for a page to load.

AJAX Frameworks and Libraries

Remote scripting can be complicated—especially considering the browser differences you'll learn about briefly in this hour—and several frameworks and libraries have been developed to simplify web application programming that leverages AJAX. Here are a few popular and feature-rich frameworks and libraries:

▶ **jQuery** (http://jquery.com) is the most popular JavaScript library in use today, with over 90% market share. It serves as the foundation for many of the AJAX functions and applications you encounter on a daily basis. The core library and the user interface extensions library allow you to rapidly build and deploy rich user interfaces and add a variety of attractive effects to existing components.

▶ **Prototype** (www.prototypejs.org) is another JavaScript library that simplifies tasks such as working with DOM objects, dealing with data in forms, and remote scripting (AJAX). Prototype is also built into the Ruby on Rails framework for the server-side language Ruby, and the Script.aculo.us library plugs in to Prototype for rapid development of visual effects and user interface elements.

▶ **Backbone.js** (http://backbonejs.org) and **Ember.js** (http://emberjs.com) are both lightweight but powerful frameworks for rapid development of AJAX-based web applications. They are especially popular for the creation of single-page web applications.

Limitations of AJAX

Remote scripting is powerful, but there are some things it can't do, and there are some things to watch out for. These are some of the limitations and potential problems of AJAX:

▶ The script and the XML data or server-side program it requests data from must be on the same domain, or steps must be taken to allow and secure cross-domain communication.

▶ Some older browsers and some less common browsers (such as some mobile browsers) don't support XMLHttpRequest, so you can't count on its availability for all users. While this is changing, it must still be accounted for.

▶ Requiring AJAX might compromise the accessibility of a site for disabled users.

▶ Users may still be accustomed to seeing a new page load each time they change something, so there might be a learning curve for them to understand an AJAX application. This, too, is changing, through heavy personal use of social media sites, which are heavy users of AJAX.

As with other advanced uses of JavaScript, the best approach is to be unobtrusive; make sure there's still a way to use the site without AJAX support if possible and use feature sensing to prevent errors on browsers that don't support it.

Using XMLHttpRequest

You will now see how to use XMLHttpRequest to communicate with a server. This might seem a bit complex, but other requests use the same process. Later, you will create a reusable code library to simplify this process.

Creating a Request

To create an XMLHttpRequest object, you use the new keyword, as with other JavaScript objects. The following statement creates a request object in some browsers:

```
ajaxreq = new XMLHttpRequest();
```

This example works with Firefox, Chrome, Internet Explorer (versions 7 and later), Microsoft Edge, and other modern browsers, but not with Internet Explorer 5 or 6. It is up to you whether you want to support these older browsers or not. Although the use percentages of the older browsers are very low, some institutions might be stuck with, for example, a lot of Internet Explorer 6 browsers installed at workstations, so your mileage may vary.

NOTE

From this point forward, the sample code supports only Internet Explorer 7 and beyond (modern browsers), and if you want to support older browsers, you have to use ActiveX syntax:

```
ajaxreq = new ActiveXObject("Microsoft.XMLHTTP");
```

Later this hour you will see how to use the correct method depending on the browser in use. In either case, the variable you use (ajaxreq in this example) stores the XMLHttpRequest object. You can use the methods of this object to open and send a request, as explained in the following sections.

Opening a URL

With the open() method of the XMLHttpRequest object, you specify the filename as well as the method in which data will be sent to the server: GET or POST (the same methods supported by web forms):

```
ajaxreq.open("GET","filename");
```

For the GET method, the data you send is included in the URL. For example, the following command opens (runs) a script file on the web server called search.php and sends the value John for the query parameter:

```
ajaxreq.open("GET","search.php?query=John");
```

Sending the Request

You use the send() method of the XMLHttpRequest object to send a request to the server. If you are using the POST method, the data to send is the argument for send(). For a GET request, you can use the null value instead:

```
ajaxreq.send(null);
```

Awaiting a Response

After the request is sent, your script continues without waiting for a result. The result could come at any time, and you can detect it with an event handler. The XMLHttpRequest object has an onreadystatechange event handler for this purpose. You can create a function to deal with the response and set it as the handler for this event:

```
ajaxreq.onreadystatechange = MyFunc;
```

The request object has a property, readyState, that indicates its status, and this event is triggered whenever the readyState property changes. The values of readyState range from 0 for a new request to 4 for a complete request, so your event-handling function usually needs to watch for a value of 4.

Although the request is complete, it might not have been successful. The status property is set to 200 if the request succeeded or an error code if it failed. The statusText property stores a text explanation of the error or OK for success.

CAUTION
_____

When using event handlers, be sure to specify the function name without parentheses. With parentheses, you're referring to the *result* of the function; without them, you're referring to the function itself.

_____

Interpreting the Response Data

When the readyState property reaches 4 and the request is complete, the data returned from the server is available to your script in two properties: responseText is the response in raw text form, and responseXML is the response as an XML object. If the data was not in XML format, only the text property will be available.

JavaScript's DOM methods are meant to work on XML, so you can use them with the responseXML property. For example, you can use the getElementsByTagName() method to extract data from XML.

Creating a Simple AJAX Library

You should be aware by now that AJAX requests can be a bit complex. To make things easier, you can create an AJAX library—a JavaScript file that provides functions that handle making a request and receiving the result, which you can reuse any time you need AJAX functions.

Listing 16.1 shows the complete AJAX library, including the special case for very old browsers.

LISTING 16.1   The AJAX library

```
// global variables to keep track of the request
// and the function to call when done
var ajaxreq=false, ajaxCallback;

// ajaxRequest: Sets up a request
function ajaxRequest(filename) {
   try {
   // Firefox / Chrome / Edge / Others
   ajaxreq= new XMLHttpRequest();
   } catch (error) {
    try {
      // IE 5 / IE 6
     ajaxreq = new ActiveXObject("Microsoft.XMLHTTP");
     } catch (error) {
     return false;
     }
   }
   ajaxreq.open("GET", filename);
   ajaxreq.onreadystatechange = ajaxResponse;
   ajaxreq.send(null);
}

// ajaxResponse: Waits for response and calls a function
function ajaxResponse() {
   if (ajaxreq.readyState !=4) return;
   if (ajaxreq.status==200) {
   // if the request succeeded...
   if (ajaxCallback) ajaxCallback();
   } else alert("Request failed: " + ajaxreq.statusText);
   return true;
}
```

To use this library, follow these steps:

1. Save the library file as `ajax.js` in the same folder that holds your HTML documents and scripts.

2. Include the script in your document with a `<script src>` tag. It should be included before any other scripts that use its features.

3. In your script, create a function to be called when the request is complete and set the `ajaxCallback` variable to the function.

4. Call the `ajaxRequest()` function. Its parameter is the filename of the server-side program or file. (This library supports `GET` requests only, so you don't need to specify the method.)

5. Your function specified in `ajaxCallback` is called when the request completes successfully, and the global variable `ajaxreq` stores the data in its `responseXML` and `responseText` properties.

The next two sections explain a bit more about the library's core functions.

The `ajaxRequest` Function

The `ajaxRequest` function handles all the steps necessary to create and send an `XMLHttpRequest` Object. First, it creates the `XMLHttpRequest` object. As noted earlier, this requires a different command for older browsers, and an error occurs if the wrong command executes, so `try` and `catch` are used to create the request. First, the standard method is used, and if it causes an error, the ActiveX method is tried. If that also causes an error, the `ajaxreq` variable is set to `false` to indicate that AJAX is not supported.

The `ajaxResponse` Function

The `ajaxResponse` function is used as the `onreadystatechange` event handler. This function first checks the `readyState` property for a value of 4. If it has a different value, the function returns without doing anything.

Next, it checks the `status` property for a value of `200`, which indicates that the request was successful. Upon success, the `ajaxResponse` function runs the function stored in the `ajaxCallback` variable. Otherwise, it displays the error message in an alert box.

Creating an AJAX Quiz Using the Library

Now that you have a reusable AJAX library, you can use it to create JavaScript applications that take advantage of remote scripting. This first example displays quiz questions on a page and prompts for the answers.

Rather than including the questions in the script, this example reads the quiz questions and answers from an XML file on the server as a demonstration of AJAX.

CAUTION

This example requires the use of a web server. It will not work on a local machine due to browsers' security restrictions on remote scripting.

The HTML File

The HTML for this example, shown in Listing 16.2, is straightforward. It defines a simple form with an Answer field and a Submit button, along with some hooks for the script.

LISTING 16.2   The HTML file for the quiz example

```
<!DOCTYPE html>
<html lang="en">
   <head>
     <title>Ajax Quiz Test</title>
     <script type="text/javascript" src="ajax.js"></script>
   </head>
   <body>
      <h1>Ajax Quiz Example</h1>
      <form method="post" action="">
      <p><input type="button" value="Start the Quiz" id="startq" /></p>
      <p><strong>Question:</strong></p>
      <span id="question">[Press Button to Start Quiz]</span></p>
      <p><strong>Answer:</strong></p>
      <input type="text" name="answer" id="answer" /></p>
      <p><input type="button" value="Submit Answer" id="submit" /></p>
      </form>
   <script type="text/javascript" src="quiz.js"></script>
   </body>
</html>
```

This HTML file includes the following elements:

► The `<script>` tag in the `<head>` section includes the AJAX library you created in the previous section from the `ajax.js` file.

► The `<script>` tag in the `<body>` section includes the `quiz.js` file, which will contain the quiz script that you'll create in a moment).

► The `<span id="question">` tag sets up a place for the question to be inserted by the script.

► The text field with the `id` value `"answer"` is where the user will answer the question.

▸ The button with the `id` value `"submit"` will submit an answer.

▸ The button with the `id` value `"startq"` will start the quiz.

You can test the HTML document at this time by placing the file on your web server and accessing it via the URL, but the buttons won't work until you add the XML and JavaScript files, which you'll learn about in the next two sections.

The XML File

The XML file for the quiz is shown in Listing 16.3. I've filled it with a few JavaScript questions, but it could easily be adapted for another purpose.

LISTING 16.3   The XML file containing the quiz questions and answers

```
<?xml version="1.0" ?>
<questions>
    <q>What DOM object contains URL information for the window?</q>
    <a>location</a>
    <q>Which method of the document object finds the
        object for an element?</q>
    <a>getElementById</a>
    <q>If you declare a variable outside a function,
        is it global or local?</q>
    <a>global</a>
    <q>What is the formal standard for the JavaScript language called?</q>
    <a>ECMAScript</a>
</questions>
```

The `<questions>` tag encloses the entire file, and the questions and answer are each enclosed in `<q>` and `<a>` tags. Remember that this is XML, not HTML; these are not standard HTML tags but tags that were created for this example. Because this file will be used only by your script, it does not need to follow a standard format.

To use this file, save it as `questions.xml` in the same folder as the HTML document. It will be loaded by the script you create in the next section.

Of course, with a quiz this small, you could have made things easier by storing the questions and answers in a JavaScript array. But imagine a much larger quiz, with thousands of questions, or a server-side program that pulls questions from a database, or even a hundred different files with different quizzes to choose from, and you can see the benefit of using a separate XML file.

The JavaScript File

Because you have a separate library to handle the complexities of making an AJAX request and receiving the response, the script for this example only needs to deal with the action for the quiz itself. Listing 16.4 shows the JavaScript file for this example.

LISTING 16.4   The JavaScript file for the quiz example

```javascript
// global variable qn is the current question number
var qn=0;

// load the questions from the XML file
function getQuestions() {
   obj=document.getElementById("question");
   obj.firstChild.nodeValue="(please wait)";
   ajaxCallback = nextQuestion;
   ajaxRequest("questions.xml");
}

// display the next question
function nextQuestion() {
   questions = ajaxreq.responseXML.getElementsByTagName("q");
   obj=document.getElementById("question");
   if (qn < questions.length) {
     q = questions[qn].firstChild.nodeValue;
     obj.firstChild.nodeValue=q;
     } else {
     obj.firstChild.nodeValue="(no more questions)";
     }
}

// check the user's answer
function checkAnswer() {
   answers = ajaxreq.responseXML.getElementsByTagName("a");
   a = answers[qn].firstChild.nodeValue;
   answerfield = document.getElementById("answer");
   if (a == answerfield.value) {
      alert("Correct!");
   }
   else {
     alert("Incorrect. The correct answer is: " + a);
   }
   qn = qn + 1;
   answerfield.value="";
   nextQuestion();
}
```

```
// Set up the event handlers for the buttons
obj=document.getElementById("startq");
obj.onclick=getQuestions;
ans=document.getElementById("submit");
ans.onclick=checkAnswer;
```

This script consists of the following:

▶ The first `var` statement defines a global variable, `qn`, which will keep track of which question is currently displayed. It is initially set to 0 for the first question.

▶ The `getQuestions()` function is called when the user clicks the Start Quiz button. This function uses the AJAX library to request the contents of the `questions.xml` file. It sets the `ajaxCallback` variable to the `nextQuestion()` function.

▶ The `nextQuestion()` function is called when the AJAX request is complete. This function uses the `getElementsByTagName()` method on the `responseXML` property to find all the questions (`<q>` tags) and store them in the `questions` array.

▶ The `checkAnswer()` function is called when the user submits an answer. It uses `getElementsByTagName()` to store the answers (`<a>` tags) in the `answers` array and then compares the answer for the current question with the user's answer and displays an alert indicating whether it was right or wrong.

▶ The script commands after this function set up two event handlers. One attaches the `getQuestions()` function to the Start Quiz button to set up the quiz; the other attaches the `checkAnswer()` function to the Submit button.

Testing the Quiz

To try this example, you'll need all four files in the same folder: `ajax.js` (the AJAX library), `quiz.js` (the quiz functions), `questions.xml` (the questions), and the HTML document. All but the HTML document need to have the correct filenames in order to work correctly, since they are referred to by name within other files. Also remember that because it uses AJAX, this example requires a web server.

Figure 16.1 shows the quiz in action, after a question has been answered.

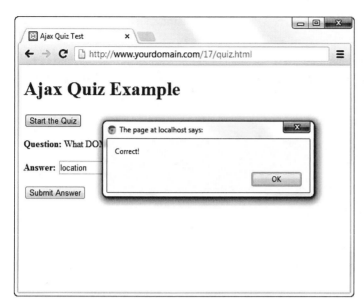

FIGURE 16.1
The quiz example loaded in a web browser.

Summary

In this hour, you've learned how AJAX, or remote scripting, allows JavaScript on the front end to communicate with scripts or data that live on a web server (the back end). You created a reusable AJAX library that can be used to create any number of AJAX applications, and you created a quiz application based on questions and answers stored in an XML file.

Q&A

Q. What happens if the server is slow or never responds to the request?

A. This is another reason you should use AJAX as an *optional* feature; whether because of the server or the user's connection, there will be times when a request is slow to respond or never responds. In such a case, the callback function is called late or not at all. This can cause trouble with overlapping requests. For example, in the live search example, an erratic server might cause the responses for the first few characters typed to come in a few seconds apart, confusing the user. You can remedy this by checking the `readyState` property to make sure a request is not already in progress before you start another one.

Q. If I use a JavaScript or AJAX framework, do I still have to use the `ajax.js` library shown here?

A. Very likely not. One of the benefits of these libraries and frameworks is that they provide commonly used code for you in ways that are very easy to use. Be sure to check the documentation of the library or framework that you choose so you know how to make AJAX requests within those frameworks.

Workshop

The quiz questions are provided for your further understanding.

Quiz

1. What does the acronym AJAX stand for?

2. What is the name of the built-in JavaScript object used to communicate with a web server?

3. Why is it important for connections to be asynchronous?

4. What are two types of back-end data formats that often contain output results that are then used on the front end?

5. True or false: When using AJAX, to support Internet Explorer 5 and 6, you must create an ActiveX object rather than an `XMLHttpRequest` object.

6. Which JavaScript library currently has the greatest market share?

7. True or false: Requiring AJAX might compromise the accessibility of a site for disabled users.

8. Which method of the `XMLHttpRequest` object specifies the file to which data will be sent on the server?

9. Which `readyState` value indicates that a request is complete?

10. Why was it important to create the basic `ajax.js` library file shown in Listing 16.1?

Answers

1. Asynchronous JavaScript and XML

2. `XMLHttpRequest`

3. Asynchronous connections provide a better user experience because the browser can continue to display information while waiting for the server to respond to other user interactions, including multiple requests at one time.

4. XML and JSON

5. True

6. jQuery

7. True

8. `open()`

9. 4

10. Since these basic functions are used every time you want to make an AJAX request and get a response, you would be typing them over and over again unless you created one file that you could just refer to each time.

HOUR 17
SQL

So far, this tutorial has covered three programming languages, which may approach syntax and commands differently but have clear similarities in approach and concepts. Thanks to these similarities, once you've learned one programming language, you have a head start on learning additional similar languages. Structured Query Language (SQL) is not as similar to the other languages you've learned about so far as they are to each other. But SQL is a tool used by a much wider group of business professionals, as it is used to retrieve data from databases and update the data as needed. Many people who would never consider themselves to be programmers employ SQL as part of their day-to-day responsibilities. They use SQL to help grab subsets of data from their company's database and make decisions based on the information. SQL is a powerful language, and you can use it to write almost all the queries you need to interact with databases by learning just a few commands.

The highlights of this hour include the following:

▸ Learning the basics of relational databases

▸ Writing basic queries in SQL

▸ Retrieving records from a database

▸ Inserting and updating records from a database

▸ Deleting records from a database

Relational Databases

In earlier hours, you learned that most computer programs deal with data entry and manipulation. Companies today have massive amounts of data that needs to be stored and accessed and analyzed. In addition, a company's data is an important asset, and it must be kept secure from both individuals outside the organization and employees who should not have access to it. Most companies use relational databases to store their key information. In fact, many companies do not utilize a singular database; rather, they employ multiple databases for different needs. For example, a store would need to keep information about its products, including inventory, price, historical sales data, and manufacturers and distributors. All that would make an excellent database. But the business would also need to store employee information, including contact info, salary, hire date, time off, and more. That would be held in a completely different database.

Data that a company stores is broken down into different databases, and it is further divided into individual tables. A *table* stores a related collection of information. In our store example, one table might be the contact information for the manufacturer of products that the store sells. A table is made up of a series of records that share common bits of information, known as *fields*. The manufacturer table probably holds the name of the company, its address, a website, a contact name, and a contact phone number. Figure 17.1 shows how such a table might look.

ManufactID	Name	StreetAddress	City	State	PostalCode	Website	ContactName	ContactPhone
1	Parts Galore!	5416 Main Street	Wabash	IN	67023	www.partsgalore.com	Jayne Forrester	(317)-555-5677
2	Smith Manufacturing	98 Valerian Drive	Sunapee	NH	07812	www.smithman.com	Tarik Davis	(603) 555-9191
3	Smith Assembly	10 10th Street	Bellvue	WA	78121	www.smithofwa.com	Brenda Roberts	(888) 555-0932
4	Jones Parts	67 Willis Avenue	Denver	CO	59808	www.jonesparts.com	Walid Basar	(800) 555-1046

FIGURE 17.1
A database table has a series of fields (represented by the top row) and a number of records (each subsequent row).

NOTE

You see that the field names in the database in Figure 17.1 have no spaces (so you get ContactName instead of Contact Name). It's accepted practice to use no spaces in field names but to capitalize each word in a multiple-word field name.

Another field not listed in the previous paragraph is the manufacturer identification number, abbreviated ManufactID in Figure 17.1. This is the primary key of the table, which is a value that is unique for each record. Almost every other field in that table can be shared; you could have multiple manufacturers with the same or similar names, addresses, or locations. All the fields in total would probably give you a unique entry, but it's better practice to have a single unique value for each record in a table. (Think of your Social Security number, employee ID, or an account number you have with a company; each of these numbers allows the company to easily look up your information and assist you.)

There's another significant use for primary keys in relational databases. Let's return to our store example and consider a second table—one that has items that are sold. Perhaps this table contains a part ID, the name of the part, a description, the cost of the good (how much it costs for the store to purchase), the net selling price (how much customers pay the store for the item), and a manufacturer ID (from which manufacturer the store purchases the part). Figure 17.2 shows an example of such a table.

PartID	Name	Description	CostOfGood	NetSellingPrice	ManufactID
1	3/8 Bolt	Package of 10 3/8 Bolts	$1.20	$1.99	1
2	1/2 Nail	Box of 100 1/2 Nails	$2.65	$5.00	2
3	1/2 Nail	Box of 100 1/2 Nails	$2.99	$5.00	4
4	1/2 Copper Wire	100 ft Roll of 1/2 Copper Wire	$12.91	$19.99	1

FIGURE 17.2
A table for part numbers, with fields across the top and unique records in the remaining rows.

You can see the value of a primary key in this table. ManufactID in this table links to the Manufacturer table, so you don't need to repeat all the details of the manufacturer for each record in the Parts table; you simply relate the data from one table to the data from another table. The table in Figure 17.2 shows another value of having a unique primary key for each record. You could easily have two manufacturers selling exactly the same item. In this example, one manufacturer does charge slightly more than the other for it, but they could easily charge the same.

Table linking doesn't have to be limited to one-on-one linking. If you built a Customer table to hold the contact information for your customers and then an Order table to store each order, the Order table could be linked to both the Customer table (to identify who purchased the order) and the Parts table (to identify what was purchased). This type of linking between tables is shown in Figure 17.3.

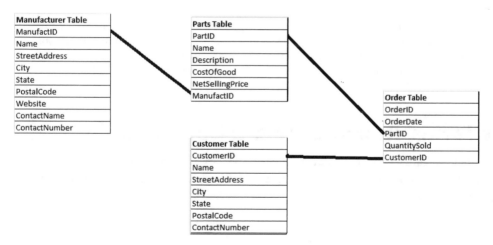

FIGURE 17.3
As your database becomes more robust, diagramming the relationships between the different tables can be extremely useful.

With each added table, your database becomes more robust and more complicated. It's easy to review a table with four records (refer to Figures 17.1 and 17.2). But what if you have 10,000 parts? You need to be able to identify subsets of data quickly and efficiently. This is where SQL comes in. You can use SQL to write queries that can either return information from your database or add, update, or delete existing records and tables.

Basic SQL Queries

Learning SQL is not difficult, particularly when you've already begun to learn multiple programming languages. SQL can be robust, but you will generally find yourself using a few commands most of the time:

- ▶ SELECT

- ▶ UPDATE

- ▶ DELETE

- ▶ INSERT INTO

- ▶ CREATE

- ▶ ALTER

- ▶ DROP

CAUTION
Be very careful when using UPDATE, DELETE, ALTER, and DROP. You could end up removing or permanently changing records you did not intend to remove or change if you type the wrong syntax for your query! If you want to experiment with SQL on a database, it's smart practice to back up your data by creating a copy of the database in question. You can always delete the copy later.

Retrieving Records from a Database

The first thing you often do with a database is retrieve records. You can do this with the SELECT statement. The simplest use of the SELECT statement is to pull all the records from a table with the following syntax:

```
SELECT columns (or *) FROM tablename;
```

The asterisk (*) means pull every single field from whatever table you specify with *tablename*. The table in Figure 17.1 is named Manufacturer, for example, so to see all the manufacturers currently stored in that table, you would type:

```
SELECT * FROM Manufacturer;
```

This query would return the following data set:

Manufact ID	Company Name	Company Street Address	Company City	Company State	Company Postal Code	Website	Contact Name	Contact Phone
1	Parts Galore!	5416 Main Street	Wabash	IN	67023	www.partsgalore.com	Jayne Forrester	(317)-555-5677
2	Smith Manufacturing	98 Valerian Drive	Sunapee	NH	07812	www.smithman.com	Tarik Davis	(603) 555-9191
3	Smith Assembly	10 10th Street	Bellevue	WA	78121	www.smithofwa.com	Brenda Roberts	(888) 555-0932
4	Jones Parts	67 Willis Avenue	Denver	CO	59808	www.jonesparts.com	Walid Basar	(800) 555-1046

You may not want all this information. Perhaps you only want the ID and company name. To get only this information, instead of using * to get all columns, you can specify what columns you wanted to see. For example, the following SQL query:

```
SELECT ManufactID, CompanyName FROM Manufacturer;
```

would return the following subset of the data:

ManufactID	Company Name
1	Parts Galore!
2	Smith Manufacturing
3	Smith Assembly
4	Jones Parts

Narrowing Your Data with WHERE

You've written your first query! But you obviously don't want to just keep retrieving entire tables. Luckily, you can further narrow the returned search results from a SELECT query by using the WHERE clause. Its syntax is as follows:

```
SELECT columns FROM tablename WHERE conditions;
```

So, if you wanted to see all the manufacturers that are based in Washington, you could use the following query:

```
SELECT * FROM Manufacturer WHERE State = "WA";
```

Your query would return the following data set:

Manufact ID	Name	Street Address	City	State	Postal Code	Website	Contact Name	Contact Phone
3	Smith Assembly	10 10th Street	Bellevue	WA	78121	www. smithofwa. com	Brenda Roberts	(888) 555-0932

When you are using a WHERE clause to narrow your expected data, you can use relational operators to select data. The relational operators are similar to elements you learned in earlier hours. Some of the most common of them are listed in Table 17.1.

TABLE 17.1 Common operators to use with the WHERE clause

Operator	Meaning
=	Equal to
>	Greater than
<	Less than
>=	Greater than or equal to
<=	Less than or equal to
!=	Not equal to

Earlier in this hour, you saw an example of using the equal sign (=), but the other operators can also be useful in decision making. For example, if you had an Inventory table with a quantity field, you could use the following query to generate a list of all products for which you have 10 or fewer in stock:

```
SELECT * FROM Inventory WHERE quantity < 10;
```

This would be a great query to run weekly to determine what you need to order before it runs out.

In addition to these mathematical operators, there are a few handy terms that can serve as effective operators as well. BETWEEN allows you to get a subset of data that falls between a lower boundary and an upper boundary. If you wanted all the products that you sell for between $10 and $20, you could write the following query:

```
SELECT * FROM Parts WHERE NetSellingPrice BETWEEN 10 AND 20;
```

This query would return a list of products that fit the specified criteria. This query also demonstrates the AND keyword, which can be used with a WHERE clause to pick items that satisfy multiple conditions. Its companion, the OR keyword, can be used with WHERE to pick items that satisfy one condition of multiple choices. If, for example, you only wanted to know which manufacturers are based on the west coast, you could write the following query:

```
SELECT * FROM Manufacturers WHERE State = 'CA' OR State = 'OR' OR State = 'WA';
```

This query would return all manufacturers based in California, Oregon, and Washington.

The third keyword, NOT, returns items that do not match the criteria.

Using SELECT with the WHERE conditional can help you focus on a specific subset of your data.

Inserting and Updating Database Records

Naturally, you don't want to just look at database records. You also need to alter your data, either adding new records to an existing database or changing the existing records. To add new records to an existing table, you use the INSERT INTO statement. The syntax follows:

```
INSERT INTO tablename (column1, column2, column3,....)
VALUES (value1, value2, value3,...)
```

You list all the table columns to which you want to add data, along with the values you want to enter in each column. You must ensure that the values are in the same order as the columns; otherwise, you will have data in the wrong fields. You do not have to list every column; if you don't include a column in the INSERT INTO statement, that field will have NULL as its value. You can then update the value later. You also do not have to list the individual columns if you are filling every value in the row; just make sure you list all the values.

NOTE

If you set the ID value (for example, PartID in Figure 17.2) to autoincrement (that is, automatically create a new ID that is one more than the previous value), you do not need to list it in the INSERT INTO statement either.

For example, to enter a new part into the Parts table, you can use the following statement:

```
INSERT INTO Parts (Name, Description, CostOfGood, NetSellingPrice, ManufactID)
     VALUES ("Packing Tape", "one roll of packing tape", $0.99, $2.49, 3)
```

Again, with all the values being entered, you could omit the parenthetical list of columns and just use the following:

```
INSERT INTO Parts VALUES ("Packing Tape", "one roll of packing tape", $0.99,
$2.49, 3)
```

Either of these statements would update your Parts table to be the following:

PartID	Name	Description	CostOfGood	NetSellingPrice	ManufactID
1	3/8 Bolt	Package of 10 3/8 Bolts	$1.20	$1.99	1
2	1/2 Nail	Box of 100 1/2 Nails	$2.65	$5.00	2
3	1/2 Nail	Box of 100 1/2 Nails	$2.99	$5.00	4
4	1/2 Copper Wire	100 ft Roll of 1/2 Copper Wire	$12.91	$19.99	1
5	Packing Tape	one roll of packing tape	$0.99	$2.49	3

To enter just a few values (perhaps because you don't have the description and net selling price yet), you can use INSERT INTO as follows:

```
INSERT INTO Parts (Name, CostOfGood, ManufactID) VALUES ("Glue Gun", $10.75, 3)
```

If you run this statement, your table now has the following data:

PartID	Name	Description	CostOfGood	NetSellingPrice	ManufactID
1	3/8 Bolt	Package of 10 3/8 Bolts	$1.20	$1.99	1
2	1/2 Nail	Box of 100 1/2 Nails	$2.65	$5.00	2
3	1/2 Nail	Box of 100 1/2 Nails	$2.99	$5.00	4
4	1/2 Copper Wire	100 ft Roll of 1/2 Copper Wire	$12.91	$19.99	1
5	Packing Tape	one roll of packing tape	$0.99	$2.49	3
6	Glue Gun	NULL	$10.75	NULL	3

Updating Existing Records

In addition to creating new records in a database, you can also update an existing record with the UPDATE statement. The syntax of UPDATE follows:

```
UPDATE tablename SET column1 = value1, column2 = value2, column3 = value3,...
   WHERE condition;
```

Just as in a SELECT statement, if you do not use a WHERE condition with this UPDATE, every record in the table will be changed by the SET part of the statement. So, if you were looking to update the Glue Gun record in the previous example because you now have a description and net selling price for the item, you would use the following statement:

```
UPDATE Parts SET Description = "A standard glue gun", NetSellingPrice = $21.99
   WHERE PartID = 6;
```

This statement finds the record with `PartID` 6 and sets its `Description` field to `"A standard glue gun"` and its `NetSellingPrice` field to $21.99. If you leave off the `WHERE` clause, every record has its `Description` and `NetSellingPrice` fields altered. This demonstrates both the real power and the possible problems associated with using SQL: If you are not careful, you can make some catastrophic changes to a database. It is always smart to back up a database before you do any heavy-duty SQL work.

Deleting Records from a Database

One way to make catastrophic changes to a database is to delete any and all records from an existing table by using the `DELETE` keyword. Its syntax is fairly straightforward and should be familiar, now that you've worked with a number of other SQL keywords:

```
DELETE FROM tablename WHERE condition;
```

Can you guess what will happen if you do not put a condition in the `DELETE` statement? You guessed it: Every record in that table will be deleted. (Good job! You are really getting the hang of SQL!) Think about how bad it would be to lose an entire table of data and make sure you delete only the records you intended to remove; otherwise, you might have to work with an older version of your database—specifically your last successful backup.

Look again at the Parts table (refer to Figure 17.3). If your store decides to stop selling packing tape, you can remove the `Packing Tape` record from the table with the following SQL statement:

```
DELETE FROM Parts WHERE Name = "Packing Tape";
```

When you create `DELETE` statements, you can use all the conditional operators covered with the `SELECT` keyword, earlier this hour.

Deleting Entire Tables or Databases

You might at some point need to remove an existing table from a database. If you wrote a `DELETE` statement with no `WHERE` clause, you would remove every row of data from the table in question, but the table would still exist. If you actually need to remove the table in question, you can use the `DROP TABLE` statement. Its syntax follows:

```
DROP TABLE tablename;
```

Again, make sure this is what you want to do, as this keyword deletes the table and all the information currently in the table.

You can take things a step further and delete an entire database. Perhaps you copied an existing database to experiment on, but you eventually want to have only the original version of the database. To delete a database, use the `DROP DATABASE` statement. Its syntax is basically the same as that of the `DROP TABLE` statement:

```
DROP DATABASE databasename;
```

You're probably getting sick of the warnings, but they're important: You don't want to use this command unless you are certain that you no longer need a particular database.

Adding, Deleting, or Modifying the Fields in an Existing Table

You may find that a table in your database needs an additional field that you hadn't considered before, or you may no longer need an existing field. For the latter issue, you might wonder why you can't just leave the extra field in the database and ignore the information in it. Performance is an important feature of databases, and the more data that is in a database, the more time it may take to process a set of SQL statements. One basic tenet is to not have unnecessary data in your database. (There are other tricks and techniques that you can learn when you continue to learn SQL to optimize your SQL work.)

Adding New Fields to a Table

You can use the ALTER TABLE statement to add a new field, remove an existing one, or modify a field to accept a different data type (more on this in a minute). Its syntax varies depending on the purpose. If you are looking to add one or more columns, use this syntax:

```
ALTER TABLE tablename ADD columnname datatype;
```

The only part of this syntax that might be a bit puzzling to you is *datatype* . Just as the variables in certain languages must be defined to hold a specific data type, when a table is created, each field has a specific data type associated with it. As in programming languages, there are types used to handle strings (blocks of letters, numbers, and other characters) and numbers. But you can also define fields specific to dates, times, and money. To make things a bit more difficult and confusing, each database implementation handles the definitions of these data types a bit differently, so you need to find out which database your organization is using (MySQL, SQL Server, Microsoft Access, and so on) and then research data types for that specific database.

In the case of our Parts database, perhaps you need to add a LastSold field so the company can track whether there are some items that haven't sold in a long time and therefore shouldn't be carried anymore. This company uses MySQL, so you would want to use the DATE field. (There is a field that stores the date and time, but a date is clear enough for the needs of this example, and as mentioned earlier in the hour, you want to be efficient when choosing what to store in your database to improve its performance.) So, to add this new field to your database, you would use the following SQL statement:

```
ALTER TABLE Parts ADD LastSold DATE;
```

Now all the records in that table will have a LastSold field, but the field will not have any data in it; the field will be set to NULL until you use UPDATE statements to fill in the data. This is an example where you actually might want to do a mass update, setting all the records to a specific date that will then be updated with the new date.

Deleting Existing Fields from a Table

If you want to remove a field from a table, you use the ALTER TABLE statement again, this time modifying it with the DROP keyword. The syntax follows:

```
ALTER TABLE tablename DROP columnname;
```

This is a little more streamlined than the ADD version of the ALTER TABLE statement because you don't need to specify a data type; the column already has a data type, although it is about to become irrelevant as the column is being dropped.

For example, say that an older table of contact information has a field for pager numbers of individuals. Because the pager is all but extinct, it would make sense to free up some space by removing that field. Assuming that the table is named Contacts, and the field is named PagerNumber, the following statement would get the job done:

```
ALTER TABLE Contacts DROP PagerNumber;
```

Again, be extremely sure you no longer need that column before dropping it!

Modifying Existing Fields on a Table

In rare situations, you might want to modify existing fields by changing their data types. For example, perhaps you decide after all that you want your Parts table to store the last day an item was sold and also the exact time. You could alter the field to be DATETIME instead of just DATE. The syntax of such a statement is not universal but can vary by database implementation. In any case, you would use the ALTER TABLE statement, but the rest of the statement would vary by database implementation. For example, to change a table, SQL Server uses ALTER COLUMN, while MySQL uses MODIFY COLUMN. If you find yourself needing to alter an existing column, research the specifics of how your database handles things before getting into it.

Summary

This brief introduction to SQL will help you understand many queries you see, but if you wish to become a SQL master querysmith, you need to study and practice the fundamentals. In particular, you need to learn how to use the JOIN keyword to combine data from multiple tables, as this introductory hour covers only pulling and changing information from a single table.

Having a working knowledge of the SQL language will help you in many job situations—even non-programming ones. To continue leaning SQL, pick up a tutorial such as *Sams Teach Yourself SQL in 24 Hours*.

Q&A

Q. Is all SQL the same, no matter the database used?

A. As mentioned this hour, different databases may handle data types and some SQL statements differently. Most SQL implementations fall under the American National Standards Institute (ANSI) guidelines. However, individual databases can extend their implementation of the languages with some customized and proprietary additions. To be ANSI compliant, all versions must be universal in their implementation and support of `SELECT`, `INSERT`, `UPDATE`, `DELETE`, and `WHERE`; therefore, your basic knowledge of these statements is universal.

Q. What's the best way to practice using SQL?

A. If possible, you can set up a database at home or use a sample database that comes with an existing database product. For example, if you have a version of Microsoft Office that comes with Access, you can write queries against its sample database to test your understanding. Or if you are feeling particularly brave, you could download the open-source database MySQL and create your own database—perhaps cataloging something you collect, like books, movies, or music. You would get hands-on experience with first the database creation and then using SQL to view and manipulate the data, which is the best way to improve your skills.

Workshop

The quiz questions are provided for your further understanding.

Quiz

1. What does SQL stand for?

2. What is the name of the field that ensures each entry in a database table is unique?

3. What SQL statement is used to return a specific data set from a table?

4. If you had a table named Employees and wanted to see all the records in that table, what SQL statement would you write?

5. If the Employees table had a field named `LastName`, and you wanted to see a list of employees with the last name Garcia, what SQL statement would you write?

For the next few questions, assume that you've built a database to catalogue your music. You have an Albums table that has five fields:

▶ **AlbumID:** The primary key, a unique identifier for each new album; this field is auto-generated when a new record is created.

▶ **Title:** The name of the album.

- ▶ **Artist:** The primary artist on the album.

- ▶ **Year:** The year the album came out.

- ▶ **Tracks:** The number of tracks on the album.

6. You add to your collection the following new album:

   Album: Astro Coast

   Artist: Surfer Blood

   Released: 2012

   Tracks: 10

   Write a SQL statement to add it to your database.

7. You were so sure you'd always listen to Nickelback—you had all their albums! But you decide to sell them and remove all traces of the band from your database. Write a SQL statement to delete your Nickelback albums.

8. You decide that you want to rate all your albums on a scale of 1 to 10, and you want to save your ratings in your Albums table. Assuming that you assign `TINYINT` as the data type (you only need 1 through 10 as values), write a SQL statement to add a `Rating` field to your Albums table.

9. What keyword do you use to delete a table or an entire database?

10. When modifying columns in an existing table, what two items might be different, depending on which database you are using?

Answers

1. Structured Query Language

2. Primary key

3. `SELECT`

4. `SELECT * FROM Employees;`

5. `SELECT * FROM Employees WHERE LastName = "Garcia";`

6. `INSERT INTO Albums (Title, Artist, Year, Tracks) VALUES ("Astro Coast", "Surfer Blood", 2012, 10);`

7. `DELETE FROM Albums WHERE Artist = "Nickelback";`

8. `ALTER TABLE Albums ADD Rating TINYINT;`

9. `DROP`

10. Both the data type and how you specify the second half of the `ALTER TABLE` statement

HOUR 18
Scripting with PHP

In 1995, a programmer named Rasmus Lerdorf created a set of scripts to help him manage some basic tasks within his own personal website, specifically around the use of HTML form data. He called this bundle of scripts "Personal Home Page/Forms Interpreter," or PHP/FI. Over the next few years, and with the help of some more developers—Zeev Suraski and Andi Gutmans—PHP/FI turned into the processing module we know today as PHP (which is now a recursive acronym that stands for "PHP: Hypertext Preprocessor"). From its humble beginnings as a server-side scripting language used for common tasks such as form handling and database interactions, PHP has grown in popularity such that almost 80% of all websites today use PHP in some way.

Often working in conjunction with a web server, the PHP processing module interprets scripts when requested by the user and produces output that is returned to the user. For example, if a user requests a web page and that web page is actually a PHP script instead of pure HTML, the PHP processing module processes that script and produces output, which, in turn, is sent back to the user as HTML and rendered in the browser.

The simplicity of the language itself makes PHP a popular language to learn—and especially a *first* scripting language to learn—but its simplicity doesn't mean it isn't powerful and feature rich. In this lesson, you'll get a whirlwind tour of the basics of the PHP language and its use.

The highlights of this hour include the following:

▶ Understanding the basic structure of PHP scripts

▶ Learning about the variables, data types, and logical control structures used in PHP

▶ Using PHP's many built-in functions

▶ Creating functions of your own to perform tasks

▶ Creating and using objects in PHP

▶ Discovering common uses for PHP scripts

What You Need for PHP Programming

Like HTML documents, PHP files are made up of plain text. You can create them with any text editor, and most popular HTML editors and programming IDEs (integrated development environments) provide support for PHP. When working with the PHP samples in this hour, you can use the same text editor you have been using to create sample code in other lessons in this book.

Beyond a simple text editor used to create PHP source files, you need access to a web server and the PHP processing module, which will interpret your source files and produce output from them. Well over 90% of all web-hosting plans offer PHP support, so it is very likely that if you have a web-hosting account, you have access to a web server and the PHP processing module.

If you do not have access to a web-hosting account and want to simply practice on your own in such a way that no one else can access your scripts, you might consider installing the Apache web server and PHP processing module on your own personal computer. While these technologies are available for Windows, Mac, and Linux, and you can download them at http://httpd.apache.org and www.php.net, respectively, a third-party installation package might prove more efficient:

▶ **XAMPP:** Installs Apache, MySQL, and PHP on Windows, Mac, or Linux. See www.apachefriends.org for more information.

▶ **WAMP:** Installs Apache, MySQL, and PHP on Windows. See www.wampserver.com for more information.

▶ **MAMP:** Installs Apache, MySQL, and PHP on Mac. See www.mamp.info for more information.

While these third-party installation packages install everything you need (and some things you didn't even know you needed, like the MySQL database server), one potential drawback to using third-party installation packages is that the versions of the core technologies that are bundled together will always be a few revision versions behind. This happens because of the work that goes into creating and testing the bundle itself, to ensure that no conflicts exist between the latest versions of the technologies; each package also has to go through a quality-assurance process. The upside of this process, however, is that when you install such a package, the upgrade process requires nothing more than running the new installer, which takes care of removing and updating all the files for you.

From this point forward in the hour, if you want to follow along with the source code, you will need access to a PHP-enabled web server either through your hosting provider or through the installation of the core technologies. If you are unsure whether your web-hosting provider is PHP enabled, or if you want to test a packaged installation, you can create a small test script like the one shown in Listing 18.1.

LISTING 18.1   A simple PHP script

```php
<?php
    echo "<h1>Hello World!</h1>";
?>
```

Type in the example shown in Listing 18.1 and save the file to the document root of your web server, using a filename something like `helloworld.php`.

If you are not working directly on the machine that will be serving your PHP script, you need to use a File Transfer Protocol (FTP) or Secure Copy (SCP) client to upload your saved document to the server. When the document is in place on the server, you should be able to access it by using your browser. If all has gone well, you should see the script's output. Figure 18.1 shows the output from the `helloworld.php` script.

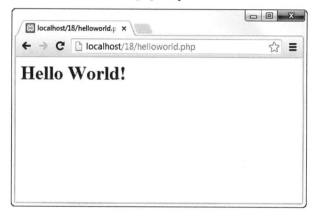

FIGURE 18.1
Success: The output from `helloworld.php`.

If you do not see similar output and instead see a replica of the code that you typed into the text file, then your web-hosting solution is not PHP enabled.

Basic Structures in PHP Scripts

When writing PHP, you need to inform the PHP-processing module that you want it to execute your commands. If you don't do this, the code you write will be mistaken for HTML and will be output directly into the browser. You can designate your code as PHP with special tags that mark the beginning and end of PHP code blocks. The most common—and standard—tag pair is `<?php` and `?>`, which is what you will see used throughout this hour.

The echo and print() Statements

You can use the echo statement to output data. In most cases, anything output by echo ends up viewable in the browser. Alternatively, you could use the print() statement in place of the echo statement. Using echo or print() is a matter of taste; when you look at other people's scripts, you might see either used, which is why both are included here.

Refer to Listing 18.1 and note that the only line of code in the listing ends with a semicolon (;). The semicolon, which informs the PHP engine that you have completed a statement, is probably the most important bit of PHP syntax you could learn at this stage.

A *statement* is an instruction to the PHP engine. Broadly, it is to PHP what a sentence is to written or spoken English, but whereas an English sentence should usually end with a period, a PHP statement should usually end with a semicolon. Exceptions to this rule include statements that enclose other statements and statements that end code blocks. In most cases, however, failure to end a statement with a semicolon will confuse the PHP engine and result in an error.

Combining HTML and PHP

The script in Listing 18.1 is pure PHP. You can incorporate it into an HTML document by simply adding HTML around the PHP start and end tags, as shown in Listing 18.2.

LISTING 18.2   A PHP script incorporated into HTML

```
<!DOCTYPE html>
<html>
<head>
    <title>A PHP script including HTML</title>
</head>
<body>
    <h1><?php echo "Hello World!"; ?></h1>
</body>
</html>
```

As you can see, incorporating PHP code into a predominantly HTML document is simply a matter of typing in that code. The PHP engine ignores everything outside the PHP open and close tags. If you were to save the contents of Listing 18.2 as helloworldagain.php, place it in your document root, and then view it with a browser, it would appear exactly as in Figure 18.1. If you were to view the document source, as shown in Figure 18.2, the listing would look just like a normal HTML document, because that's all the output actually is; the PHP processor simply places some text within an <h1> element before it gets to your web browser.

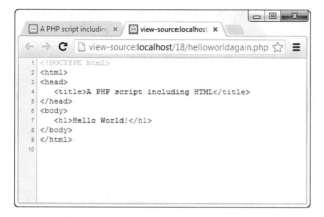

FIGURE 18.2
The output of `helloworldagain.php` as HTML source code.

You can include as many blocks of PHP code as you need in a single document, and you can intersperse them with HTML as required. Although you can have multiple blocks of code in a single document, they combine to form a single script. Any variables defined in the first block will usually be available to subsequent blocks.

Adding Comments to PHP Code

A *comment* is text in a script that is ignored by the PHP engine. Comments can make code more readable or annotate a script. Single-line comments begin with two forward slashes (//)—the preferred style—or a single hash or pound sign (#). The PHP engine ignores all text between these marks and either the end of the line or the PHP close tag:

```
// this is a comment
# this is another comment
```

Multiline comments begin with a forward slash followed by an asterisk (/*) and end with an asterisk followed by a forward slash (*/):

```
/*
this is a comment
none of this will
be parsed by the
PHP engine
*/
```

Flow Control Functions

It is common for scripts to evaluate conditions and change their behavior accordingly. These decisions are what make your PHP pages dynamic—that is, able to change output according to circumstances.

Like most other programming languages, PHP enables you to control the logical flow with statements such as the `if` statement, among others that you'll learn about in a moment.

The `if` statement evaluates an expression that appears between parentheses:

```
if (expression) {
    // code to execute if the expression evaluates to true
}
```

If this expression results in a `true` value, the statement is executed. Otherwise, the statement is skipped entirely. This functionality enables scripts to make decisions based on any number of factors.

When working with an `if` statement, you might want to define an alternative block of code that should be executed if the expression you are testing evaluates to `false`. You can do this by adding `else` to the `if` statement followed by a further block of code:

```
if (expression) {
    // code to execute if the expression evaluates to true
} else {
    // code to execute in all other cases
}
```

Using an `else` clause in conjunction with an `if` statement allows scripts to make decisions about code execution. However, your options are limited to an either-or branch: either the code block following the `if` statement or the code block following the `else` statement.

You can use an `if...elseif...else` clause to test multiple expressions (the `if...elseif` portion) before offering a default block of code (the `else` portion):

```
if (expression) {
    // code to execute if the expression evaluates to true
} elseif (another expression) {
    // code to execute if the previous expression failed
    // and this one evaluates to true
} else {
    // code to execute in all other cases
}
```

If the initial `if` expression does not evaluate to `true`, the first block of code is ignored. The `elseif` clause presents another expression for evaluation. If it evaluates to `true`, its corresponding block of code is executed. Otherwise, the block of code associated with the `else` clause is executed. You can include as many `elseif` clauses as you want; if you don't need a default action, you can omit the `else` clause.

Using the `switch` statement is an alternative way of changing flow, based on the evaluation of an expression. Using the `if` statement in conjunction with `elseif`, you can evaluate multiple expressions, as you've just seen. However, a `switch` statement evaluates only one expression in a list of expressions, selecting the correct one based on a specific bit of matching code. Whereas the result of an expression evaluated as part of an `if` statement is interpreted as either `true` or `false`, the expression portion of a `switch` statement is subsequently tested against any number of values, in hopes of finding a match:

```
switch (expression) {
    case result1:
        // execute this if expression results in result1
        break;
    case result2:
        // execute this if expression results in result2
        break;
    default:
        // execute this if no break statement
        // has been encountered hitherto
}
```

The expression used in a `switch` statement is often just a variable. Within the `switch` statement, you find a number of `case` statements, each of which tests a value against the value of the `switch` expression. If the `case` value is equivalent to the expression value, the code within the `case` statement is executed. The `break` statement ends the execution of the `switch` statement altogether.

If the `break` statement is omitted, the next `case` statement is executed, regardless of whether a previous match has been found. If the optional `default` statement is reached without a previous matching value having been found, its code is executed.

CAUTION

It is important to include a `break` statement at the end of any code that will be executed as part of a `case` statement. Without a `break` statement, the program flow continues to the next `case` statement and, ultimately, to the `default` statement. In most cases, this results in unexpected behavior—likely incorrect!

Finally, the `?:` operator—called the *ternary* operator—is similar to the `if` statement, except that it returns a value derived from one of two expressions, separated by a colon. This construct provides you with three parts of the whole—hence the name *ternary*. The expression used to generate the returned value depends on the result of a test expression:

```
(expression) ? returned_if_expression_is_true : returned_if_expression_is_false;
```

If the test expression evaluates to `true`, the result of the second expression is returned; otherwise, the value of the third expression is returned.

Looping

So far, you've looked at decisions that a script can make about what code to execute. Scripts can also decide how many times to execute a block of code. Loop statements are specifically designed to enable you to perform repetitive tasks because they continue to operate until a specified condition is achieved or until you explicitly choose to exit the loop.

The while statement looks similar in structure to a basic if statement but has the ability to loop:

```
while (expression) {
        // do something
}
```

Unlike an if statement, a while statement executes for as long as the expression evaluates to true—over and over again if needed. Each execution of a code block within a loop is called an *iteration*. Within the block, you usually change something that affects the while statement's expression; otherwise, your loop continues indefinitely. For example, you might use a variable to count the number of iterations and act accordingly. Listing 18.3 creates a while loop that calculates and prints multiples of 2 up to 24.

LISTING 18.3 A while **statement**

```php
<?php
$counter = 1;
while ($counter <= 12) {
    echo $counter." times 2 is ".($counter * 2)."<br />";
    $counter++;
}
?>
```

This example initializes the variable $counter in line 2 with a value of 1. The while statement in line 3 tests the $counter variable so that as long as the value of $counter is less than or equal to 12, the loop continues to run. Within the while statement's code block, the value of $counter is multiplied by 2, and the result is printed to the browser. In line 5, the value of $counter is incremented by 1. This step is extremely important because if you did not increment the value of the $counter variable, the while expression would never resolve to false, and the loop would never end.

If you put these lines of code into a text file called while.php, place this file in your web server document root, and access the script through your web browser, you see the following output:

```
1 times 2 is 2
2 times 2 is 4
3 times 2 is 6
4 times 2 is 8
5 times 2 is 10
6 times 2 is 12
```

```
7 times 2 is 14
8 times 2 is 16
9 times 2 is 18
10 times 2 is 20
11 times 2 is 22
12 times 2 is 24
```

A do...while statement looks a little like a while statement turned on its head. The essential difference between the two is that the code block is executed *before* the truth test and not after it:

```
do {
 // code to be executed
} while (expression);
```

This type of statement is useful when you want the code block to be executed at least once, even if the while expression evaluates to false.

The while statement is useful, but using a for statement is often a more efficient method of achieving the same effect. In Listing 18.3, you saw how a variable was initialized outside the while statement and then tested within its expression and incremented within the code block. With a for statement, you can achieve this same series of events but in a single line of code:

```
for (initialization expression; test expression; modification expression) {
 // code to be executed
}
```

This structure allows for more compact code and makes it less likely that you will forget to increment a counter variable, thereby creating an infinite loop.

NOTE

Infinite loops, as the name suggests, are loops that run without bounds. If your loop is running infinitely, your script is running for an infinite amount of time. This behavior is very stressful on your web server and renders the web page unusable.

The expressions within the parentheses of the for statement are separated by semicolons. Usually, the first expression initializes a counter variable, the second expression is the test condition for the loop, and the third expression increments the counter. Listing 18.4 shows a for statement that re-creates the example in Listing 18.3, which multiplies 12 numbers by 2.

LISTING 18.4 Using the for statement

```php
<?php
for ($counter=1; $counter<=12; $counter++) {
      echo $counter." times 2 is ".($counter * 2)."<br />";
}
?>
```

The results of Listings 18.3 and 18.4 are the same, but the `for` statement makes the code in Listing 18.4 more compact. Because the `$counter` variable is initialized and incremented at the beginning of the statement, the logic of the loop is clear at a glance.

TIP

Loops can contain other loop statements, thus creating nested loops, as long as the logic is valid and the loops are tidy.

The Building Blocks of PHP: Variables, Data Types, and Operators

Now that you have learned of the basic structures of PHP scripts, this section introduces you to more of the building blocks you'll use in those scripts. Many of these basic concepts are similar to concepts in other programming languages you might already have encountered, or will encounter, later in this book.

Variable Naming and Scope

In PHP, a variable consists of a name of your choosing, preceded by a dollar sign ($). Variable names can include letters, numbers, and the underscore character (_), but they cannot include spaces. A variable name must begin with a letter or an underscore. The following list shows some legal variables:

```
$a;
$a_longish_variable_name;
$_453;
$sleepyZZZZ;
```

A semicolon (;)—also known as the *instruction terminator*—is used to end a PHP statement. The semicolons in the previous fragment of code are not part of the variable names but are used to end the statement that declares the variable as "alive and kicking," if you will. To declare a variable, you need only include it in your script. When you declare a variable, you usually assign a value to it in the same statement, as shown here:

```
$num1 = 8;
```

```
$num2 = 23;
```

These lines declare two variables and use the assignment operator (=) to assign values to them. After you assign values to your variables, you can treat them exactly as if they were the values themselves. In other words, this:

```
echo $num1;
```

is equivalent to this:

```
echo 8;
```

as long as $num1 is assigned a value of 8.

In addition to the rules for naming variables, there are rules regarding the availability of variables. In general, the assigned value of a variable is present only within the function or script where it resides. For example, if you have scriptA.php, which holds a variable called $name with the value joe, and you want to create scriptB.php that also uses a $name variable, you can assign to that second $name variable the value jane without affecting the variable in scriptA.php. The value of the $name variable is *local* to each script, and the assigned values are independent of each other.

However, you can also define the $name variable as *global* within a script or function. If the $name variable is defined as a global variable in both scriptA.php and scriptB.php, and these scripts are connected to each other (that is, one script calls the other or includes the other), there will be just one value for the now-shared $name variable.

In addition to using global variables of your own creation, you can use PHP's predefined variables, called *superglobals*. These variables are always present, and their values are available to all your scripts. Each of the following superglobals is actually an array of other variables:

▶ $_GET contains any variables provided to a script through the GET method.

▶ $_POST contains any variables provided to a script through the POST method.

▶ $_COOKIE contains any variables provided to a script through a cookie.

▶ $_FILES contains any variables provided to a script through file uploads.

▶ $_SERVER contains information such as headers, file paths, and script locations.

▶ $_ENV contains any variables provided to a script as part of the server environment.

▶ $_REQUEST contains any variables provided to a script via GET, POST, or COOKIE input mechanisms.

▶ $_SESSION contains any variables that are currently registered in a session.

Using superglobals is crucial in creating secure applications because they reduce the likelihood of user-injected input to your scripts. By coding your scripts to accept only what you want, in the manner defined by you (from a form using the POST method or from a session, for example), you can eliminate some of the problems created by loosely written scripts.

Data Types

Different types of data take up different amounts of memory and may be treated differently when they are manipulated by a script. Some programming languages therefore demand that the programmer declare in advance which type of data a variable will contain. By contrast, PHP is *loosely typed*, meaning that it automatically determines the data type at the time data is assigned to each variable.

Table 18.1 shows the eight standard data types available in PHP.

TABLE 18.1   **Standard data types**

Type	Example	Description
Boolean	`true`	One of the special values `true` or `false`
Integer	5	A whole number
Float or double	`3.234`	A floating-point number
String	`"hello"`	A collection of characters
Object		An instance of a class
Array		An ordered set of keys and values
Resource		Reference to a third-party resource (a database, for example)
NULL		An uninitialized variable

TIP

PHP provides the function `settype()`, which is used to change the type of a variable. To use `settype()`, you place the variable to change and the type to change it to between the parentheses and separate the elements with a comma, like so:

```
settype($variabletochange, 'new type');
```

PHP also allows you to change the type of an existing variable by *casting*; this produces a copy, leaving the original variable untouched. To change type through casting, you indicate the name of a data type, in parentheses, in front of the variable you are copying:

```
$newvar = (integer) $originalvar
```

Operators and Expressions

With what you have learned so far, you can assign data to variables, and you can even investigate and change the data type of a variable. A programming language isn't very useful, though, unless you can manipulate the data you have stored. *Operators* are symbols used to manipulate data stored in variables; they make it possible to use one or more values to produce a new value, to check the validity of data to determine the next step in a condition, and so forth.

The following sections describe the operators commonly used in PHP programming.

The Assignment Operator

You have seen the assignment operator in use each time a variable has been declared in an example; the assignment operator is an equal sign (=). The assignment operator takes the value of the right-side operand and assigns it to the left-side operand:

```
$name = "John";
```

In this example, the variable $name now contains the string "John".

Arithmetic Operators

The *arithmetic operators* do exactly what you would expect: They perform arithmetic operations. Table 18.2 lists these operators and provides examples of their use and results.

TABLE 18.2 Arithmetic operators

Operator	Name	Example	Sample Result
+	Addition	10+3	13
−	Subtraction	10−3	7
/	Division	10/3	3.3333333333333
*	Multiplication	10*3	30
%	Modulus	10%3	1

The addition operator adds the right-side operand to the left-side operand. The subtraction operator subtracts the right-side operand from the left-side operand. The division operator divides the left-side operand by the right-side operand. The multiplication operator multiplies the left-side operand by the right-side operand. The modulus operator returns the remainder of the left-side operand divided by the right-side operand.

The Concatenation Operator

The concatenation operator is represented by a single period (.). Treating both operands as strings, this operator appends the right-side operand to the left-side operand. So this:

```
"hello"." world"
```

returns this:

```
"hello world"
```

Note that the space between the words occurs because there is a leading space in the second operand (" world" rather than "world"). The concatenation operator literally smashes together two strings without adding any padding. So, if you try to concatenate two strings without leading or trailing spaces, they will be smashed together. For example, with this:

```
"hello"."world"
```

you will get this as your result:

```
"helloworld"
```

Regardless of the data types of the operands used with the concatenation operator, they are treated as strings, and the result is always of the string type.

Combined Assignment Operators

Although there is only one true assignment operator, PHP provides a number of combination operators that transform the left-side operand and return a result while also modifying the original value of the variable. As a rule, operators use operands but do not change their original values. However, combined assignment operators break this rule.

A combined assignment operator consists of a standard operator symbol followed by an equal sign. Combination assignment operators save you the trouble of using two operators in two different steps within your script. For example, if you have a variable with a value of 4, and you want to increase this value to 4 more, you might see this:

```
$x = 4;
$x = $x + 4; // $x now equals 8
```

However , you can also use a combination assignment operator (+=) to add and return the new value, as shown here:

```
$x = 4;
$x += 4; // $x now equals 8
```

Each arithmetic operator, as well as the concatenation operator, also has a corresponding combination assignment operator. Table 18.3 lists these new operators and shows examples of their use.

TABLE 18.3 Some combined assignment operators

Operator	Example	Equivalent To
+=	$x += 5	$x = $x + 5
-=	$x -= 5	$x = $x - 5
/=	$x /= 5	$x = $x / 5
*=	$x *= 5	$x = $x * 5
%=	$x %= 5	$x = $x % 5
.=	$x .= " test"	$x = $x." test"

Automatically Incrementing and Decrementing an Integer Variable

When coding in PHP, you will often find it necessary to increment or decrement a variable that is an integer type. You usually need to do this when you are counting the iterations of a loop. You have already learned two ways of doing this—either by incrementing the value of $x using the addition operator:

```
$x = $x + 1; // $x is incremented by 1
```

or by using a combined assignment operator:

```
$x += 1; // $x is incremented by 1
```

In both cases, the new value is assigned to $x.

Because expressions of this kind are common, PHP provides some special operators that allow you to add or subtract the integer constant 1 from an integer variable and assign the result to the variable itself. These are known as the *post-increment* and *post-decrement* operators. The post-increment operator consists of two plus symbols appended to a variable name:

```
$x++; // $x is incremented by 1
```

This expression increments the value represented by the variable $x by 1. Using two minus symbols in the same way decrements the variable:

```
$x--; // $x is decremented by 1
```

If you use the post-increment or post-decrement operators in conjunction with a conditional operator, the operand is modified only after the first operation has finished:

```
$x = 3;
$y = $x++ + 3;
```

In this instance, $y first becomes 6 (the result of 3 + 3), and then $x is incremented.

In some circumstances, you might want to increment or decrement a variable in a test expression before the test is carried out. PHP provides the pre-increment and pre-decrement operators for this purpose. These operators behave in the same way as the post-increment and post-decrement operators, but they are written with the plus or minus symbols preceding the variable:

```
++$x; // $x is incremented by 1
--$x; // $x is decremented by 1
```

If these operators are used as part of a test expression, incrementing occurs before the test is carried out. For example, in the next fragment, $x is incremented before it is tested against 4:

```
$x = 3;
++$x < 4; // false
```

The test expression returns `false` because 4 is not smaller than 4.

Comparison Operators

Comparison operators perform comparative tests using their operands and return the Boolean value `true` if a test is successful or `false` if the test fails. This type of expression is useful when using control structures in your scripts, such as `if` and `while` statements.

Table 18.4 lists the comparison operators.

TABLE 18.4 Comparison operators

Operator	Name	Returns True If...	Example ($x Is 4)	Result
==	Equivalence	left is equivalent to right.	`$x == 5`	false
!=	Nonequivalence	left is not equivalent to right.	`$x != 5`	true
===	Identical	left is equivalent to right, and they are the same type.	`$x === 4`	true
===	Non-equivalence	left is equivalent to right, but they are not the same type.	`$x === "4"`	false
>	Greater than	left is greater than right.	`$x > 4`	false
>=	Greater than or equal to	left is greater than or equal to right.	`$x >= 4`	true
<	Less than	left is less than right.	`$x < 4`	false
<=	Less than or equal to	left is less than or equal to right.	`$x <= 4`	true

These operators are most commonly used with integers or doubles, although the equivalence operator is also used to compare strings. Be very sure to understand the difference between the == and = operators. The == operator tests equivalence, whereas the = operator assigns value. Also, remember that === tests equivalence with regard to both value and type.

Creating Complex Test Expressions with the Logical Operators

Logical operators test combinations of Boolean values. For example, the `or` operator, which is indicated by two pipe characters (||) or simply the word `or`, returns the Boolean value `true` if either the left or the right operand is true:

```
true || false
```

This expression returns `true`.

The `and` operator, which is indicated by two ampersand characters (&&) or simply the word `and`, returns the Boolean value `true` only if both the left and right operands are true:

```
true && false
```

This expression returns the Boolean value `false`.

It's unlikely that you will use a logical operator to test Boolean constants because it makes more sense to test two or more expressions that resolve to a Boolean. The following example:

```
($x > 2) && ($x < 15)
```

returns the Boolean value `true` if $x contains a value that is greater than 2 and smaller than 15. Parentheses are used when comparing expressions to make the code easier to read and to indicate the precedence of expression evaluation.

Table 18.5 lists the logical operators.

TABLE 18.5 Logical operators

Operator	Name	Returns True If...	Example	Result
`||`	Or	left or right is true.	`true || false`	`true`
`or`	Or	left or right is true.	`true or false`	`true`
`xor`	Xor	left or right is true, but not both.	`true xor true`	`false`
`&&`	And	left and right are true.	`true && false`	`false`
`and`	And	left and right are true.	`true and false`	`false`
`!`	Not	left single operand is not true.	`! true`	`false`

Why are there two versions of both the `or` and the `and` operators? That's a good question. The answer lies in operator precedence, which we examine next.

Operator Precedence

When you use an operator within an expression, the PHP engine usually reads the expression from left to right. For complex expressions that use more than one operator, though, the PHP engine could be led astray without some guidance. First, consider a simple case:

```
4 + 5
```

There's no room for confusion here; PHP simply adds 4 to 5. But what about the following example, which has two operators:

```
4 + 5 * 2
```

This presents a problem. Should PHP find the sum of 4 and 5 and then multiply it by 2, providing the result 18? Or does it mean 4 plus the result of 5 multiplied by 2, resolving to 14? If you were simply to read from left to right, the former would be true. However, PHP attaches different precedence to different operators, and because the multiplication operator has higher precedence than the addition operator, the second solution to the problem is the correct one: 4 plus the result of 5 multiplied by 2.

However, you can override operator precedence by putting parentheses around your expressions. In the following fragment, the addition expression is evaluated before the multiplication expression:

```
(4 + 5) * 2
```

Whatever the precedence of the operators in a complex expression, it is a good idea to use parentheses to make your code clearer and to prevent errors such as applying sales tax to the wrong subtotal in a shopping cart situation. The following is a list of the operators covered in this section, in precedence order (those with the highest precedence listed first):

```
++, --, (cast)
/, *, %
+, -
<, <=, =>, >
==, ===, !=
&&
||
=, +=, -=, /=, *=, %=, .=
and
xor
or
```

As you can see, `or` has a lower precedence than `||`, and `and` has a lower precedence than `&&`, so you can use the lower-precedence logical operators to change the way a complex test expression is read.

The order of precedence is the only reason that both `&&` and `and` are available in PHP. The same is true of `||` and `or`. In most circumstances, the use of parentheses makes for clearer code and fewer bugs than code that takes advantage of the difference in precedence of these operators.

Constants

Variables offer a flexible way of storing data because you can change their values and the type of data they store at any time during the execution of your scripts. However, if you want to work with a value that must remain unchanged throughout your script's execution, you can define and use a *constant*. You must use PHP's built-in `define()` function to create a constant, which subsequently cannot be changed unless you specifically define it again. To use the `define()` function, place the name of the constant and the value you want to give it within parentheses and separated by a comma:

```
define("YOUR_CONSTANT_NAME", 42);
```

The value you want to set can be a number, a string, or a Boolean. By convention, the name of the constant should be in all capital letters. Constants are accessed with the constant name only; no dollar symbol is required.

PHP automatically provides some built-in constants for you. For example, the constant __FILE__ returns the name of the file that the PHP engine is currently reading. The constant __LINE__ returns the current line number of the file. These are just two examples of "magic constants," which are not statically predefined and instead change depending on the context in which they are used. For a complete list, see www.php.net/manual/en/language.constants.predefined.php.

Using and Creating Functions in PHP

A *function* is a self-contained block of code that can be called by a script. When called, the function's code is executed and performs a particular task. You can pass values to a function, which then uses the values appropriately—storing them, transforming them, displaying them, whatever the function is told to do. When finished, a function can also pass a value back to the original code that called it into action.

Functions come in two flavors: those built in to the language and those you define yourself.

Using Built-in Functions

PHP has hundreds of built-in functions, ranging from simple string manipulation to mathematical operations to database interactions—and many, many things in between. To get a feel for the functions that PHP includes, browse the list in the online function reference at www.php.net/manual/en/funcref.php.

Using built-in functions in your scripts is often as simple as typing the function name and passing an argument to it. For example, take a look at the following snippet:

```
strtoupper("Hello Web!");
```

This example calls the built-in strtoupper() function and passes it the string "Hello Web!". The function then goes about its business of changing the contents of the string to uppercase letters.

A function call consists of the function name (strtoupper in this case) followed by parentheses. If you want to pass information to the function, you place it between these parentheses. A piece of information passed to a function in this way is called an *argument*. Some functions require that more than one argument be passed to them, separated by commas:

```
some_function($an_argument, $another_argument);
```

`strtoupper()` is typical for a PHP function in that it returns a value. Most functions return some information after they've completed their task; they usually at least tell whether their mission was successful. `strtoupper()` returns a string value, so its usage requires the presence of a variable to accept the new string, such as the following:

```
$new_string = strtoupper("Hello Web!");
```

You can now use `$new_string` in your code, such as to print it to the screen:

```
echo $new_string;
```

This code results in the following text on the screen:

```
HELLO WEB!
```

You can call user-defined functions in exactly the same way that you have been calling built-in functions.

Defining a Function

You can define your own functions by using the `function` statement:

```
function some_function($argument1, $argument2)
{
      //function code here
}
```

The name of the function follows the `function` statement and precedes a set of parentheses. If your function requires arguments, you must place comma-separated variable names within the parentheses. These variables are filled by the values passed to your function. Even if your function doesn't require arguments, you must nevertheless supply the parentheses.

NOTE

The naming rules for functions are similar to the naming rules for variables, described earlier in this hour. Names cannot include spaces, and each name must begin with a letter or an underscore. As with variables, your function names should be meaningful and consistent in style. The capitalization of function names is one such stylistic touch you can add to your code; using mixed case in names, such as `MyFunction()` or `handleSomeDifficultTask()`, makes your code much easier to read. You may hear this naming convention referred to as CamelCase or lower camelCase, depending on whether the first character is capitalized.

Listing 18.5 declares and calls a function of your own making.

LISTING 18.5   Declaring and calling a function

```php
<?php
function bighello()
{
    echo "<h1>HELLO!</h1>";
}
bighello();
?>
```

The script in Listing 18.5 simply outputs the string "HELLO!" wrapped in an HTML <h1> element.

Listing 18.5 declares a function, bighello(), that requires no arguments. Because of this, the parentheses are left empty. Although bighello() is a working function, it is not terribly useful. Listing 18.6 creates a function that requires an argument and actually does something with it.

LISTING 18.6   Declaring a function that requires an argument

```php
<?php
function printBR($txt)
{
    echo $txt."<br/>";
}
printBR("This is a line.");
printBR("This is a new line.");
printBR("This is yet another line.");
?>
```

NOTE

Unlike variable names, function names are not case sensitive. In Listing 18.6, the printBR() function could have been called as printbr(), PRINTBR(), or any combination thereof, with success.

The output of this script is three lines of text with an HTML linebreak after each line, which would not automatically be there otherwise.

Returning Values from User-Defined Functions

The previous example outputs an amended string to the browser through the use of the printBR() function. Sometimes, however, you will want a function to provide a value that you can work with yourself. If a function has transformed a string that you have provided, you might want to get the amended string back so that you can pass it to other functions. A function can return a value by using the `return` statement in conjunction with a value. The `return` statement stops the execution of the function and sends the value back to the calling code.

Listing 18.7 creates a function that returns the sum of two numbers.

LISTING 18.7   A function that returns a value

```php
<?php
function addNums($firstnum, $secondnum)
{
     $result = $firstnum + $secondnum;
      return $result;
}
echo addNums(3,5);
//will print "8"
?>
```

The `return` statement can return a value or nothing at all. How you arrive at a value passed by `return` can vary. The value can be hard-coded:

```php
return 4;
```

It can be the result of an expression:

```php
return $a/$b;
```

It can be the value returned by yet another function call:

```php
return another_function($an_argument);
```

Variable Scope in Functions

A variable declared within a function remains local to that function. In other words, it is not available outside the function or within other functions. In larger projects, this can save you from accidentally overwriting the contents of a variable when you declare two variables with the same name in separate functions.

From within one function, you cannot (by default) access a variable defined in another function or elsewhere in the script. Within a function, if you attempt to use a variable with the same name, you will only set or access a local variable. Let's put this to the test in Listing 18.8.

LISTING 18.8 Variables defined outside functions are inaccessible from within a function by default

```php
<?php
$life = 42;
function meaningOfLife()
{
    echo "The meaning of life is ".$life;
}
meaningOfLife();
?>
```

If you run this script, the output will be:

```
The meaning of life is
```

As you might expect, the meaningOfLife() function does not have access to the $life variable in line 2; $life is empty when the function attempts to print it. On the whole, this is a good thing because it saves you from potential clashes between identically named variables, and a function can always demand an argument if it needs information about the outside world.

Occasionally, you might want to access an important variable from within a function without passing it in as an argument. This is where the global statement comes into play. Listing 18.9 uses global to restore order to the universe.

LISTING 18.9 Accessing global variables with the global statement

```php
<?php
$life=42;
function meaningOfLife()
{
    global $life;
    echo "The meaning of life is ".$life;
}
meaningOfLife();
?>
```

If you run this script now, the output will be:

```
The meaning of life is 42
```

When you place the global statement in front of the $life variable when it is declared in the meaningOfLife() function (line 5), it refers to the $life variable declared outside the function (line 2).

You need to use the `global` statement within every function that needs to access a particular named global variable. Be careful, though: If you manipulate the contents of the variable within the function, the value of the variable changes for the script as a whole.

You can declare more than one variable at a time with the `global` statement by simply separating each of the variables you want to access with commas:

```
global $var1, $var2, $var3;
```

CAUTION

Usually, an argument is a copy of whatever value is passed by the calling code; changing it in a function has no effect beyond the function block. Changing a global variable within a function, however, changes the original and not a copy. Use the `global` statement carefully.

Working with Objects in PHP

Programmers use objects to store and organize data. Object-oriented programming (OOP) is a type of programming in which the structure of the program (or application) is designed around these objects and their relationships and interactions. OOP structures are found in many programming languages, including PHP. In fact, many PHP programmers—especially those coming from a highly OOP background—choose to develop PHP applications in an object-oriented way.

However, in PHP, it is not required that you write your scripts in an object-oriented manner. Many PHP scripts are procedural and functional rather than object oriented. That is to say, the emphasis is on stepping through the use of variables, data and control structures, and subroutines and functions in the course of creating a program. Regardless of which method you choose for writing your PHP scripts, it's important to understand a little bit about objects in PHP.

Creating an Object

Although it's easy to visualize a scalar variable, such as `$color`, with a value of `red`, some people have a difficult time visualizing objects. For now, try to think of an object as a little box with inputs and outputs on either side of it. The input mechanisms are *methods*, and methods have properties. Throughout this section, we look at how classes, methods, and properties work together to produce various outputs.

An object exists in a structure called a *class*. In each class, you define a set of characteristics. For example, suppose you have created an `automobile` class. In the `automobile` class, you might have `color`, `make`, and `model` characteristics. Each `automobile` object uses all the characteristics, but each object initializes the characteristics to different values, such as `silver`, `Mazda`, and `Miata`, or `red`, `Porsche`, and `Boxster`.

The whole purpose of using objects is to create reusable code. Because classes are so tightly structured but self-contained and independent of one another, you can reuse them from one application to another. For example, suppose that you write a text-formatting class for one project and decide you can use that class in another project. Because a class is just a set of characteristics, you can pick up the code and use it in the second project, reaching into it with methods specific to the second application but using the inner workings of the existing code to achieve new results.

Creating an object is simple; you just declare it to be in existence:

```
class myClass {
     //code will go here
}
```

When you have a class, you can create a new instance of an object:

```
$object1 = new myClass();
```

Listing 18.10 provides proof that your object exists, even though there's nothing in it—it's just been named.

LISTING 18.10   Proof that your object exists

```php
<?php
class myClass {
    //code will go here
}
$object1 = new myClass();
echo "\$object1 is an ".gettype($object1).".<br/>";

if (is_object($object1)) {
    echo "Really! I swear \$object1 is an object!";
}
?>
```

The output of this script is:

```
$object1 is an object.
Really! I swear $object1 is an object!
```

This is not a particularly useful class because it does absolutely nothing, but it is valid and shows you how the class template works in lines 2 to 5. Lines 8 to 10 use the is_object() function to test whether something is an object; in this case, the *something* is $object1. Because the test of is_object() evaluates to true, the string within the if statement is printed to the screen.

Properties of Objects

The variables declared inside an object are called *properties*. It is standard practice to declare your variables at the top of the class. These properties can be values, arrays, or even other objects. The following snippet uses simple scalar variables inside the class, prefaced with the `public` keyword:

```
class myCar {
    public $color = "silver";
    public $make = "Mazda";
    public $model = "Miata";
}
```

NOTE

If you use the keyword `public`, `protected`, or `private` before the variable name, you can indicate whether the class member (the variable) can be accessed everywhere (public), within the class itself or a parent class or an inherited class (protected), or only by the class itself (private).

Now when you create a `myCar` object, it will always have those three properties. Listing 18.11 shows how to access properties after they have been declared and values have been assigned to them.

LISTING 18.11   Showing object properties

```
<?php
class myCar {
    public $color = "silver";
    public $make = "Mazda";
    public $model = "Miata";
}
$car = new myCar();
echo "I drive a: ".$car -> color." ".$car -> make." ".$car -> model;
?>
```

The output of this script is:

```
I drive a: silver Mazda Miata
```

Object Methods

Methods add functionality to objects. No longer do your objects just sit there, holding on to their properties for dear life; they can actually do something! Listing 18.12 shows how it works.

LISTING 18.12   A class with a method

```php
<?php
class myClass {
    function sayHello() {
      echo "HELLO!";
    }
}
$object1 = new myClass();
$object1 -> sayHello();
?>
```

Running this code produces the following output:

```
HELLO!
```

A method looks and acts like a normal function but is defined within the framework of a class. The -> operator is used to call the object method in the context of your script. If there are any variables stored in the object, the method is capable of accessing them for its own purposes, as illustrated in Listing 18.13.

LISTING 18.13   Accessing class properties within a method

```php
<?php
class myClass {
    public $name = "John";
    function sayHello() {
        echo "HELLO! My name is ".$this->name;
    }
}
$object1 = new myClass();
$object1 -> sayHello();
?>
```

Running this code produces the following:

```
HELLO! My name is John
```

The special variable $this is used to refer to the currently instantiated object, as you see on line 5. Any time an object refers to itself, you must use the $this variable. Using the $this variable in conjunction with the -> operator enables you to access any property or method in a class—within the class itself.

Common Uses of PHP

Because PHP is relatively simple to work with and has a low barrier to entry—since the vast majority of web-hosting providers offer PHP support—you can imagine that web application developers use PHP in many different ways. This is one reason that PHP contains hundreds of built-in functions grouped together into many different categories (see www.php.net/manual/en/funcref.php): When it comes to working with strings, dates, files, images, databases, and everything in between, there aren't a lot of basic functions that are unique, so the language just includes a lot of these functions right out of the box.

What you *do* with these functions may be unique, but as a general-purpose scripting language, PHP tries to cover all the bases so you can just get down to the business of scripting with built-in functions rather than reinventing the wheel. This feature of PHP is also one reason it has detractors: Some people think the language contains too much built-in functionality and is too forgiving (for example, PHP allows developers to "get away with" too many imperfections in the code, where scripts in other languages would simply error and fail). While this and other points about the overall value of the language are debatable, that PHP is widely used *cannot* be debated. Following are some of the ways in which PHP is used by developers every day:

▶ **Processing form data:** As mentioned earlier in this lesson, PHP includes superglobal variables that hold all the values sent in an HTML form. Using either the $_POST or $_GET superglobal, you have at your fingertips all the information you need from a user, and you can manipulate it as necessary—by processing text (see www.php.net/manual/en/book.strings.php), performing mathematical functions (see www.php.net/manual/en/book.math.php), or just sending an email (see www.php.net/manual/en/book.mail.php), among many, many other functions.

▶ **Setting and reading cookies and user sessions:** The primary way to track a user through your application is to set and maintain cookies that store pieces of data in the browser and are accessed and used by the application. PHP has built-in functions for handling both cookies (see www.php.net/manual/en/features.cookies.php) and user sessions (see www.php.net/manual/en/book.session.php).

▶ **Interacting with databases:** It would be difficult for you to come up with a database product that PHP cannot access. Whether through an abstraction layer or through vendor-specific database functions, you can use PHP to put or retrieve data from your database and your application's custom database schema (see www.php.net/manual/en/refs.database.php).

If you look at these three points, you might think "that's all?" But think for a moment about how web applications are put together. Typically, you perform one of four operations when interacting with a web application and its underlying data: creating, reading, updating, and deleting (commonly referred to as CRUD operations). When creating, updating, and deleting data, you typically interact with a database through some sort of form action, which may or may not include custom string input. When reading information, you are also interacting with a database to retrieve that information, and thus the strings likely have some sort of manipulation happening between their raw state in the database and what you see on your screen.

PHP is a powerful general-purpose scripting language that contains multitudes of useful functions. Some may argue that the most complicated aspect of using PHP is not the tactical application of the language itself but instead in deciding which of the many approaches and functions are best suited to solving any given problem.

Summary

This brief lesson has not made you an expert in PHP; as with anything, you need to do thousands of hours of practice to become a PHP expert. But you should now have a solid understanding of the fundamentals of the PHP language and how it can be used to solve basic programming problems, especially in web application development.

Continue to practice with the variables, data types, logical structures, and built-in functions that PHP offers you and create functions of your own that provide unique solutions. To learn a *lot* more about the PHP language and how to develop PHP-based applications using the MySQL database, take a look at *Sams Teach Yourself PHP, MySQL, and Apache All-in-One,* 5th edition.

Q&A

Q. What editors should I avoid when creating PHP code?

A. Any plain-text editor will do. Do not use word processors that format text for printing (Microsoft Word, for example). Even if you save files created using this type of editor in plain-text format, hidden characters are likely to creep into your code.

Q. Should I learn the operator precedence table or memorize *any* of the intricate details of the PHP language?

A. There is no reason you shouldn't memorize the operator precedence table, but I would save the effort for more useful tasks. By using parentheses in your expressions, you can make your code easy to read while defining your own order of precedence. As for memorizing *any* of the details of the PHP language, I would recommend knowing the basics about variables, data types, operators, and logical structures, and over time you will begin to remember the syntax of the functions you use frequently. As with any other new language (programming or otherwise), repetition and practice will help the knowledge stick, but you can turn to the PHP Manual online at www.php.net should you need to refer to it.

Workshop

The quiz questions are provided for your further understanding.

Quiz

1. What are the standard opening and closing tags used in PHP scripts?

2. Which of the following statements contains an operator?

   ```
   4;
   is_int(44);
   5/12;
   ```

3. Which of the following variable names are not valid, and why?

   ```
   $a_value_submitted_by_a_user
   $666666xyz
   $xyz666666
   $_____counter_____
   $the first
   $file-name
   ```

4. True or false: If a function doesn't require an argument, you can omit the parentheses in the function call.

5. What is the output of the following PHP code?

   ```php
   <?php
   $number = 50;

   function tenTimes() {
       global $number;
       $number = $number * 10;
   }
   tenTimes();
   echo $number;
   ?>
   ```

6. Create a `while` statement that increments through and prints every odd number between 1 and 49, with an HTML line break after each.

7. Convert the answer from question 6 into a `for` statement that does the same.

8. When creating a function of your own design, what is the limit to the number of arguments you can pass?

9. How can you ensure that a variable is accessible by multiple functions?

10. Which PHP superglobal variable would you use to extract form values sent via the `POST` method?

Answers

1. `<?php` and `?>`

2. The statement `5/12` contains a division operator.

3. The variable name `$666666xyz` is not valid because it does not begin with a letter or an underscore character. The variable name `$the first` is not valid because it contains a space. `$file-name` is also invalid because it contains a nonalphanumeric character (-).

4. False. You must always include the parentheses in your function calls, whether or not you are passing arguments to the function.

5. `500`

6.
```
$num = 1;
while ($num <= 49) {
    echo $num."<br />";
    $num += 2;
}
```

7.
```
for ($num = 1; $num <= 49; $num += 2) {
    echo $num."<br />";
}
```

8. There is no limit to the number of arguments you can pass, but you might want to limit the number to a handful for your own sanity and ease of maintenance.

9. Declare it as a global variable.

10. `$_POST`

Programming with C and C++

C is one of those programming languages that most programmers never predicted would take off. Designed as a highly efficient, somewhat cryptic language used to write an operating system named *UNIX*, C is a language designed by systems programmers. In the late 1980s, the same decade after its primary release, virtually every program on the store shelves was written in C. C, followed by its successor C++, quickly replaced the popular Pascal language in the 1980s and despite the fact that a much broader set of programming languages are available today for different development jobs, C and C++ still remain viable programming choices. C's impact on the programming world cannot be stressed enough.

Many consider C++ to be a better language than C. C++ offers full support for object-oriented programming (OOP). (Remember that both Java and Python are also object-oriented programming languages.) You'll learn in this hour how and why C++ provides strong OOP support and how the mechanics of C++ provide for more flexible, maintainable, and efficient programming than its predecessor, C.

The highlights of this hour include the following:

- ▶ Understanding why C is so efficient
- ▶ Recognizing C commands and operators
- ▶ Outputting with C's `printf()` function
- ▶ Using C++ to build on C programming skills
- ▶ Using C++ classes
- ▶ Using inheritance to decrease programming time

Introducing C

C is highly efficient, and C's developers required such efficiency because before C came along, programmers used *assembly language*, a language just above the machine language level, to write operating systems. Only assembly language had the efficiency needed for systems programs.

C brought the advantage of a higher-level language to the table when developers used C for operating systems. Along with the efficiency of a low-level language, C has the high-level-language advantage of being more maintainable, and programmers were more easily able to update the operating system and produce accurate code. Assembly language doesn't lend itself very well to proper program maintenance.

To achieve its efficiency, C does have one drawback that other high-level languages don't: C is more cryptic than most other programming languages. Its cryptic nature comes in the form of a huge collection of operators and a small number of keywords. Table 19.1 lists C's keywords. In the standard C language, there are only 32 keywords, which is an extremely small number compared to other languages, such as Java and PHP.

TABLE 19.1   32 supported C command keywords

auto	double	int	struct
break	else	long	switch
case	enum	register	typedef
char	extern	return	union
const	float	short	unsigned
continue	for	signed	void
default	goto	sizeof	volatile
do	if	static	while

CAUTION

Notice that C's keywords all appear in lowercase. C's built-in functions also require lowercase names. C is *case sensitive*, so if you use an uppercase letter anywhere inside a keyword or function, your program will not compile properly.

You should recognize some of C's commands because the Python language that you learned about in earlier lessons borrows heavily from C and C++.

C has more operators than any other programming language, with the exception of the scientific APL language that is rarely, if ever, used anymore. Of course, languages derived from C, such as Java and C++, often have as many or more operators than C. Because you have already studied Java, you understand many of C's operators.

What You Need for C and C++ Programming

To program in C, you need a C compiler. Almost any C compiler you use today is a C++ compiler as well. Therefore, you get two languages for one, although C++ is really just an extension of the C language. In the early days, you often needed to purchase a compiler, usually from Borland or Microsoft. Now, there are a number of options available for free download. These are powerful packages that include an integrated development environment (IDE), compiler, debugger, and other helpful development tools.

If you plan on developing in multiple languages, including C (or C++), Microsoft's development tools can be an excellent choice, as the IDE for C/C++ is similar to the one for Visual Basic and other .NET languages. Developers created Visual Basic from the beginning to be a Windows programming system. C, on the other hand, began in the world of text-based computers. Therefore, nothing is embedded in the C or C++ programming languages to support a graphical interface.

Looking at C

Let's begin this section with an illustrative example.

TRY IT YOURSELF ▼

Listing 19.1 contains a short but complete C program.

LISTING 19.1   C is cryptic and requires several elements that other languages do not

```c
/* Prints a message on the screen */
#include <stdio.h>
main()
{
    printf("C is efficient.\n");
    return 0;
}
```

If you were to enter the program in Listing 19.1 in your C compiler's editor, compile the program, and run it, you would see this message on the screen:

```
C is efficient.
```

You can test this program by using Visual C++ or any of the many C and C++ compilers available on the Internet.

The program required seven lines to output one simple sentence—so why is C considered an efficient language? Actually, C is an efficient language, but it you will need to get into C and write more complex programs to really take advantage of the power of C; the language was written by programmers for programmers. To take advantage of C's compiled efficiency and power, you need to master the nuances of the language.

Listing 19.1 contains three sets of grouping symbols: angled brackets (<>), braces ({ }), and parentheses (( )). Be extremely careful when typing a C program because the correct and exact symbol is important. C doesn't handle ambiguity very well, and if you type the wrong symbol, C won't work properly.

Using the `main()` Function's Format

The cornerstone of every C program is the `main()` function. Because `main()` is a function and not a command, the parentheses after it are required. A C function, just like a Python function, is a section of code that does something. The `main()` function is required because execution of a C program always begins in its `main()` function. Programmers use `main()` to control the rest of the program. The `main()` function often includes a series of procedure calls.

The code for `main()`, as with all C functions (except the built-in functions, whose code you never see), begins after the opening brace ({), and `main()` continues until the closing brace, (}), where `main()` terminates and other functions often begin. Other sets of braces, always in pairs, may appear within a function such as `main()` as well.

As in JavaScript, many of C's (and C++'s) statements end with a semicolon (;). The more you work with C, the more familiar you'll become with which statements require the semicolon and which don't. Full statements require the semicolon. In Listing 19.1, the line with `main()` doesn't require a semicolon because `main()` doesn't terminate until the final closing brace in the last line. The brace requires no semicolon because it is a grouping character and does nothing on its own.

NOTE

The next few sections concentrate on the fundamental C language, but the material here is applicable to C++ also. C++'s strength over C is its OOP capability, as you'll see later in this hour.

Using the `#include` Statement

You'll never see `#include` in a list of C commands because `#include` is not a C command. Statements in a C program that begin with the pound sign are called *preprocessor directives*. The compiler analyzes the directive and, instead of compiling the statement, acts upon the statement immediately during compilation.

The #include preprocessor directive tells the compiler to insert another file that resides in source code form at the location in the program where the directive resides. (The #include directive is similar to the import() command in Python.) Therefore, before the program is actually compiled, more code is inserted, at the programmer's request, at the place where #include occurs. That code is compiled along with the programmer's code.

The stdio.h file is a source code auxiliary file that helps a C program perform input/output (I/O) properly. C files that end with the .h extension are called *header files*, whereas C program source code files end with the .c filename extension. All C programs perform some kind of I/O, and the most common header file used to help C with its I/O is stdio.h. As you learn more about C, you'll learn about additional header files that can be helpful, such as the time.h header file, which includes definitions that help with time and date conversions.

C Data

C supports data formats that work much like Python's data formats. For example, C supports the following kinds of data:

- ▶ Character

- ▶ Integer

- ▶ Floating point (decimal numbers)

C supports several types of integers and floating-point data, such as long and short integers, as well as single-precision and double-precision floating-point decimal data.

Unlike Python, C does *not* support a string data type. Although C has some built-in functionality to handle strings in some situations, generally the C language leaves it to the programmer and functions to handle strings. C doesn't support an intrinsic string data type. Therefore, the only text-based data type that C supports is a single character.

NOTE

The fact that C doesn't include support for a built-in string data type isn't a huge problem because ample built-in functions are available in the language to work with string data. Also, C does allow for string *literals*, such as strings that you type directly in the code—just not string variables. Unlike Python, however, C does not inherently support string data, which sometimes makes for some interesting programming.

Listing 19.1 includes a string literal. String literals (remember that there is no string variable) are always enclosed in quotation marks. Therefore, the following are string literals:

```
"C is efficient"
"3"
"443-55-9999"
```

TIP

Given the cryptic nature of C, you should add comments to your code as much as possible. You will need the comments when you later make changes to the program. You'll be happy to know that the style of comments used in C is exactly the same as in JavaScript—enclose comments between /* and */ or precede them by //, as shown in the statements below:

```
/* Ask how old the user is */
    printf("How old are you? "); // Ask for the age
    scanf(" %d", &age); /* Ampersand required */
```

When you declare variables in C, you need to be more specific about the type of variable you need than in Python. Consider the following section of a main() function:

```
main()
{
    char initial;
    int age;
    float amount;
...// more code here

}
```

This code declares three variables: initial, age, and amount. They hold three different types of data: a character, an integer, and a floating-point value. These variables are local to the function and cannot be used outside main(). (You can declare variables before main(), and those variables would be global to the whole program, but global variables are not recommended, as you already know.)

The assignment statement works just as it does in Python. You can initialize variables like this:

```
initial = 'G';
age = 21;
amount = 6.75;
```

C Functions

C is built on a foundation of functions—both functions that you write and functions supplied by C. The next two sections should help you understand the nature of C functions.

Using Built-In Functions

Unlike just about every other programming language in the world, C has *no* input or output statements. Look through Table 19.1 once more. You don't see a `print` statement or anything else that might be considered an I/O statement.

C performs all its I/O through functions that your C compiler provides. By letting the compiler makers implement I/O in functions, the C language is highly *portable*, meaning that a C program that runs on one kind of computer should run on any other computer that is capable of running C programs. A C program written for a Mac will work on a PC without change, assuming that you compile the program using each computer's own C compiler.

The `printf()` Output Function

The most common I/O function is the `printf()` function. `printf()` outputs data to the screen in most cases (although the programmer can route the output to other devices, if needed, through operating system options). Here is the format for `printf()`:

```
printf(controlString [, data]);
```

controlString determines how the output will look. *controlString* formats any data values that you specify (separated by commas if more than one value is output) in the *data* area. Consider the following `printf()`:

```
printf("Read a lot");
```

This `printf()` doesn't include a data list of any kind. *controlString* is the only argument to this `printf()`. When you use a string of text for the *controlString* value, C outputs the text directly to the screen. Therefore, the `printf()` produces this onscreen when the user runs the program:

```
Read a lot
```

CAUTION

Unlike in Python, in C you need to use the \n character if you want output to force the cursor to the next line. If the previous `printf()` were followed by this `printf()`:

```
printf("Keep learning");
```

the output would look like this:

```
Read a lotKeep learning
```

Obviously, the second `printf()` should have used the \n character, like this:

```
printf("\nKeep learning");
```

With \n, subsequent `printf()` output would appear on the next line.

When you print numbers and characters, you must tell C exactly how to print them. You indicate the format of numbers with *conversion characters* that format data. The conversion characters format data in functions such as `printf()` (see Table 19.2).

TABLE 19.2 C's most-used conversion characters

Control Character	Description
%d	Integer
%f	Floating point
%c	Character
%s	String

When you want to print a value inside a string, insert the appropriate conversion characters in `controlString`. Then, to the right of `controlString`, list the value you want printed. Figure 19.1 shows how a `printf()` can print three numbers—an integer, a floating-point value, and another integer.

print["%d roses cost %f per %d.\n" , 24, 19.95, 12];

24 roses cost 19.95 per 12

FIGURE 19.1
Conversion characters determine how and where the output appears.

Strings and characters have their own conversion characters as well. You don't need `%s` to print strings by themselves because strings included inside `controlString` that don't have the formatting percent sign before them print exactly as you type them. Nevertheless, you might need to use `%s` when combining strings with other data.

The following `printf()` prints a different type of data value, using each of the conversion characters from Table 19.2:

```
print("%s %d %f %c\n", "Sams", 14, -8.76, 'X');
```

This `printf()` produces the following:

```
Sams 14 -8.760000 X
```

The string `Sams` needs quotation marks, as do all other string literals, and the character `X` needs single quote marks, as do all other characters. C formats the floating-point numbers with full precision—hence the four zeros at the end of the value. You can limit the number of places printed by using format specifiers. If the `printf()`'s conversion characters for the floating-point number had been `%5.2`, the `-8.76` would have been output in five spaces, with two of those five spaces used for the decimal portion. Therefore, the following `printf()`:

```
printf("%s %d %5.2f %c\n", "Sams", 14, -8.76, 'X');
```

would yield this output:

```
Sams 14 -8.76 X
```

Working with Strings

Although C doesn't support string variables, there is a way to store strings. C represents every string with a null zero character at the end of the string. This null zero has an ASCII value of zero. When C encounters the null zero, the end of the string is reached. You never see this null zero on a string, but it is there, internally, at the closing quotation mark. You never add the null zero; C adds it.

If a string includes a 0 as part of its text, as in the address 190 S. Oak Road, the embedded zero is not the null zero because the embedded zero is a regular ASCII character for zero (ASCII number 48).

Figure 19.2 shows how the string `"Sams"` is stored in memory as a string. The `\0` character is C's representation for the null string. The length of a string includes the characters within the string but never includes the null zero.

Memory

FIGURE 19.2
A string always terminates with a null zero character.

C uses a character array to hold a string, including the string's null zero. All of C's data types can appear in their own arrays, but when a character array appears and a null zero is included at the end of the data, C treats that character array just like a string. C uses brackets instead of parentheses for array subscripts. To define a character array that will hold a 10-character string, you could declare the following array:

```
char month[10]; /* Defines a character array */
```

The month array can hold 10 individual characters or a string if the string includes the null zero. Always leave room for the null zero in the array. C uses zero-based arrays, so month can hold a 10-character string in elements 0 through 9 and the null zero in element 10. You can initialize a string when you define the array, like this:

```
char month[10] = "September"; /* Declare and initialize the string */
```

You can also assign the array at runtime by using a special `strcpy()` function, like this:

```
strcpy(month, "September"); /* Assigns September to the month array */
```

To use `strcpy()`, you must include the header file named `string.h` in the same area of the program where you include `stdio.h`.

CAUTION

The only data `printf()` doesn't format is string data. Therefore, if you use `printf()` to print anything other than a single string, you must supply a conversion code.

The `scanf()` Input Function

Getting keyboard input is much more difficult than producing output on the screen. Use `scanf()` to accept keyboard input. `scanf()` is fairly simple now that you understand `printf()`, but `scanf()` does behave strangely at times. Here is the format for `scanf()`:

```
scanf(controlString [, data]);
```

Understand the following rule, and `scanf()` should work for you every time:

Prefix each variable inside the `scanf()` with an ampersand unless that variable is an array.

Therefore, the following `scanf()` gets an age value entered by the user:

```
scanf(" %d", &Age);
```

CAUTION

Do you see the blank before the `%d` in `scanf()`'s *controlString*? Always include the blank because the input of values works better with it.

The following `scanf()` gets the user's first name into a character array as a result of the user following the prompting `printf()`:

```
printf("What is your first name? ");
scanf(" %s", name); /* Get the name */
```

The `scanf()` function is a mirror-image function to `printf()`. Often, you will write programs that ask the user for values with a `printf()` and get those values with `scanf()`. When your program gets to `scanf()`, C stops and waits for the user to type values. The variables listed inside `scanf()` (following the *controlString* argument) accept whatever the user types, and `scanf()` quits receiving input when the user presses Enter.

CAUTION

When the user types a space, `scanf()` also stops getting input! Therefore, `scanf()` is good for getting only one word at a time in a string.

Despite its problems, scanf() is useful because it allows you to practice getting user input. There are many other ways to get user input in C and C++, and often they work better than scanf(), but scanf()'s similarity to the simpler printf() makes scanf() an acceptable keyboard-input function for beginners.

Listing 19.2 shows a complete program that prompts for user input and gets output. You can study the program to gain a better understanding of the material covered so far in this lesson.

LISTING 19.2 Use scanf() and printf() for input and output

```c
#include <stdio.h>
main()
{
    int age;
    float weight;
    char first[15], last[15]; /* 2 char arrays */

    printf("\nWhat is your first name? ");
    scanf(" %s", first); /* No ampersand on char arrays */
    printf("What is your last name? ");
    scanf(" %s", last);

    printf("How old are you? ");
    scanf(" %d", &age); /* Ampersand required */
    printf("How much do you weigh? ");
    scanf(" %f", &weight); /* Ampersand required */

    printf("\nHere is the information you entered:\n");
    printf("Name: %s %s\n", first, last);
    printf("Weight: %3.0f\n", weight);
    printf("Age: %d", age);
    return 0; /* Always best to do this */
}
```

▼ Here is a sample execution of Listing 19.2:

```
What is your first name? Joe
What is your last name? Harrison
How old are you? 41
How much do you weigh? 205


Here is the information you entered:
Name: Joe Harrison
Weight: 205
Age: 41
```

Writing General Program Functions

As with a Python program's collection of functions and event procedures, C programs are modular and are composed of many functions. Although you *can* put all of a C program's code in the main() function, main() was intended to be used as a controlling function for the rest of the program. Listing 19.3 illustrates the outline of a C program that has proper form.

LISTING 19.3   Use main() to control the rest of the program

```c
#include <stdio.h>
main()
{
   getNums(); /* Get a list of numbers */
   sortNums(); /* Sort the numbers */
    printNums(); /* Print the list */
    return 0; /* End the program */
}
getNums()
{
   /* Body of function goes here
     that gets a list of values
     from the user */
}
sortNums()
{
    /* Body of function goes here
      that sorts the values */
}
```

```
printNums()
{
   /* Body of function goes here
      that prints the values */
}
```

The `main()` function is composed of a series of function calls to three separate procedures. (The code bodies of the procedures are not included in this example.) The `main()` function, and hence the entire running program, terminates when the `return 0;` statement is reached. The `return` often appears at the end of a function when the function is returning a value to the calling function. Here the `main()` function is returning a 0 to the operating system. 0 is a standard return value that the operating system can check.

C Operators

C's collection of operators matches those you learned in Python. For example, the plus sign works exactly as it does in Python. In addition, C supports the increment and decrement operators, `++` and `--`, which add and subtract 1 from whatever variable you apply them to. The following statements each add 1 to the variables a, b, and c:

```
a++;
b++;
c++;
```

The following statements decrease a, b, and c by 1:

```
a--;
b--;
c--;
```

C Control Statements Mimic Python

Actually, C came first (just not in this book), so it's accurate to state that Python's control statements mimic those of C (and C++). For example, C supports an `if...else` statement such as this:

```
if (age < 18)
  { printf("You cannot vote yet\n");
    yrs = 18 - age;
    printf("You can vote in %d years.\n", yrs);
  }
else
  {
    printf("You can vote.\n");
  }
```

C also supports several kinds of looping statements that use the relational operators. For example, the following code shows a `while` loop that continues as long as the relational expression evaluates to `true`:

```
while (amount < 25)
  {
    printf("Amount is too small.\n");
    wrongVal++; /* Keep track of number of problems */
    printf("Try again... What is the new amount? ");
    scanf(" %d", &amount);
  }
```

Learning C++

Much of a C++ program looks like pure C code, which it is. The C++ language introduces some new language elements, but the keywords and structure are similar to those of C. Most of C++'s change over C is a result of injecting OOP technology into C. The primary differences between C and C++ don't lie in commands and keyword differences but rather in how the language supports the use of objects.

C programs use the `.c` filename extension, and C++ programs use the `.cpp` filename extension. Not all C++ compilers support programming in the Windows environment, but most PC-based C++ compilers sold today do provide full Windows programming support, including support for a visual interface such as a toolbox with controls, just as Visual Basic provides.

Object Terminology

You learned a bit about OOP in Part III, "Java and Object-Oriented Programming," earlier in this tutorial. OOP is laden with terminology that might seem daunting at first. The actual implementation of OOP is fairly easy to understand, and with the quick introduction you've already had, you are already somewhat acquainted with terms such as these:

▶ **Abstraction:** The situation when internals of an object do not always have to be known by the programmer to use an object.

▶ **Class:** The definition of a related group of objects.

▶ **Inheritance:** The ability to create a new class of objects from an existing class. By inheriting a new class of objects, you can create new objects with new behaviors and characteristics based on existing objects and classes.

▶ **Message:** A command that acts on specific objects as opposed to the other language commands that are not tied to specific objects.

▶ **Object:** A collection of characteristics and behaviors, perhaps even two or more variables treated as a single unit, that appears in OOP programs.

▶ **Polymorphism:** A name given to the ability of different objects to respond differently to the same commands (called *messages*).

▶ **Reusability:** The ability of the language to utilize objects defined in other programs.

Fundamental Differences Between C and C++

Some of the new language features that C++ provides over C have nothing directly to do with OOP. The following sections preview some of the non-OOP language differences that you'll find between C and C++.

Name Differences

Some differences between C and C++ are simple changes. For example, instead of C's `#include <stdio.h>` directive, C++ programs almost always include the following directive:

```
#include <iostream>
```

As with the C header files, C++ programmers include many other header files in addition to `iostream.h`, but `iostream.h` is the most commonly included file. `iostream.h` is the header file that defines basic input and output.

I/O Differences

C++ includes several new operators. The two most common C++ operators are >> (the *insertion* operator) and << (the *extraction* operator) for input and output. These operators are usually combined with the two *stream objects* `cout` and `cin`. `cout` always represents an output device and defaults to the screen. `cin` always represents an input device and defaults to the keyboard. You can redirect `cout` and `cin` to other devices through the operating system and through compilers such as Visual C++ if you ever have the need. Your program considers these stream objects to be nothing more than a series of data values that are being input or output.

A few examples will quickly show you how to combine the insertion and extraction operators with stream objects. The following statement sends a string and a number to the screen (typically the output stream goes to the screen, although you can change that destination to a different device):

```
cout << "Here is the total: " << 1000.00;
```

If you want to write several lines of output, you can do so by embedding the newline character in the output stream. The following line:

```
cout << "Line 1" << '\n' << "Line 2" << '\n' << "Line 3" << '\n';
```

produces this output:

```
Line 1
Line 2
Line 3
```

Generally, C++ programmers don't use the newline character, \n, at the end of a statement with
cout. They use a special object called endl, which not only produces a newline character but
also empties the output buffer if you send data to a device that buffers output, such as a printer.
Therefore, the following statement would be more likely than the one shown before this tip:

```
cout << "Line 1" << '\n' << "Line 2" << '\n' << "Line 3" << endl;
```

C++ combines the cin input stream with the >> extraction object to support keyboard input. As
with scanf(), keyboard-based input with C++ is fairly simple to understand and implement, but
C++'s input capabilities are limited when you use cin >> just to start with a way to get keyboard
input quickly. However, keep in mind that more advanced and better input methods exist that you
will master if you pursue the C++ language.

To get a keyboard value into an integer variable named intAge, you could use the following:

```
cin >> intAge;
```

Of course, you would probably prompt the user first with a cout, so the I/O would more likely
look like this:

```
cout << "How old are you? ";
cin >> intAge; // Get the age
```

Introducing C++ Objects

To declare a C++ object, you first must declare a class. A class is not an object but rather a description
of an object. The C++ language includes the class keyword that you use to define a class.

Consider the following class declaration:

```
class Person {
    char strLastName[25];
    int intAge;
    float flSalary;
};
```

Here the class name is Person. The class is said to have three *members*. The member names are
strLastName, intAge, and flSalary. This class, therefore, describes objects that contain
three members. Individually, each member could be considered a separate variable, but taken

together (and C++ will *always* consider the members to be part of the class) the members form the class. The members are not objects but parts of objects that you can define with this class.

CAUTION

Remember that a class is a description of an object but not the object itself. In a way, int is a keyword that defines a class; int is a data type that describes a type of numeric value or variable. Only after you define integer variables do you have an integer object.

Declaring Object Variables

Without your help, C++ would have no idea what the Person class would be because Person is not some internal class native to C++. Therefore, the multilined class statement shown earlier tells C++ exactly what the class's characteristics are like. After you define the class, you then can declare variables, or, more accurately, objects of the class. The following statement declares a Person object called Mike:

```
Person Mike;  // Declares an instance of the Person class
```

Figure 19.3 shows what the object (or variable or instance of the class) looks like. The object named Mike is a three-part object. The characteristics are as follows: Mike is an object that begins with a 25-character array, followed by an integer, followed by a floating-point value.

FIGURE 19.3
The object named Mike internally contains three members.

All Person objects that you declare from the Person class will look like Mike, but they will have different names, just as integer variables in a program have different names. In addition, the objects will have local or global scope, depending on where you declare them.

TIP

Generally, programmers place the class definition globally or even stored in a header file that they include in subsequent programs. After the class definition appears globally (such as before the main() procedure), any place in the rest of the program can declare object variables from the class. The variables might be global, but they will probably be local if the programmer follows the suggested standards and maintains only local variables to a procedure. As with any other variables, you can pass object variables between procedures as needed.

Any place in the program can declare additional object variables. The following statement would declare three additional objects that take on the characteristics of the Person class:

```
Person Judy, Paul, Terry;
```

Accessing Members

You use the dot operator (a period) to access members in an object. For example, the following assignment stores a value in the Mike object's intAge member:

```
Mike.intAge = 32; // Initialize the member named age
```

As long as you qualify the member name with the object name, C++ knows which object to assign to. Therefore, if several Person objects are declared in the program, the object name before the member informs the program exactly which object member you want to initialize. Anywhere you can use a variable, you can use a member name, as long as you qualify the name with the object. For example, you cannot directly assign a string literal to a character array in C++ (or in C), but you can use the strcpy() function, like this:

```
strcpy(Mike.strLastName, "Johnson"); // Assign the name
```

You could print one of the members like this:

```
cout << Mike.intAge; // Display the age
```

If you wanted to print the three members, you might do so like this:

```
cout << Mike.strLastName << ", " << Mike.intAge << ", " << Mike.flSalary << endl;
```

Adding Behavior to Objects

Until now, you've only seen how to add characteristics to a class by defining the class members. You can also define the class behaviors. The behaviors describe what objects in the class can do. Adding behaviors to a class requires much more time to cover than the rest of this hour will allow. But by seeing an example or two of a class with defined behavior, you will begin to see how objects begin to take on a life of their own—something that simple variables cannot do.

The following Person class definition is more complete than the previous one because it defines not only the characteristics (the members and their data types) but also the behaviors (called *member functions*):

```
class Person {
   char strLastName[25];
   int intAge;
   float flSalary;
   // Member functions appear next
   void dispName( void )
     { cout << "The last name is ";
```

```
        cout << strLastName << endl;
      }
    void compTaxes(float taxRate)
      { float taxes;
        taxes = taxRate * flSalary;
        cout << "The taxes are ";
        cout << taxes << endl;
      }
    char * getName ( void )
      { return strLastName; }
    int getAge ( void )
      { return intAge; }
    float getSalary ( void )
      { return flSalary; }
};
```

Just as a member can be an instance of a variable, a member can also be a function. The embedded function, the member function, applies only to objects declared from this class. In other words, only `Person` objects behave exactly this way but those `Person` objects can perform the operations defined by the member functions. In a way, the objects are smart; they know how to behave, and the more member functions you supply, the more the objects know how to do.

Many programmers elect to use function declarations (the declaration, or first line of a function, is called the function's *prototype*) in the `class` statement but then define the function code later. By placing function prototypes after the `class` itself, you keep the class cleaner, like this:

```
class Person {
    char strLastName[25];
    int intAge;
    float flSalary;
    // Member functions appear next
    void dispName( void );
    void compTaxes(float taxRate);
    char [] getName( void );
    int getAge ( void );
    float getSalary ( void );
};

void Person::dispName( void )
    { cout << "The last name is ";
      cout << strLastName << endl;
    }
void Person::compTaxes(float taxRate)
    { float taxes;
      taxes = taxRate * flSalary;
      cout << "The taxes are ";
      cout << taxes << endl;
    }
```

```
char [] Person::getName( void )
   { return strLastName; }
int Person::getAge ( void )
    { return intAge; }
float Person::getSalary ( void )
    { return flSalary; }
```

The `class` statement is more compact because only prototypes—and not member function code—appear in the definition. The member function code could appear elsewhere in the program or, more likely, would be included from a file you or another programmer created that contains the member functions you need to call. Notice that if you place the function's definition later in the program, you must preface the definition with the class name followed by the `::` operator. The class name qualifies the function because different classes may have member functions with the same name as other classes in the program.

Before you see how to apply the member functions to objects, you need to understand how scope affects objects and their member functions.

Working with Class Scope

As you know, the `class` statement defines a class and its members and member functions. However, special consideration must be given to the scope of individual data and function members. In the previous class definition, all members were *private*, meaning no code outside the class could access the data members. You can override the default privatization of members by using special `public` and `private` qualifiers to make the class available to code.

Consider this modified `Person` class definition (with the member function code omitted for brevity):

```
class Person {
   char strLastName[25];
   int intAge;
   float flSalary;
   // Member functions appear next
public:
   void dispName( void );
   void compTaxes(float taxRate);
   char [] getName( void );
   int getAge ( void );
   float getSalary ( void );
};
```

All members are considered to be private unless you precede them with the `public` keyword. All members before `public` are private, but you can optionally place `private:` before the first member so other programmers know your intention is for the class members up to the next `public` keyword to remain private. All members (both data members and function members) that follow `public:` are public.

Being private means that any program that uses the class can *never access private members*. This is critical for the data protection that the class provides. Earlier in this hour you saw the following statement:

```
cout << Mike.intAge; // Display the age
```

Actually, this statement will not work in the program because the program does *not* have access to the `intAge` data member. The `intAge` data member is private, so no code outside the class can access `intAge`. By protecting data members, you keep an object intact and ensure that only predefined functions available in the class can access the age. That's why you often see member functions that begin with `get` (for example, the `getAge()` function shown earlier in this lesson). Because `getAge()` is in the public section of the class, any program that defines `Person` objects *can* use the `getAge()` function. Therefore, you cannot display `intAge` directly, but you can call the `getAge()` function like this:

```
cout << Mike.getAge(); // Display the age
```

Notice that when you apply the member function to the object, you use the dot operator just as you do for data members. Other class objects may be defined and also have functions named `getAge()`, so you must qualify the member function by letting the program know you want the `getAge()` function applied to one specific object variable in the program named `Mike`.

Keep in mind that complete college courses and huge texts exist that teach OOP in C++. You're getting only an overview here, although the overview is actually rather complete. After mastering this introductory hour, you should be able to understand the early portions of a course or text on C++ much more easily.

Things to Come

Given the introduction to C++ that you've now had, you can better understand the advantages that C++ provides over more traditional, non-OOP languages. One of the benefits of OOP is that you can create your own operators. More accurately, you can change the way an operator works when the program uses that operator with one of your objects.

By writing special *operator overloading* member functions, you can make any C++ operator work on your own objects. For example, a plus sign is the addition operator, which automatically works on all numeric values. However, the plus sign cannot work on a `Person` object such as `Mike`. Therefore, if you wanted to add two `Person` objects together to get a total of the salaries, you could write a function to add the salaries of two or more `flSalary` data members. When you apply the totaling function members to objects, you can produce the total of the salaries, but you can also overload the plus sign operator so that plus works not only for two numbers but also for two `Person` objects, like this:

```
totalSals = Mike + Terry; // Possible by overloading the +
```

You could never ordinarily use a plus sign between two `Person` objects such as `Mike` and `Terry` because they are objects you created, and they contain three data members of different data types. But once you overload the plus operator to add the appropriate values inside `Person` objects, you can add their values easily.

NOTE

You saw an example of operator overloading when you learned Python earlier in this tutorial. When the plus sign (+) is used with two numbers in Python, it adds the values, but when it is used with two strings, it concatenates them into one larger string. It's one operator, but it can perform different jobs.

Such operator overloading allows you to simplify a program's code. Instead of using a function to simulate a common operation, you can actually use the operator itself, applied to your own objects. The member function that describes the operator overloading determines exactly which data members are affected and used by the operation.

NOTE

The overloading of operators is how you can use the << and >> to input and output complete classes of objects with multiple members and even use Windows-based controls such as text boxes to receive or initiate the special I/O.

The concept of polymorphism makes the overloading of operators possible. For example, the same operator applied to an integer variable behaves much differently if you apply that operator to a class object that you define.

In addition to overloading operators, you can create your own data types. Keep in mind that a class simply defines a collection of data that is composed of data members that conform to an ordinary data type. You could, for example, create a `String` class whose only data member is a character array. By overloading the appropriate operators, you can make C++ behave like Java and support string-like variables.

The `String` class is just one example of the many classes you and others can write to support object reuse later on. Over time, you will build a large library of classes that you can use for future programs. As you build classes, the amount of code that you have to write should decrease, and you should complete applications more quickly. In addition, as you build and debug object class libraries, your programs should become more maintainable. Using operator overloading and other OOP advantages means that your code will be less bulky. When you need an object, you can simply create one from one of your class libraries just as you add new stereo components when you want to expand your music system.

One of C++'s most productive features is inheritance. When you or someone else writes a class that you use, you are not limited to objects of that class. The C++ language supports inheritance so that you can derive new classes and create new objects that have all the benefits and features of their parent classes but with additional features as well.

Summary

Are you a C or C++ expert after one hour's lesson? No way. Do you understand the fundamentals of C and C++? You'd be surprised at how well you now already understand the language, especially with your Java introduction earlier. You could not master OOP with C++ in one hour either, but you've already learned the fundamentals of how C++ works. At its most basic level, the C++ language offers language improvements over C even if you don't use OOP. When you begin to use OOP, you will learn to create classes that define objects that seem to take on lives of their own. The objects understand how to perform some duties based on their member functions, and you can extend the objects through inheritance to derive new classes that you can use later.

Q&A

Q. Why is `#include` **not a C command?**

A. `#include` is a preprocessor directive and is not part of the C language. `#include`, and all other lines that begin with `#`, such as `#define`, control how C compiles a program instead of controlling the way that a C program executes.

Q. Can a programmer extend a class by adding functionality if a class does not quite contain enough power?

A. Certainly. That's where the power of class inheritance comes into play. A programmer can include a class and then inherit a new class from the existing class. The inherited class contains all the data members and member functions of the parent class without requiring the programmer doing anything special. Then, the programmer can add additional data members and member functions (both private and public) to the class to make the class operate as needed. Such inheritance makes the reuse and extension of objects extremely easy and should improve the efficiency of programmers as more object libraries are written and distributed.

Workshop

The quiz questions are provided for your further understanding.

Quiz

1. How is C more efficient than Python?

2. What is a header file?

3. What function do all C programs begin with?

4. True or false: C supports string literals.

5. What is wrong with the following statement?

```
if (sales < 2500.00);
   {
      printf("You need to work harder.\n");
   }
```

6. What included header file defines I/O in most C++ programs?

7. Where do you define an object's data members and member functions?

8. What two operators and system objects do C++ programmers often use for input and output?

9. What OOP term is related to operator overloading?

10. How does inheritance improve a C++ programmer's efficiency?

Answers

1. C compiles into a more efficient language than Python, often because of its heavy use of operators instead of commands.

2. A header file brings in extra routines and library definitions and is brought in with the `#include` statement, not unlike the Java `import` command.

3. All C programs start with `main()`.

4. True.

5. The semicolon should not appear after the `if`'s closing parenthesis.

6. `<iostream>` defines the I/O routines for most C++ programs.

7. You define an object's data members and member functions inside the object's class definition.

8. C++ programmers often use `cin>>` and `cout<<` for input and output.

9. Polymorphism allows for operator overloading.

10. Programmers do not have to repeat all the code when defining inherited objects; programmers only have to write code that adds or changes functionality.

Programming with Visual Basic 2019

Unlike with many other programming languages, much of the work of a Visual Basic programmer doesn't lie in code but in the design of the application's visual elements, such as the controls that the programmer places on forms at design time. These controls allow interaction both to and from the user. The code that the programmer places behind the controls handles the events as well as data calculations and manipulations that produce the information required by the program.

This lesson is intended to introduce you to Visual Basic and Microsoft's Visual Studio environment. As in other lessons in this section, you will only be getting a taste of the language, but if you like it, you can dive deeper into Visual Basic with a tutorial book such as *Sams Teach Yourself Visual Basic 2015 in 24 Hours*, from Sams Publishing.

The highlights of this hour include the following:

- ▶ How to set control property values

- ▶ How to embed code within a Visual Basic application

- ▶ How to place and size controls so they look correct on the form

- ▶ What kind of code appears in a Visual Basic application

Reviewing the Visual Basic Screen

Unlike most other programming languages, Visual Basic is and always has been a Windows programming language. When you learn to write programs with Visual Basic, you learn not only the language but also its environment. Visual Basic is part of Microsoft's Visual Studio, a shared integrated development environment (IDE) where you can develop in Visual C++, Visual C#, Java, JavaScript, Python, and F#. The advantage to a shared IDE like this is that once you learn the ins and outs of using the editor and tools of one programming language, you've got a head start on your next language. Before you can do anything in Visual Basic, you must understand the Visual Basic screen.

NOTE
_____
This hour assumes that you've installed the Visual Studio environment and focuses on using Visual Basic 2019. If you need help installing Visual Studio, you can find many online resources to help.
_____

Figure 20.1 shows the Create a New Project screen with Visual Basic Windows options selected. This screen offers a rich variety of options, and across the top of the window, you can filter by language (Visual Basic in the sample screen), Platform (Windows in this example, but you can also choose Android, Azure, iOS, Linux, MacOS, tvOS, or Xbox), and Project Type (All Project Types in this case). In addition, there are more template choices, depending on the languages and the submenu (for example, Windows, Web, Office). You can always select Empty Project and build your offering from scratch, but a template gets things started for you. Much of what you do with Visual Basic is Windows based, so Blank App (Universal Windows) is a common starting point.

FIGURE 20.1
When you start a new Visual Basic project, you have a rich variety of options.

A Windows application is often composed of several files, including the following:

▶ **Form files:** This type of file contains a form and its description, controls, and related event procedure code.

▶ **Code modules:** These modules hold general-purpose code.

▶ **Other files:** Other files contain elements needed by the application.

The Project window keeps track of all items within an application.

The term *project* is used to describe a collection of all files that compose a single Windows application. (The Project window is often called the Project Explorer window because of its tree-structured nature that mimics the Windows Explorer program.) The Form Layout window lets you determine, by dragging with your mouse, the location of the current form on the user's screen when the user runs the program.

CAUTION
_____

Depending on the version of Visual Studio you have, you may see slightly different screens from the ones presented here. Figure 20.1 shows the project options in Visual Studio 2019 Professional. Other versions of Visual Studio have fewer options to select. Don't worry, though. Windows Form Application, covered in this hour, is a universal option in all Visual Studio installations.
_____

The latest versions of Visual Basic include tools that go far beyond those available in most other languages. However, creating a Visual Basic application from scratch involves little more than these steps:

1. Design the application by stating its goals and detailing its requirements.

2. Place graphics controls on the application's Form window. (This is the output definition design stage.) As you place the controls, you'll assign many of the initial properties to the controls.

3. Add event procedures that handle control events.

4. Add any other code needed to tie the controls together and process data as required by the application.

5. Test and distribute the application to users.

As you'll see in the next section, Visual Basic can greatly help reduce the time it takes to complete steps 2 through 4.

Creating a Simple Application from Scratch

With just a single lesson on Visual Basic, you might as well take the plunge into the creation of a program from scratch. However, if you don't have access to a Visual Basic programming environment, reading through this section still has some value. You can follow along to get an idea of what Visual Basic requires when you create applications.

This first application you'll create in this lesson displays a picture and a command button. The program will change the picture when you click the command button. Follow these steps to create this simple application:

1. After starting Visual Studio, select Create a New Project to display the New Project list (refer to Figure 20.1).

2. Type **Windows Form** in the search bar and highlight Visual Basic as the language and Windows as the platform. Make sure Windows Form App is highlighted and click the Next button.

3. Enter **TYBeginProgVB** as the project name—or feel free to name it something more clever. You can also change its location from the current default if you wish.

4. Click Create. Visual Basic adds a single form (currently named Form1) for you to start building your project.

NOTE

The small white squares that appear on the right side, bottom, and bottom-right corner of the form are sizing handles that you can use to change the width or length of your form. Notice that the Properties window in the bottom right displays properties of the form.

5. Drag the form's lower-right sizing handle down and to the right. As you drag the form, notice the changing width and height measurements at the right of the toolbar. Size the form so that it measures about 740×520 pixels. If you want to be exact in the size of the form and you are finding that stretching the form with the sizing handles is too difficult, click the plus sign next to the Size information in the Properties window. Two lines, Width and Height, appear. You can then type the specific data you want, and the window instantly resizes to the size you specified. Figure 20.2 shows the screen.

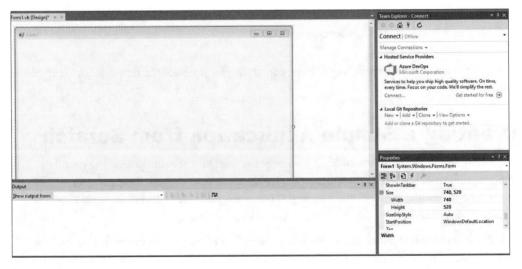

FIGURE 20.2
When you resize the form window, you are resizing your application's program window.

NOTE

The size of the window is measured in pixels, a refreshing change from early Visual Basic versions that used twips. Twips were screen units used commonly during programming screen controls. The number of twips was somewhat dependent on hardware, but the general calculation of a twip was approximately 1/1,440 of an inch. That is, there were 1,440 twips to an inch. Switching to pixels made much more sense as pixels are a more universal measurement to computers in general.

6. To see how to work with the Properties window, assign a better name than `Form1` to the form. In the Design section, a property called `(Name)` (enclosed in parentheses to keep the name at the top of the alphabetical property list) holds the selected form's name. (In the future, this lesson omits the parentheses from around the `Name` property.) Scroll up the Properties window, if necessary, until you see the `Name` value and notice that the `Name` value is currently assigned `Form1`.

7. Click the form's `Name` property and type **frmMyFirst** for the form name.

TIP

You change and assign all properties inside the Properties window the same way you just changed the form's name. Scroll to a property, click the property, and enter (or select for those properties with drop-down list boxes) a new property value. Notice that the name `frmMyFirst` is more descriptive than Visual Basic's default form name, `Form1`. Get in the habit of changing the default object names to make them more representative of what they label. Better naming makes your program easier to maintain.

8. Change the form's title bar from its original value to Hat Picture Application by selecting the `Text` property in the Appearance section and typing **Hat Picture Application**. The `Text` property determines what appears in the form's title bar when the user runs the program. The new name appears in both the Properties window and the form's title bar and helps describe the picture this application will produce.

9. Now that the application's background is complete, you are ready to add the details by putting controls on the form.

Adding the Details

Adding controls to a form typically involves one or more of these steps:

1. Select the control from the toolbox.

2. Place the control in its proper location.

3. Size the control.

4. Set the control's properties.

5. Activate the control with Visual Basic code, if needed.

In the steps that follow, you'll quickly learn how to place controls on the form you've already created. Generally, you perform these steps in one of two ways:

▶ Double-click the control's icon on the toolbox. Visual Basic places that control in the center of the form. You can then drag the control to its proper location and size the control by dragging its sizing handles in or out.

▶ Click the control's icon on the toolbox and move the resulting crosshairs mouse cursor to the form where the control is to be placed. Click and hold your mouse button where the control is to start. As you drag the mouse, Visual Basic draws the control's outline on your form. When you've drawn the control at its proper location and size, release the mouse button to place the control.

Follow these steps to spruce up the application you began in the previous section:

1. Double-click the Label control so that Visual Basic places the label in the center of your form. The Label control contains the letter *A*. (ToolTips pop up to let you know what a toolbox icon is for.) The label is now the selected tool on your Form window editing area, so the sizing handles appear around the label. In addition, the Properties window changes to show the label's properties, and the toolbar's location and size coordinate pairs now reflect the label's measurements. A label displays text on a form. This new label will hold a title banner for your application.

2. Drag the label up the form until it rests approximately 340 pixels from the left edge of the form window and 20 pixels from the top of the form. Again, you can use the Location values in the Properties window to type in exact values if you don't want to mess with dragging it around.

3. In the Properties window, scroll down to the text control and type your title. The default font and size are a little bland, but you can use the font properties to alter its style, size, and any effects, much as you would do in a word processor. If the text for this box has caused the box to lose its centering, feel free to go back and tweak the positioning of the label.

4. Click the Toolbox button in the upper-left corner to bring back the choices and double-click the toolbox's Button control to place a button in the center of your form. The icon on each choice in the toolbox should illustrate the purpose of the button. You can also point to any button to see a ToolTip pop up at the mouse pointer that shows the name of the button. Use the other properties to alter the size of the button and the style and size of the font for the button's text label that you can change from Button1 by typing in the words in the Text Property box.

5. Locate the toolbox's PictureBox control. Instead of double-clicking to place the control as you did with the label, click the control's icon once. Move your mouse to the Form window and draw the Image control, trying to first anchor the image at 260 pixels from the form's left edge and 210 from the form's top edge. Size the image at approximately 220 pixels wide and 190 pixels high. Again, you can do this by meticulously dragging the handles so that Visual Basic's ScreenTips pop up, showing you the coordinates of the image. When the coordinates appear at their proper size, release your mouse button to place the image at that size. Or you can type the information into the Location and Size property boxes. (I find the latter option to be much easier.) Figure 20.3 shows the screen at this point. The PictureBox control displays a graphics image when you run the program.

FIGURE 20.3
Your application is taking shape.

TIP

The sample application is not exactly centered at this point. You can use some simple math to center align your controls if you wish. Simply divide the size of the form in two. (In this case, the form is 740 pixels, so half would be 370.) Then take the size of your controls, divide them in half, subtract that number from the number you calculated as half the form size, and that should be the first number of the location of your form. It sounds complicated, but when you do it a couple times, it gets easy. So if the label is 300 pixels wide, it should start at 220 pixels in order to be centered.

NOTE

Location pixel coordinates and size pixel coordinates are always specified in pairs. Often, you'll see such coordinate pairs specified inside parentheses, as in a location value of (250, 280). For the coordinates, such a pair of values would signify that the width is 250 pixels, and the height is 280 pixels.

Now that you're more familiar with setting property values for controls, even though you may not understand many of the properties yet, you are equipped to set additional properties for the form and controls to finalize the look of the application. After you set appropriate property values, you will add code to connect the controls and make them work together.

Table 20.1 contains a list of properties that you would need to set for the form and the three controls in order to match. Remember that you must select the form or specific control before you can change property values for that form or control. To select the form, click anywhere inside the form or title bar—but not over any of the controls. The Properties window will change to display the form's properties. Click either the label, command button, or image to select the control, and then you can change one of that control's properties by clicking the property name and typing the new value.

TABLE 20.1 Property values to set for the application's form and controls

Control	Property	Property Value
Form	MaximizeBox	False (open the drop-down list box to see values)
Label	AutoSize	False (open the drop-down list box to see values)
Label	Name	FranPlace
Label	Text	Welcome to Fran's Place
Label	Font	Showcard Gothic
Label	Font.Bold	True
Label	Font.Size	11.25
Label	Location	220,30
Label	Size	250,20
Image	Name	ProductPicture
Image	Location	240,140
Image	Size	220,190
Command Button	Name	FranPic
Command Button	Text	Pick a Product

Finalizing with Code

You can add Visual Basic programming statements to turn your creation into a working, although simple, application. Visual Basic automatically adds the opening and closing statements needed when you write a subroutine, as you'll see in the following steps:

1. Double-click the command button to open the Code window. A set of beginning and ending statements appears for a new procedure related to the command button that looks like this:

```
Private Sub FranPic_Click() Handles FranPic.Click
End Sub
```

These lines are two of the three lines needed for code required by the command button. The Code window works like a miniature text editor, in which you can add, delete, and change statements that appear in your program code.

NOTE

All code appears in procedures, and every procedure requires beginning and ending lines of code that define the procedure's start and stop locations. Visual Basic automatically adds the first and final lines of many procedures.

2. Press the spacebar three times and type the following line between the two lines that Visual Basic provided for you (specifying your own directory path as it will probably not match the one below):

```
ProductPicture.Image = Image.FromFile("C:\Documents\TY Begin 24\product1.jpg")
```

As soon as you type `Image.FromFile`, Visual Basic offers pop-up help with the statement's format. Some Visual Basic statements, especially those with parentheses, such as the ones you see in this statement, require that you type one or more values. Visual Basic pops up the format of these required values so you know how many to enter. You'll learn more about why these values are required if you decide to pursue the language in more depth. Visual Basic is a large language, and this help comes in handy.

3. Run the program and click the command button. A picture appears, as shown in Figure 20.4. You have successfully completed your first Visual Basic application. You've created an application that displays a picture when you click the command button. The application contains code, and its controls all have property values that you've set.

4. Click the Close window button to terminate the program. Be sure to save your project before you exit Visual Studio.

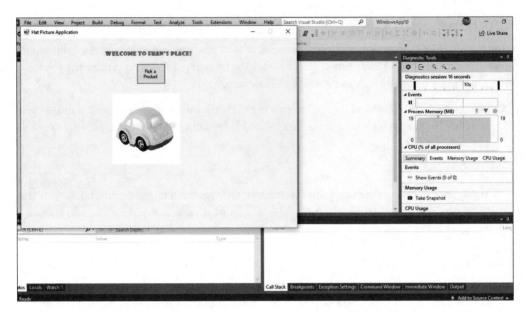

FIGURE 20.4
Your application produces a graphics image when you click the command button. *(Credit: Pavel Losevsky/123RF)*

Other Visual Basic Programming Considerations

This hour approaches the Visual Basic language differently from most other languages discussed in these 24 hours. Instead of walking you through specific programming language commands, this hour walks you through the steps required to create a sample application from start to finish. If you look back through this lesson, you'll notice that very little of the discussion includes actual programming language statements. Visual Basic does a lot just using a visual environment, and adding code sometimes seems like an afterthought.

Even adding menus to the Visual Basic applications that you create from scratch is relatively simple because of a tool called the MenuStrip control (see Figure 20.5). The MenuStrip control lets you build a menu bar and the pull-down options from that menu bar by selecting and specifying options. No code is required as you add the menu options to your application, but after you use the MenuStrip control to add the options, you have to specify event code procedures for the menu options. When the user selects a menu option, a `Click` event for that menu option occurs, and each event procedure that you write tells Visual Basic how to respond to that event.

FIGURE 20.5
Use the MenuStrip control in the toolbox to add menu options to your Visual Basic application.

Understanding Procedures

Consider the following event procedure for the File, Exit menu option:

```
Private Sub ExitToolStripMenuItem_Click(sender As Object, e As EventArgs)
    Handles ExitToolStripMenuItem.Click
        ' Terminates The Program
        End
    End Sub
```

By studying this simple procedure, you can learn quite a bit about all event procedures. The `Private` keyword indicates that the procedure is *local* to the current form and cannot be called by other form modules. Therefore, if several forms exist in the current Windows application, selecting File, Exit from this form will execute this specific event procedure and not one outside the scope of this form. The opposite of `Private` is `Public`, and public procedures are available to any code in the entire application. Such public procedures are known as *global* procedures because any procedure in the application can call them.

The keyword `Sub` or `Function` always follows the `Private` (or `Public`) keyword and indicates the type of the procedure. A subroutine is a procedure that always performs work and then returns control to whatever code was executing before the event took place. A function is a procedure that always performs its job when the event takes place and then returns a value to another place in the program that might need that value.

The name of the event procedure specifies exactly which control and event this procedure responds to. The body of the procedure may consist of several lines, but this one happens to include only two lines: a remark and the `End` statement, which stops the running program. Every procedure ends with an `End Sub` or `End Function` statement. The parentheses that follow the procedure name indicate that the code begins a new procedure; sometimes, when one procedure must pass data values to another, you list one or more values separated by commas inside the parentheses. Even if you don't pass data, you must type the parentheses after every procedure declaration.

Understanding the Language Behind Visual Basic

The language behind Visual Basic has significant differences from the Python you've learned to this point, but the concepts are similar: You just need to understand the tweaks you must make to the syntax of loops, conditional expressions, and assignments. Visual Basic also includes several statements that are unique to the Windows environment.

One of the ways that Visual Basic is unique, however, is in its distribution of procedures across different areas of an application. You now know that several small event procedures reside in a form's Code window to handle any events that occur on that form. Other forms can exist as well, and code appears in them to handle events that occur there. In addition, other files might be part of a complex application. A *code module* is a file, separate from any form and the form's associated code, that holds code that you might use in more than one application. Suppose that you write a procedure that prints your company logo at the top of a page. Such a logo would appear before any report that you produce, before any accounting statement, and before anything you print. You could use this procedure in many different applications.

Instead of typing the procedure in every application that needs it, you can put the code in a general-purpose code module that you then can copy into a new code module for all applications that need to produce the logo. You can, from anywhere else in the application, call a `Public` general procedure with a `Call` statement such as this:

```
Call logoPrint    ' Detour to the procedure
```

When the `Call` statement finishes, execution returns to the statement that follows `Call`.

Your Next Step

This hour offers only a walkthrough of the steps that you take to create a Visual Basic application, and it provides some insight into the nature of Visual Basic programming. Although Visual Basic is probably the easiest programming tool available for creating Windows applications, Visual Basic is vast compared to simpler languages such as JavaScript. Therefore, an hour's lesson could not hope to cover more than what is included here. Nevertheless, you now have a firm grasp of what it takes to write Windows applications in Visual Basic.

TIP

If you want more in-depth Visual Basic programming coverage, pick up a copy of *Sams Teach Yourself Visual Basic 2015 in 24 Hours*, from Sams Publishing, which explores Visual Basic programming and takes a beginning Visual Basic programmer to advanced levels in 24 lessons.

Summary

Visual Basic is more than a language; it is part of a complete Microsoft programming environment called Visual Studio. Other languages are available for Visual Studio, such as Visual C#. Visual Basic was the first language to use the Visual Studio environment. When you create a Visual Basic application, you first create the visual elements of the program by placing the controls from the Toolbox window onto the form. As you place the controls, you set the properties and then write event procedure code to activate the controls when certain events take place.

The next hour describes another language within Visual Studio, C#, as well as Microsoft's overall .NET strategy.

Q&A

Q. Could I allow users to pick an image instead of displaying a specific image when they click a button?

A. Absolutely. With Visual Basic you can use most controls you see in Windows-based programs, so you can trigger a dialog box that lets users browse their hard drive and select an image of their choice instead of using a predetermined file.

Q. Do all Visual Basic applications contain code in addition to event procedures?

A. Some Visual Basic applications contain code that forms event procedures only, but most other Visual Basic applications contain other kinds of code. Most applications have more than events going on. Data must be processed, calculations must be performed, reports must be printed, and files must be read and written. The code behind these specific tasks often appears in a code module separate from the form module.

Workshop

The quiz questions are provided for your further understanding.

Quiz

1. How much code do you have to write to add Internet access to a Visual Basic application?

2. What toolbox control would you use to add menus to a form?

3. Why is it a good practice to change the names of controls from their default names that Visual Basic assigns?

4. What happens when you double-click a toolbox control?

5. What tool do you use to create menus for Visual Basic applications?

6. How does Visual Basic determine which control properties appear in the Properties window?

7. Name one advantage to running a Visual Basic application inside Visual Basic's environment as opposed to running a compiled application from Windows.

8. Which runs faster: a Visual Basic application running inside Visual Basic's environment or a compiled Visual Basic application running outside Visual Basic's environment?

9. What information can you gather from the following Visual Basic procedure's declaration line?

```
Private Sub scrMeter_Change()
```

10. True or false: All Visual Basic procedures reside in the application's form module.

Answers

1. You don't have to write any extra code to add Internet access to a Visual Basic application.

2. You use the `MenuStrip` control.

3. The default names are not meaningful, and when your application uses several controls, you should name those controls with names that you will recognize when maintaining the program so you modify the correct controls when needed.

4. The toolbox control appears in the center of your Form window.

5. The Menu Editor helps you build and test menus.

6. The control you place on a form determines which properties appear in the Properties window.

7. You can debug the application inside the Visual Basic environment.

8. A compiled Visual Basic application is faster than an application run inside the Visual Basic environment.

9. The procedure is private, which means only the enclosing program can access the procedure, the procedure is a subroutine so it does not return any values, and no arguments are passed to the procedure.

10. False. Some procedure code can appear in code modules.

C# and the .NET Core

Microsoft's .NET framework, and its successor .NET Core, are some of the most important technologies for developing applications and web services. Now almost 20 years old, .NET continues to evolve, incorporating new standards that allow developers to create full-featured Windows applications; version 4.8 was released in 2019 in parallel with Visual Studio 2019. .NET is not new technology, but it provides a way to approach new technology. .NET consists of today's software and hardware tools as well as tomorrow's more advanced ones. Microsoft's .NET development environment, Visual Studio, was introduced in the last hour. With it, you can create programs in a variety of languages, including C#, which will be touched upon in this hour.

The concepts behind the .NET Framework and .NET Core are complicated, so don't be discouraged if the material in this hour doesn't immediately make sense. But if you wish to take your rudimentary knowledge gained throughout this book to the next level, .NET is an excellent place to go.

The highlights of this hour include the following:

▶ Understanding why developers use the .NET Framework and .NET Core

▶ Breaking down the elements of the .NET Framework and .NET Core

▶ Defining the C# language

▶ Writing your first C# program

▶ Creating a C# Windows application

Understanding the Purpose of .NET

In this tutorial, you have seen ways to tackle online programming, including using Python, Java, HTML, CSS, JavaScript, and PHP. Microsoft's .NET is a centralized approach to online and networked technology. For the past nearly two decades, Microsoft has developed an approach to online programming and encapsulated that approach into an umbrella of multiple technologies called .NET.

Microsoft wants .NET to address the needs of users who live in an always-on and connected online world. Developers who use .NET are looking to build next-generation, platform-independent products. With the significant changes occurring in the computing space, platform independence has become more crucial than ever before; programmers today need to worry about multiple operating systems, a host of mobile environments and devices, and cloud-based services as well. Code written for either the .NET Framework or .NET Core is called *managed code* (and it can be easily be shared, thanks to the Common Intermediate Language [CIL], covered later in this hour). Code written in languages such as C and C++ that is compiled into machine code tied specifically to the computer on which it was compiled is known as *unmanaged code*.

TIP

If you are looking to create managed code in C or C++, that option is available when you use Visual C++ in Visual Studio.

The .NET Framework and .NET Core create simplified software deployment agnostic of platform, thanks to the common language runtime (CLR), the Framework Class Library (FCL), the parallel computing platform, and the dynamic language runtime (DLR).

The Common Language Runtime

The heart of the .NET Framework and .NET Core is the common language runtime (CLR and CoreCLR). The CLR allows multiple languages to share objects and methods and cuts down on memory leak problems, thanks to garbage collection.

CLR and CoreCLR might sound difficult to understand at first, but they are simple. A .NET-compatible language such as Visual Basic, Visual C++, or C# will not compile to a specific machine, as has historically been the case for computer languages; rather, it compiles to a common machine language. Every .NET-based operating system emulates this common language. So, in theory, a single program written in C++ could run, unaltered, on a PC, on a Windows phone, and as a web service.

TIP

If a programmer learns a language that compiles to a CLR, that program runs on any device that supports .NET. A different compiler and a different language no longer have to be developed for each kind of computing device.

The key components of the CLR include the following:

▶ **The Common Type System:** As you have probably noticed during your survey of languages throughout this book, while most programming concepts and syntaxes are fairly universal, there are subtle differences (like dialects within a shared language) that can cause problems if you attempt to integrate multiple languages. The Common Type System (CTS) allows all languages within the .NET framework to share type definitions, preventing problems that could arise if an incompatible piece of data is assigned to a type. The CTS also sets rules that allow types written in different programming languages to interact with each other. These rules are enforced by the CLR.

▶ **The Common Intermediate Language:** As discussed in earlier lessons, other languages covered in this book, like C and C++, compile their code into machine language that is unreadable and also specific to the platform and machine on which it was compiled—and that is not a great start in creating platform-independent applications and services. The CIL creates a middle step of low-level instructions called an assembly, which when combined with the metadata that describes the types, members, and references in the code, allows your code to run on a variety of platforms; it just needs to be put through a just-in-time compiler (JIT) to run on your specific hardware platform.

▶ **Garbage collection:** Although it was not covered in great detail in Hour 19, "Programming with C and C++," an effective programming practice is to declare only the memory you need for your programs and then release the memory back to the system when you are done with it. Inefficient memory use can slow both your program and your entire system. The .NET Framework introduced garbage collection, an automatic memory management feature that prevents you from worrying about these issues. This isn't to say you are completely free from any involvement in memory management; in fact, if you pursue development in .NET, you should learn how garbage collection works.

TIP

If you want to know more about .NET, its strengths, and the C# language, pick up *Sams Teach Yourself C# 5.0 in 24 Hours*, from Sams Publishing. It covers in excellent detail the subjects touched upon in this hour.

The Framework Class Library

There is little sense in reinventing the wheel. While writing your own code from scratch is always a bit gratifying, using existing code as a foundation helps you build more robust code. The .NET Framework's FCL includes a number of reusable classes, interfaces, and types. There are thousands of classes in the FCL, and you can find detailed information on some of the most commonly used classes at msdn.microsoft.com/en-us/library/gg145045.aspx.

One of the lowest-level FCL offerings is the Base Class Library (BCL), which you use for string manipulation, working with streams, file input and output, and more.

With these thousands of classes, .NET uses namespaces to avoid ambiguity between type names and to clarify hierarchical groupings. The website listed earlier in this section has a robust table that lists several dozen of the most common namespaces, many of which fall in the `system` grouping. Specific namespaces use the dot operator to clarify the levels of the hierarchy (for example, `system.collections`). If you click on the `system.collections` element in the table on Microsoft's website, you get a listing of the base namespaces and four others within the collections hierarchy. Clicking on any of them gives you their classes, interfaces, structures, and more. Effective use of the elements in the FCL will save you considerable development time and add impressive power to your programming abilities.

Parallel Computing Platform

Developers looking to speed up the execution of their programs have turned to multithreaded and asynchronous applications. While these methodologies can greatly increase the speed of programs, they also can lead to problematic, error-filled programs. The .NET Framework simplifies creation of these apps with the parallel computing platform, which allows developers to write code that can take advantage of multiple processors. This is a topic far beyond your knowledge and experience at this point, but it is a key feature of the .NET Framework that you should know about in case you want to head in that direction.

Dynamic Language Runtime

JavaScript, covered in Part IV, "Web Development with HTML and JavaScript," is considered a dynamic language, as are many other scripting languages you may have heard of, like Python (covered in Part I, "Start Programming Today," and Part II, "Programming Fundamentals") and Ruby. These languages have subtle differences from languages like C and Visual Basic. One example you may remember is that you don't have to specify a type for your variables. You can declare a variable `culture` and have it first hold a floating-point number like `14.5` and then assign it a string like `"breakfast cereal"`. Other languages don't allow this because they want to ensure that variables aren't used improperly. This is known as *type safety*. Obviously, you don't want any interactivity problems to arise when a statically typed language like Visual Basic or C# interacts with a dynamic language, and the DLR covers these potential problems, allowing you as a developer to choose whatever language you feel suits your development purposes best.

The C# Language

C# was developed specifically for .NET, to act as a scripting language for applications and web pages. C#, like Java, is based on the C and C++ programming languages. Also like Java and

C++, C# is an object-oriented language; it and supports classes, inheritance, polymorphism, encapsulation, and abstraction.

If you installed Visual Studio in order to follow along with the Visual Basic examples in the previous lesson, you already have your C# integrated development environment (IDE) ready to go. To build a C# (also called Visual C#) program, you select New Project, just as you did in the last hour. This time, though, you click on one of the Visual C# choices from the language list on the right side, of the window shown in Figure 21.1. Notice that there are numerous language choices, including several languages covered in this book, such as Python, Java, JavaScript, and C++.

NOTE

Your dialog boxes and choices may look a bit different than what you see here, depending on what version of Visual Studio you have installed.

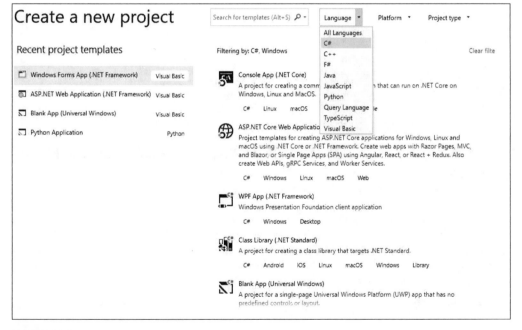

FIGURE 21.1
Much as with Visual Basic, the project choices for Visual C# are quite diverse.

▼ TRY IT YOURSELF

In the previous lesson, with Visual Basic, you selected a Windows Form App. You could do the same here to get the same setup with a form on which you could drag and drop controls and then add lines of underlying code to activate them. Here you should select instead Console App so you can create a simple program to display the area of a circle. After you've selected Console App, you need to name your project as you did for the Visual Basic project in the last hour, and you should get the screen shown in Figure 21.2.

FIGURE 21.2
When you create a new application, Visual C# creates much of the baseline code your application needs.

You have yet to write a line of code, but you are already seeing the power of the .NET Framework. Several of the namespaces from the FCL are listed in the first five lines of your program. This is a signal to your compiler that you can use the classes and other objects of these namespaces in your program. If you found yourself wanting to use others, you would just need to add a `using` line at the top of the code listing.

Type the code in Listing 21.1 into your Visual C# window.

LISTING 21.1 A simple C# program to calculate the area of a circle when given the radius

```
using System;
using System.Collections.Generic;
using System.Linq;
```

```csharp
using System.Text;
using System.Threading.Tasks;

namespace ConsoleApplication1
{
    class Program
    {
        static void Main(string[] args)
        {
            string enteredRadius;
            double radius, area;

            //Get the number from the user
            Console.WriteLine("Enter the radius of the circle: ");
            enteredRadius = Console.ReadLine();


            // The entered value, currently a string, must be turned into
            // a number
            radius = double.Parse(enteredRadius);

            // Once you have the radius, multiply it by itself and PI (3.14)
            // to get the area of the circle
            area = 3.14 * radius * radius;

            //Now output the answer
            Console.WriteLine("The area of a circle with a radius of "
                              + radius );
            Console.WriteLine("is " + area);

            //Your code window will just disappear if
            //you don't add these lines
            Console.WriteLine("Press any key to continue");
            Console.ReadKey();

        }
    }
}
```

When you run this program, you get the results shown in Figure 21.3.

FIGURE 21.3
Your first C# program accomplishes the same goal as one of your first Python programs.
(Remember way back then?)

This should be a fairly easy program to follow by this point in the book. Generally, first programs are "Hello World" examples, but working on a program with not just output but input and variables can be a bit more instructive.

The most confusing part of the program is probably the first few lines. As mentioned earlier, these `using` lines instruct the compiler to let you use the classes and objects associated with the namespaces that follow. Frankly, you don't really need any of them except `System`, and if you comment out the next four (by adding the double slashes `//` at the beginning of each line) and rebuild the project, it will work just fine. Remember that these lines were generated automatically when you selected your project.

From the previous paragraph you should see a similarity that C# has with C, C++, and JavaScript. You use `//` to create comments, telling the compiler to ignore anything that appears to the right of the slashes. As emphasized throughout the book, it is good programming practice to use comments frequently. Some would argue that this listing has too many comments, and that's a fair point; you don't want to overdo things and state the obvious. But undercommenting is far worse, particularly if you have to return to a piece of code you wrote months, or even years, earlier and have to waste time piecing together what the code is accomplishing.

Input and output are the staples of any programming language, and for C#, `Console.Readline` and `Console.Writeline` are great starting points. A secondary input function, `Console.Readkey`, is also being used in this example, although its value is not being assigned to a variable. This is just a way to keep the output window from disappearing after it calculates the area and presents the result onscreen. Without that line waiting for you to input any single character (press any key), the program will output the value of the area and then end, making the window go away before you have time to read it properly. To see what I mean, comment out those last two lines and rebuild and rerun the program.

Taking Advantage of the Visual Nature of Visual C#

The example you just saw in Listing 21.1 and Figure 21.3 is easy to follow and demonstrates the use of C# code in an old-school way. However, one of the advantages of Visual Studio is being able to create Windows applications, so let's look at how easy it is to make a Windows form that does the same radius calculation. Save your previous project and select a new C# project, this time by first clicking a Windows Form App. Visual Studio sets things up for you and gives you the work area shown in Figure 21.4.

FIGURE 21.4
Visual C# Windows-based applications should be easy to understand if you've read through the introduction to Visual Basic in the previous lesson.

This should look familiar to you, as it is virtually identical to the application you saw for Visual Basic in Hour 20, "Programming with Visual Basic 2019." The controls in the toolbox are also similar. The underlying code you write for the application will be where Visual Basic and Visual C# truly diverge.

Open your toolbox and place two labels and two text boxes on your form. It's easy to align them, as once you start dragging one text box under the other, a blue guideline appears to ensure that you place one under the other. These guidelines appear both vertically and horizontally, as shown in Figure 21.5.

FIGURE 21.5
Guidelines can help you with alignment.

Highlight the two labels and rename their text properties in the properties box to Radius (the top label) and Area (the bottom label). While you're at it, click the form and give it the name "Radius to Area Calculator".

Now you need to reopen the toolbox and add a button to your form. Align it to the two text boxes and then change the button's text property to calculate. Your form should look like the one shown in Figure 21.6.

Next, you need to highlight the text box to the right of Radius and name it enteredRadius.

TIP
When you have a variable name made up of multiple words, capitalizing the first letter of the second word (and all following words) is common practice; this convention is known as *camel notation* because it is like you are creating little camel humps within your word.

FIGURE 21.6
Your area calculator should be coming along nicely.

You need to take similar steps for the area text box. Name it `enteredArea`. (I understand that the area is being calculated, not entered, but consistency in naming can be a good thing.)

Now all that is left to do is to put some code behind the calculate button. If you double-click on the button, you bring up the code section. Between the two braces following `private void calculate_Click`, enter the following code:

```
double radius, area;

radius = double.Parse(enteredRadius.Text);
area = 3.14 * radius * radius;

enteredArea.Text = area.ToString();
```

Your code should look as shown in Figure 21.7.

The first three lines of code are similar to your console version. You declare two variables named `radius` and `area`. The information entered by the user into the `enteredRadius` text box is considered a string, so you need to parse it into a number before you do math with it. Then you use the radius of the circle to calculate the area. But before you can display the calculated area in its text box, you must turn the number back into a string, which is easy enough with the `ToString` method. Now your control is ready to go. Build it and run it. If you enter the same radius as you did in the console example, you should get the same area, as shown in Figure 21.8.

FIGURE 21.7
Just as with Visual Basic, once you set your controls, you enter code to get the controls to do what you want.

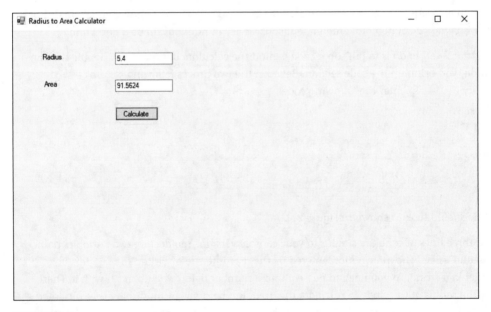

FIGURE 21.8
Now you can calculate circle areas whenever you want!

This isn't the sexiest example, but it has shown you text-based and Windows-based versions of the same program. This lesson obviously just scratches the surface of what you can do with C#. As with the other languages you've learned so far, you can do loops, conditional statements, object-oriented programming (OOP), and much more with C#. There's almost no limit to the power of C#, particularly when you learn to use it in conjunction with the other tools of Visual Studio.

Summary

This 30,000-foot-view of Microsoft's .NET Framework terrain should give you some idea of where you can take your programming knowledge next. The world of application and web service development continues to splinter into different devices and platforms, and the ability to create solutions that work regardless of platform is crucial. In addition, it makes little to no sense to learn multiple development environments as well as languages; the commonality of tools and editor in Visual Studio can save you time and effort and allow you to focus on solving the business issues at hand.

This lesson completes the survey of other languages and environments. The next part (Part VI, "The Business of Programming") takes a three-hour look at the business of programming, giving you some understanding of where the skills you are acquiring can be used in the corporate world.

Q&A

Q. Is using .NET the only way to develop platform-independent applications and services?

A. Not at all. Some people initially thought that .NET and C# were going to replace Java, but as you saw in Part III, "Java and Object-Oriented Programming," Java is still going strong. In addition, new cloud-based programming methods, such as Infrastructure as a Service (IaaS) and Software as a Service (SaaS), can also deliver applications that are largely platform independent. Microsoft's size and marketing muscle will keep .NET in the game, but there are other options as well.

Q. Is it best to use a particular programming language with .NET?

A. While Visual Studio offers a suite of programming languages and tools, there are certain advantages to using C#. It was developed specifically for the .NET Framework. Its similarities to C, C++, and Java make it easy to pick up for anyone who has any experience with those other languages, and it incorporates the strengths of both object-oriented and component-oriented languages. However, if you prefer VB or C/C++, you can use those options in Visual Studio as well.

Workshop

The quiz questions are provided for your further understanding.

Quiz

1. What is the IDE that developers use to create .NET applications?

2. What are the components of the .NET framework?

3. What does CIL stand for?

4. True or false: The power of the FCL is that it has just a few dozen classes, so they are easy to memorize.

5. What is garbage collection in .NET?

6. What language is an example of a dynamic language?

7. What other languages is C# is similar to?

8. Why is it not wise to immediately do math with numbers entered by users in C#?

9. How do you add comments to your code in C#?

10. What is the purpose for the CLR?

Answers

1. Visual Studio

2. The components of the .NET Framework are the CLR, the FCL, the parallel computing platform, and the DLR.

3. Common Intermediate Language

4. False. The power of the FCL is that it has hundreds of classes that cover a number of programming needs.

5. Garbage collection is automatic memory management.

6. JavaScript and Python are examples of dynamic languages.

7. C# is similar to C and C++ (as well as Java).

8. You should parse entered values into numbers before doing math, or C# may assume that the value is a string, and you won't get the result you expect.

9. You can either create single-line comments with the double slash (/ /) or multi-line comments enclosed in (/ * and * /), just as you do in JavaScript, C, and C++.

10. The CLR allows all computers with a CLR compiler to be .NET compatible.

HOUR 22
How Companies Program

The goal of this hour is to give you an idea of how companies program computers. While the focus here is on larger companies working on data processing or enterprise application development, you will also learn about working with smaller companies and even technology startups.

Regardless of size, companies must coordinate their programming efforts to make the best use of their resources. This doesn't always mean that every program wanted by every person gets written. Actually, the allocation of programming talents is one of the primary tasks of a software development manager (or other similar supervisory position). You will learn about some of the different types of available jobs and their common titles and how those people interface with one another. After this hour, you will better understand the wording of the employment ads for computer professionals, and you will have an idea of the experience needed to obtain the different jobs in the computer industry.

Highlights of this hour include the following:

▶ Learning about typical computer-related departments in large companies

▶ Schooling behind programming: which programming degree may give you a boost on the job market

▶ Getting computer experience without a degree or training

▶ Understanding programming-related jobs

▶ How programming teams perform structured walkthroughs of their work

Data Processing and Information Technology Departments

In large companies, core aspects of computer programming might not happen in a department labeled as such. This is especially true in companies that do not actually develop commercial software products. Instead, a large company might have a sort of data processing department known as *data processing*, *information services*, *information systems*, or *management information systems* (*MIS*). Or this function could be subsumed within a greater *information technology* (*IT*) department, which would also include desktop hardware, communications, servers, and networking (among other things).

No matter what the company's employees call this sort of department, it is commonly in the center of almost every major new project the company takes on. When a company expansion, acquisition, or merger is about to take place, this department must prepare for the additional computing resources needed. When an internal engineering project begins, this department supplies engineers and analysts to perform tasks.

As Figure 22.1 shows, a data processing or internal software development department writes programs for every other department in the company. Unless the company itself is a software-writing company (such as Microsoft), the company's main focus is not going to be software development. The company has other objectives, but there is a data processing and IT department that supplies the computer systems and programming resources needed to keep the other departments working as effectively as they can.

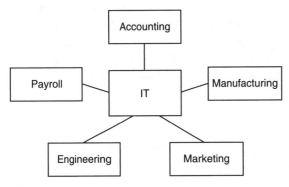

FIGURE 22.1
An IT department manages and maintains programs for the rest of the company.

Such a corporate setup is natural. In the early years of business computing, the computer department was placed in the accounting department and governed by the accounting staff. The problem with putting the computer department under direct control of accounting is that accounting will tend to write computer systems it needs, and the engineering, marketing, and upper management departments might take a backseat. This doesn't mean that the accounting department would selfishly hoard the computer resources, but the accounting bias would be natural because part of the accounting department's own budget was set aside for the computers and their people.

Organizations began to realize in the late 1960s that the data processing department was not directly tied to any one department, such as accounting, but, instead, computer people worked for the entire company because they developed programs that the entire company used. Therefore, standalone computer departments started appearing on companies' organizational charts. Organizations began viewing their computer departments as individual cost centers that required their own budgets and autonomy. Figure 22.2 shows how the typical data processing or IT department fits into today's organizational charts. As you can see, the IT department is located on the same level as accounting, payroll, engineering, and the rest of the departments.

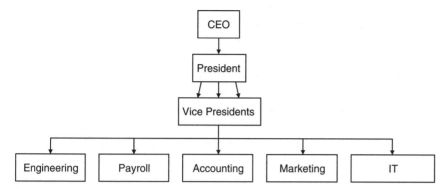

FIGURE 22.2
The IT department is evenly ranked with the company's other departments.

Despite the fact that the data processing or IT department is now autonomous in most companies, that autonomy still doesn't ensure proper allocation of computer resources. A data processing department's resources consist of the hardware, peripheral material (such as paper and cables), and people. The people are the most expensive resource in a data processing department. Their office spaces, desks, supplies, personal computer equipment, telephones, benefits, and payroll costs all add up to a tidy sum.

CAUTION

No matter how much money a company makes, it cannot allow unlimited spending for the computer resources just described. There must be some checks and balances applied to the money spent in data processing. Unlike other departments, whose worth is measured in dollars received by outside customers, the company itself is the only customer of its data processing department. (Many accounting-related departments, such as payroll, often have a similar setup, where they work for the rest of the company and produce no outside income of their own.) That is, each department's budget includes a little extra for overhead expenses (lights, desks, paper, telephones, faxes, copying, secretarial, and data processing usage). By collecting some of each department's overhead budget, the company can pay for the data processing resources.

This overhead method of paying for data processing costs doesn't always work well. Overhead is fine for departments such as the accounting department's general ledger group, but the data processing department's skills are more in demand than are other departments. Without checks and balances of some kind, all the other departments will want programs written with little regard to cost; after all, they've already paid their share of the overhead expense. The information technology or internal software development department can't hire an unlimited supply of programmers just because it receives endless requests for programs.

Not all computer programmers work at the company's location. This is increasingly true for companies that are wholly focused on creating and distributing software as a product or service, where programmers and analysts make up the bulk of the employee roster. As technology improves, companies are learning that some jobs, such as programming, can be performed from any location, including the employee's own home. For some companies—even large companies—partial-week telecommuting is available to staff members who want to work from home. These employees must still come into the office for meetings and team evaluation and review, but the bulk of their work can be done from a PC with an Internet connection. Other companies allow full telecommuting, using video conferences to substitute for meetings, such that remote employees might work for a company several time zones away from their home locations. Telecommuting can save money for a company because the company no longer has the expense of the office space and other support services for each employee. Telecommuting can also make for happier employees, especially those who thrive in their own environment (as opposed to spending time commuting and being in a sterile office environment every day).

Understanding the Chargeback Approach

Companies have been turning away from the overhead approach to another approach, called *chargeback*. With chargeback, the data processing center or IT department is given no funds from the overhead account—which immediately lowers the overhead expenses for all the other departments. When a department needs a program written, that department requests the program from the internal group, which estimates the cost of writing the program and sends that estimate back to the original department.

It is then up to the requesting department to accept or reject the charge for the programming resources. If the department wants the program badly enough and has the funds in its budget, that department's management can transfer those funds to the data processing department's budget, and work begins.

One of the biggest advantages of the chargeback method is that a department cannot ask for the world unless it is willing to pay for it. A department's own limited resources keep it from requesting more than it really needs.

NOTE

The money being transferred is sometimes referred to as *funny money*. It is made up of internal funds that already belong to the company that are being passed from department to department. The company is still out the cost of the computing resources, but when it comes directly from the requesting department's budget, that department puts its own check-and-balance system in place to determine whether its data processing requests are reasonable.

The nice thing about chargeback is that one department works like a miniature company within the parent company, supplying services as long as those services are paid for. The company doesn't have to worry about skyrocketing costs; after all, if the money is already in a department's budget and that department wants to spend it on internal computer programming projects, there is nothing wrong with that. The department will not have those funds to spend on other things, and departments have the right to determine how they spend their own budgets.

Often, the computer programming or IT department hires contract programmers, analysts, and systems administrators when the company's requests grow. If the department predicts that its workload will increase for a short time, such as when another company is bought by the parent company, or a specific project needs to be completed on an aggressive deadline, *contract programmers* are hired to program for a fixed time period. Whether the time is six months, a year, or longer is negotiable.

Generally, contract programmers are paid a large salary because the company doesn't have to pay for the contract programmers' benefits and retirement. There are software companies that hire programmers full time, giving them benefits and insurance, and there are companies that do nothing but hire out their programmers to other companies that need contract programming. Don't rule out an opportunity for contract programming if you are looking for a job. The pay is good, the experience is often better (or at least more varied), and often a company eventually hires contract programmers full time as permanent employees if they turn out to be productive workers.

Computer-Related Jobs

Several times a year, media outlets list the job outlook for the coming year, 5 years, and 10 years. For the past 25 years, computer-related jobs have been high on the lists for the best job environments, highest pay, long-term stability, and so forth. That trend will continue for many years. Despite advancements, computer technology is still in its infancy because there are a lot more programs to write than have already been written.

Companies—especially startups and small to mid-size companies—often allow computer programmers and managers to work in more relaxed conditions than are allowed in other departments. Whereas a company's accounting department reports in at 8:00 a.m., clocks out for exactly 60 minutes for lunch, and leaves at 5:00 p.m. on the dot, the software development staff might not all arrive and leave at a uniform time, if they even work on-site at all.

The reason working conditions can be more relaxed is that programmers and analysts often need to pursue a problem or programming task until its conclusion, even if that means staying awake in the computer room for 20 hours straight. Many programmers love to burn the midnight oil. As you now know, programming is not a science yet, and it might never be one. A large part of programming reflects a person's style and involves a personal commitment to a project. There is a creative side to programming that programmers often find addictive. A programmer who drags in at 11:00 a.m. might be doing so because he stayed up until 4:30 a.m. trying to debug some code for the company.

Managers understand that the creative spirit that programming brings often comes in spurts. When a programmer gets involved on a programming project, she spends more voluntary overtime than any other type of worker would consider. The trade-off seems to be worth the relaxed attitude in many programming organizations.

NOTE

Another primary advantage of the programming field over many others is its equal opportunity. Because the business computer industry didn't really begin until the mid-1960s—when the idea of equal pay for equal work was coming into acceptance—equal opportunity was already a part of the computer industry. There are many female, minority, and physically challenged employees in technical fields, and the norm has always been for the jobs and salaries of all workers in the field to be equal.

Job Titles

You should understand the kinds of jobs that are out there for programmers. Then when you look at employment ads online, you'll have an idea of the qualifications and experience needed for the different jobs that are advertised.

CAUTION

The titles described in this section are common in the computer industry, but they are by no means universal. Whereas the title for a job in one company might be *programmer analyst*, another company might give the same duties the title *senior programmer*. The specific titles mentioned here, although open to change and interpretation, are common enough to describe most of the responsibilities and titles you will see in larger companies.

Degrees and Certificates

Most jobs in technical fields require some kind of degree or certification; whether or not this degree or certification is *useful* is a common topic for debate. There is also a debate as to whether a two-year associate degree or a four-year bachelor's degree is best. The four-year degree is always better in one respect: You are more grounded in the theory behind how computers work and will be able to learn new computer skills faster because of it. However, a four-year degree keeps you out of the workforce two years longer than a two-year degree, and two years is a long time in the rapidly changing field of computers. However, a two-year programming degree simply doesn't give you enough time to learn much about foundational computing theory. In two years, a college will teach you as many hands-on skills as possible. You'll become familiar with one or two programming languages but likely not have extended time to hone your skills by doing group projects or advanced work. While you may find you can enter the programming marketplace at the same job rank and get paid just as much as someone with a four-year degree (at the entry level), a two-year degree in many companies will be a limiting factor to progression in your job.

Perhaps the best of both worlds is possible. You can get a two-year degree, go to work for a company in an entry-level programming job, and go the last two years part time to finish a four-year degree. (Most four-year colleges give credit for classes taken for a two-year degree, with only a few exceptions here and there.) Often a company will pay for, or at least supplement, its employees' continuing education.

TIP

If you have time and money to spare, and who doesn't (seriously, though, there are always scholarships, grants, and loans), consider getting a second degree, either an additional two-year degree or a master's in a field other than programming. A second degree will augment your programming skills. In addition to understanding programming, you will be able to apply those programming skills more readily to an area such as accounting or engineering.

Certification

Another kind of "degree" in the computing scene is not a degree at all. Instead of a degree, a technical certificate shows that you are well skilled in a specific area of computing. Microsoft, Amazon, Oracle, and several other companies offer certification training classes and certifications for their product offerings. After you pass the certification test for a specific area, you are certified by the corporation offering the certificate. In some fields, job applicants in the computing industry are in much greater demand if they are certified. Unlike a college degree, a certificate demonstrates a specific, measurable ability in a high-demand area of computing, such as networking or operating systems.

CAUTION

Certification tests are rigid and difficult. That's a good thing (if you pass one) because it demonstrates true proficiency in a particular subject. With a certificate, your minimum skill level is known in advance by those hiring.

Data Entry

Some computer-related jobs don't require any programming skills. On the low end of the computer ranks are the *data entry clerks* (often called *data entry operators*). Data entry clerks typically need only a high school diploma or its equivalent and some keyboarding skills. Data entry clerks, except for the ones who have been with a company for a long time and have often received pay raises, make the lowest salaries of any of those in computer jobs in a company.

The life of a data entry clerk is simple; he sits in front of a computer screen, typing data into the computer. Typically, as Figure 22.3 shows, all the data entry clerks type on terminals (keyboard and screen combinations) attached to a central computer, usually a mainframe. Eight hours a day, five days a week, the data entry department enters data.

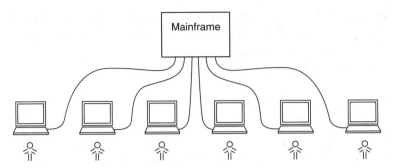

FIGURE 22.3
Data entry clerks normally enter data into the same computer.

A company's data entry requirements are massive. Payroll figures, sales figures, government figures, competing statistics, market trends, industry trends, projections, and so forth all must be factored into the company's working atmosphere. The computer programs that process a large amount of data need it to be entered somehow. The larger the organization, the larger the data needs: Some companies have hundreds of full-time data entry clerks.

At first glance, you might want to stay away from such a job. A data entry position, however, can be a powerful first step into a computing career for some people. People with little or no computer training who need experience can begin as data entry operators. While with the company, they can show a positive attitude, meet others within the company, and receive the typical company insurance and benefits. If a clerk pursues the proper training, she can move into higher programming positions, such as data analyst or database administrator.

TIP

As mentioned earlier, a company will often pay for some or all of an employee's part-time education. Therefore, a data entry clerk with no programming background at all may be able to take night classes to begin training in programming skills. After he finishes a degree or is trained adequately, the company can move him into one of the entry-level programming jobs. Such a person might never have been able to get a programming job if he had not started out in data entry.

Programming

A person with knowledge of programming, either a self-taught programmer who has a degree in another area, a person who received programming training in a two-year or four-year institution, or a certified programmer, will bypass data entry jobs and move straight into a job actually related to programming. The first job title given to a new programmer hired fresh out of college (or one with little professional programming experience) is usually *junior programmer* (or *junior software developer* or *programmer I*). Junior programmer is generally considered the entry-level job for anyone without experience as a programmer in another company.

A person typically doesn't remain a junior programmer for more than a year or two. Often, a junior programmer does not create new code but instead focuses entirely on programs others have written, often doing routine program maintenance. During this initial period, a junior programmer learns how the company operates, gets acquainted with other team members and the team's coding styles, and generally learns the ropes of the company's working environment.

After a person stays in the junior programmer role for a while, he is usually promoted to *programmer* and given a small raise and a pat on the back. The programmer title means that the company expects good things in the coming years and has trust in the person. It is rare for a person to hold a junior programmer title for several years and still be with the same company.

A programmer's primary job is to collaborate on new features as well as work on programs written by others, both maintaining them and modifying them when the need arises. The programmer's supervisor will begin to have the programmer write programs from scratch. Of course, the specifications of the program (the flowchart, output definition, and possibly pseudocode) will already be done, and the programmer has to implement only those specifications into a new program. After a while, the programmer's attitude and on-the-job learning can justify moving into a more advanced job with the title *senior programmer*.

A senior programmer is primarily responsible for writing new programs after being given specifications to follow and sometimes advises other teams during the creation of specifications. In some companies, the senior programmer doesn't have to worry much about maintaining older code because the new junior programmers and mid-level programmers take care of that, but many times a senior programmer also acts as a team leader and mentor to less experienced colleagues, and in that role, the senior programmer will revisit old code with them.

The senior programmer title usually commands a pay raise and maybe an office of his own instead of an office shared with other programmers. A person is a senior programmer for a few years, writing code and getting to know the workings of the company, its users' needs, and the base of programs already in existence. Senior programmers may eventually move into managerial roles, or they may remain senior programmers for as long as the work remains interesting to them. Another option for experienced programmers is to move laterally into systems analysis and design.

Analysis and Design Staff

In many companies, *systems analysts* never write programs, but they will have done so in the past. These skills help them efficiently and thoroughly analyze and design programs that others write.

NOTE
_____

Isn't it strange that you train for a long time to be a computer programmer and work hard at programming for several years, just so you don't have to program anymore? Actually, the programming experience is a must for a high-level systems analyst. Without the understanding that programming brings, one cannot design systems for others to program.

A systems analyst is often a liaison between the users and the other departments who need data processing work performed. As Figure 22.4 shows, a systems analyst talks to both the users and the programming staff. The users don't understand computer requirements; they only know what they want (or what they think they want). The users must work with the systems analyst to design the needed computer system. The systems analyst has worked in the company for many years. The systems analyst understands the needs of the programmers and the needs of the users in the company. The programmers might appear too technically oriented to the users; sometimes the users themselves don't even know what they want. The systems analyst must be able to produce the output definition and logic design through numerous conversations with the users.

Some companies reward years of excellent performance by promoting a systems analyst to *senior systems analyst*. A senior systems analyst often participates in higher-profile projects and works on many projects at once. In addition, there may be managerial aspects to the position.

Users ⇔   SA (Systems Analyst)   ⇔ Programmers

FIGURE 22.4
A systems analyst is a go-between for users and programmers.

NOTE

In smaller programming departments (or companies), one person might wear lots of hats, but that person's job title doesn't accurately reflect the range of jobs performed. For example, some companies have only two or three people in the entire software development or IT department. All of them might program and also perform systems analysis and design duties. Smaller companies give you the opportunity to perform a wider range of programming tasks, improve your skills, and gain an understanding of the responsibilities of lots of job titles. Larger companies usually offer better benefits, pay, and job security, but it will take you longer to broaden your skills.

Internet- and Network-Related Jobs

The online world has created its own set of job positions, many of which overlap those you've read about in this hour. "Programmers" for web development agencies, companies that produce web applications, and even mobile application developers might make a distinction between "front end" and "back end" programming, specializing in one or the other. You might also hear the term "full stack" developer, which indicates that a company is hiring programmers who have skills and ability to program both the user interface (UI) of a software application and the underlying logic and systems interactions. You may see the same junior/senior distinction in job titles as you do with traditional programmers, or you may see the distinction only in the specialization, such as *front end* or *UI developer, back end developer, mobile developer,* and so on.

The huge collection of networked computers generates its own set of jobs as well. You will see jobs with titles such as LAN designer and WAN specialist, as well as managers of these positions and technologies, including security officers who patrol the network for unauthorized access. *LAN* is an acronym for *local area network*, a network that links two or more computers in the same area, floor, or building, usually by direct wiring or wireless technology. *WAN* is an acronym for *wide area network*, which is a network that spans more territory than the usual one-building network.

Demand plays a big role in the pay scales and corporate levels of all computer-related jobs. For example, in the last half of the 1990s, when the Internet was still gaining popularity and use by leaps and bounds, people with Internet-related skills received a bonus that boosted their pay levels higher than they would have traditionally earned based on seniority. This was due to the demand for workers with those types of skills. While there is still a demand for workers in the programming and technology fields in general, to some extent, salaries have leveled because there is now a different baseline for technological competency in a position. That is to say, basic familiarity with computer technology is no longer a differentiating factor between applicants.

The higher salaries offered in the computer field can be a mixed blessing. When you've been in data processing for a few years, your salary becomes much higher than that of others who have been with other departments for the same amount of time. A person who becomes a systems analyst and then decides that computers are no longer a challenge often finds it difficult to move to another position within that company. Companies rarely let people move to a position that requires a pay cut; such employees soon miss the money they were used to, and they start looking elsewhere for a job.

Often, upward moves for computing professionals include a move into management. One of the first management-level job titles is *team lead* or *supervisor*. A lead or supervisor manages a small group of programmers and analysts, directing projects from a management point of view (making sure the group has adequate resources to do the jobs, gets properly evaluated for raises, and so forth). Companies normally prefer their leads and supervisors to have experience similar to those they are managing, and so managers are often promoted from within.

From a supervisory position, you might next move into a position with *director* in its title and be responsible for several supervisors and their projects. The director may be even in rank with the vice presidents in other departments of the firm.

Structured Walkthroughs

A programmer may generally follow these steps after completing a programming task:

1. The programmer tests the program at her desk and tries to get as many bugs out as possible.

2. The programmer passes the program on to the user for testing (often, parallel tests are performed).

3. The user puts the program into use.

Now that you are more familiar with the roles of the programming staff, you might be interested to know about an extra step that often takes place between steps 1 and 2. When the programmer is satisfied that the program is as accurate as possible, he prepares for a structured walkthrough. A structured walkthrough is a review of a newly written program by some of the programming staff.

Once you have a job as a programmer in a corporate environment, you should soon learn the norms adhered to by your colleagues. These norms and standards within the company are most often in focus during a walkthrough, which you may participate in on a regular basis.

In a structured walkthrough, several other programmers and systems analysts get together with the source code of the program, with the programmer in the room, and they pick apart the program in detail, trying to find errors, weak spots, broken standards, and poor documentation. Along the way, they make suggestions on how to improve the code. You might also find this process called a *code review* in some companies, and it may occur frequently (even daily).

NOTE

A structured walkthrough often produces what is known in the industry as *egoless programmers*. Programmers are often known for their egos; a good structured walkthrough often shows that a program is not as well written as the original programmer might have first thought.

A structured walkthrough is not an attempt to point fingers. Its purpose is to produce the best code possible. The other programmers are not going to be critical of the programmer personally; after all, they are going to be at the center of future structured walkthroughs themselves.

After a programmer implements many of the suggestions from the structured walkthrough, the programmer usually finds that he agrees that the program is better written than it was originally. After many such walkthroughs, the programmer develops better programming skills, and the company acquires better programs.

Putting a Program into Production

Figure 22.5 shows one version of the steps needed to get a program into use by the user. When the user is finally convinced that the program works as well as originally asked for, and the user is convinced that the parallel testing went smoothly, the program is then moved into production.

When a program moves into production, it is considered complete. The user begins to use the program in a working, non-test environment. The program's results are considered reliable within reason. (Over time, a program's reliability improves as it is used and continues to work well.)

Being in production hardly implies that the program needs no changes and updates over the years. Nevertheless, a production program is one that is considered fixed and usable until a user makes a request to update the program or scrap it for a completely new one. If changes are made to a program that is in production, the systems analyst may go back to user interviews and determine what the user wants. The entire systems analysis and design stage is then repeated for the revised program.

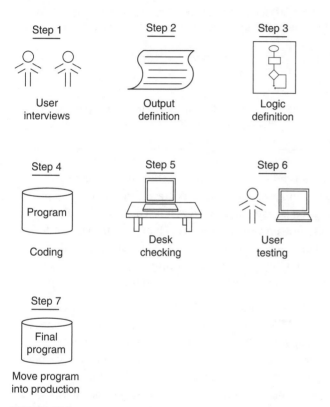

FIGURE 22.5
Common steps for designing, writing, and installing programs.

Depending on the extent of the changes, a program's revision might take more or less development time than its ancestor program took to write. As you have read throughout this tutorial, the maintenance of programs is critical in our ever-changing world. If you write your code better—by supplying more documentation and closely following your company's programming standards—you will have a better chance at locking in your career in the computer field.

"I Want Job Security!"

Job security is an overused term. Often, you hear programmers jokingly talk about the cryptic code they write so that "only they will be able to understand it." Modern programmers are only too aware of the fact that the better employers seek programmers who write clear, clean code, are more concerned with proper programming, and follow as many of the company's programming standards as possible.

Some people can write programs very quickly, but the spaghetti code they produce is unreadable for future maintenance. Don't fall into the trap of thinking that speed is more important than clear programs.

TIP

Version control keeps strict track of versions of each piece of source code that goes into programs, as programmers update them. You'll learn more about version control in Hour 23, "Distributing Applications."

Some systems don't enable programmers to change a program once the system is instructed to treat that source program as a production program. Programmers are able to make copies of the program's source code, but the program is read-only and cannot be changed. If an update has to be made, the programmer copies the source code and makes changes to the copy. After the updates are made and the new version is ready for production, the production records are changed to reflect the new source code. From that point, the production system treats the new version of the code as the production version, but the original remains in place as a backup.

This tight control over production source code enables a company to ensure that it always has an unmodified copy of every program used by every user in the company. Without such control, a programmer could write a program, compile and test it, and install it on the user's system. When installed, the programmer might inadvertently change the program. Because it is virtually impossible to reproduce source code from compiled code, the data processing department would have no way to generate the original source code if the users wanted a change made to the program they are using.

Consulting

Many programmers, systems analysts, and other IT professionals find enriching lives as computer consultants. Too many businesses and individuals buy a computer system or software package thinking all their problems will be solved, and they don't realize the amount of training that is often needed to use the computer effectively. There has been a growing niche for computer consultants for more than a decade, and you might find success as a consultant yourself.

As a consultant, you can be a hero or a heroine to your clients. Many times, computer consultants rush to help someone with a problem getting a report completed, only to find that the client has turned off the Wi-Fi connection or forgot to update the firmware on the printer. The computer is still a mystery to many people.

As a consultant, you can take on as much or as little work as you want. Many programmers moonlight as consultants, sometimes finding that their consulting business grows enough to do it full time. They might give up the benefits that a company can provide, but they like having full say over what they do.

Getting started as a consultant takes little more than word-of-mouth coverage. Offer to help your accountant, attorney, or anyone you know who uses a computer or needs a website with a little interactivity. Tell the person that you'd like to start doing some consulting and that you'd be glad to give them an hour or two free of charge just to see how they like the work (and how you like the work). Often, these initial free calls turn into long-term propositions that are good for both parties.

Summary

You now have an understanding of some common types of computer departments and the people in them. There are many jobs in the computer industry, both for entry-level and advanced programmers and analysts. A computer job is a fun, well-respected, and needed occupation; you'll be glad you're a part of the computer industry.

Understanding the job levels and job promotions can be confusing, especially because many companies follow a unique promotion and title scheme. Nevertheless, the general order of jobs that a programmer follows from the beginning to the end of her career is similar across many companies. The online and networking worlds have increased the nature of jobs and demand, which makes the roles of programmers even more interesting.

Q&A

Q. Can I get a programming job without a college degree?

A. Many people will argue that one does not need a college degree to be a good programmer and a solid employee, as many programmers are in fact self-taught in their areas of expertise. However, it is often difficult to get through human resources screening without a college degree on your resume, regardless of what that degree is in. For example, you might find many holders of liberal arts degrees among a company's programmer ranks; it wasn't their degree (or even their skillset) that got them the job, but it did get them in the door. Focus on honing your skills and producing programs that people can see and use when evaluating your candidacy for employment. Some companies, especially small companies and startups, are often more willing to look at programmers with nontraditional backgrounds who nevertheless have produced good work.

Workshop

The quiz questions are provided for your further understanding.

Quiz

1. What does MIS stand for?

2. Who do data processing or IT department programmers write programs for?

3. True or false: Computer programmers may find that they have the luxury of flexible working hours and telecommute options.

4. What is one downside of a four-year college degree in a computing field?

5. What does a junior programmer typically do?

6. What does a systems analyst do?

7. What is a structured walkthrough?

8. How can computer programming personnel ensure job security?

9. What is a contract programmer?

10. Is management always the next step for a senior programmer?

Answers

1. Management information systems

2. Any department in the company that requests (and potentially pays for) their assistance

3. True

4. What you learn during the course of your degree may be obsolete by the time you begin working in the real world.

5. Junior programmers often work only on code produced by others and doing routine maintenance tasks.

6. A systems analyst acts as a go-between for users and programmers and often designs the rules around the input, output, and logical features of programs.

7. A structured walkthrough, or code review, is a collaborative session to review a program for potential issues.

8. Computer programming personnel can ensure job security by following good coding practices and internal coding guidelines and always enhancing skills by learning on their own.

9. A contract programmer is hired on a temporary basis to perform specific tasks over a period of time and often paid more to make up for the lack of benefits.

10. No. Some programmers do not see management as a step up but rather as a completely different step altogether that holds no interest for them. Some senior programmers may become analysts, but that is also a lateral move.

Distributing Applications

After you write a program, test it, and debug it, you must get the program into the hands of those who will use it. If you are developing software for Windows, Mac, Linux/UNIX, or mobile devices, or even if you're deploying web applications, you'll have different processes and procedures for distribution, from both technical and commercial perspectives. You want to be sure that your users have an easy time installing or accessing the programs you write. In addition, those programs have to work after they are installed. This hour introduces you to some of the issues associated with software distribution.

The highlights of this hour include the following:

▶ Learning why installation issues can be complex

▶ Using build tools to simplify the creation of installation routines

▶ Understanding why compiling an application is critical to proper installation

▶ Using version control

▶ Distributing open-source software

Issues Surrounding Software Distribution

One of the easier aspects of software distribution is finding an outlet to sell a product. More computer-related online stores are open today than ever before. Even discount stores and warehouse chains carry some commercial software products, since software has become a staple item in the daily lives of many people. Software companies are always looking for new titles to distribute and new programmers to write the code, and the business of computers today gives you many avenues in which to market a software product.

Of course, you don't have to charge money for a software program. You can distribute freeware or shareware software via download links on your own website or on websites that aggregate such software for distribution rather than sale. *Freeware* is typically closed-source software that is distributed without a cost to the consumer; *shareware* is also typically closed-source software distributed without a cost to the consumer, but it is available only for a trial period or on some other limited basis. In addition, you can distribute open-source software, which means providing all the source code so that it can be modified by the consumer. Open-source software is typically free, though it doesn't have to be.

Just because you wrote a program that works on your computer with your software settings does not mean the program will work on others' computers. To make your users happy, you must make sure that your program installs on the users' computers and ensure that the program will run after it's installed. You may choose to provide cross-platform versions of software, provide software for only one operating system such as Windows or Mac, or choose some other option in between.

Application Compilation and Packaging

The process for compiling and packing applications for distribution depends entirely on the target installation platform. That is to say, compiling applications for Windows requires one set of tools, while compiling applications for Mac, Linux, mobile devices, or web applications requires completely different tools. In addition, the language that you develop in will require different tools for different platforms. For example, if you develop Java applications to distribute to Windows users, you will use a different set of tools than if you are developing Ruby applications to deploy to a web server. Because each combination provides a range of options, this section describes the process in an abstract way.

All the resource files (source code, libraries, graphics, and so on) for your application will be maintained in a project or code repository with version control applied to it. (You'll learn more about version control later in this hour.) In addition to developing the source code that makes up the core of the program you are developing, you will likely also include an *installation script* that controls the full installation process initiated by the user (if it is a distributed application) or you (if you are deploying to a web server, for example).

In many instances of distributing applications, you will be distributing the compiled version of the source code. With compiled code, you create a single executable file that, when run, extracts and installs individual files. Using Windows as an example, you have probably run into setup files with an .exe file extension; these are compiled executable files. All the related Windows application modules and forms work together to form an executable file.

NOTE

A compiled application is more secure than a distributed-source project. If you distribute the source code (that is, a project and its related files), anyone with skills in the language can modify your work—which might be what you want in an open-source project, but not in a closed-source project. However, most people won't be able to do anything with the source code; therefore, a compiled file is not only secure but necessary so that all can use your application.

CAUTION

Before you finish compiling your application for distribution, make sure that you've debugged it as much as is feasible to eliminate as many bugs as possible.

Once you have a compiled a project for your platform of choice (or all the platforms), you can begin the manufacturing process if you wish to distribute it on CD-ROM or DVD, or you can place it online for sale or free distribution through one of the many software "stores," such as download.com. These days, most software is delivered online—in fact, most computers sold these days do not even come with an optical drive (either CD-ROM or DVD) standard. Instead, the computer connects to the Internet and downloads and installs any needed software. Either the entire software package is placed on the computer or the user can connect to the cloud and run the software that way.

Cloud Computing

The term *cloud computing* refers to storing and accessing data and programs over the Internet instead of from a computer's hard drive. The cloud is just a metaphor for the Internet, really, but the term *cloud computing* implies not having dedicated network-attached storage (NAS) hardware or a server in residence. With large-scale intelligence and data available, programmers must consider threat detection, and their response must be smarter and faster, with security signals and security operations. In addition, it is possible to deliver updates to existing software more quickly if users receive the software via the cloud.

Private Cloud Storage

Private cloud storage is a system designed for one person or company that is specific to that individual's or company's needs. Private cloud storage comes in two formats: on-premises and externally hosted. Private cloud storage enables more administrative control and can be designed to accomplish particular business needs.

Public Cloud Storage

Public cloud storage involves few administrative controls and can be accessed online by anyone who has the proper authorization. It provides the same security as a private cloud, but your company doesn't need to maintain the system as much as it would with a private cloud. A public cloud doesn't need a rigid integration with your business needs, and generally you don't have the same storage concerns as you do with a private cloud solution.

Cloud Services

Users employ four main cloud services today: Infrastructure as a Service (IaaS), Platform as a Service (PaaS), Software as a Service (SaaS), and Function as a Service (FaaS). Together, these services are sometimes called the *cloud computing stack* because they build on top of one another. If you are writing programs to distribute to users, you are most likely going to be in the SaaS space, but developers are needed in all areas.

Mobile Application Distribution

The process for distributing mobile applications is slightly different from the process for distributing desktop applications, as software distribution typically goes through the specific store for the mobile operating system. For example, if you develop an application for iOS, that application is distributed through Apple's App Store; if you develop an Android application, it is distributed through Google Play. The same concept holds true for developers of Windows Phone applications, which go through the Windows Phone Store.

While it is not required that developers distribute applications through the respective stores, users *expect* to find new and updated applications for their devices in the stores for those devices, so it is in the developer's best interest to participate in the platform-specific programs. Each of these developer programs (one for iOS, one for Android, and so on) typically charges an annual fee for participation and provides access to additional documentation and development toolkits that are not otherwise available to the public. Each store also maintains guidelines for inclusion and reviews submissions to ensure that applications are not full of viruses or (in some cases) potentially objectionable content.

Distributing Open-Source Software

You might decide that you want to create and distribute applications under one of several different open-source licenses. These licenses allow for the entire source code, and not just a compiled executable file, to be shared under specific terms, including terms that limit reuse and what is to be done with modifications to the software. Open-source software is often free to consumers, but some developers sell additional versions (such as customized compiled binaries) or support contracts to consumers in lieu of specifically charging money for the software itself.

One of the most important factors when distributing open-source software is determining which license to use. Some developers are concerned primarily with maintaining ownership in the case of patents, others want to ensure that any external modifications in the source code are shared with others, and some developers are not concerned with either (or any) of these issues. There are at least 10 different variations of open-source licenses in use today; you can learn more about licenses and how to choose one at the informative website choosealicense.com.

Using Version Control

During the course of software development, you will likely use version control to maintain your source code and other application resources. Although there are several different version control systems available for use—some free and open source and some proprietary—two of the most popular systems are Subversion (http://subversion.apache.org) and Git (https://git-scm.com). If you have a web hosting service that enables you to install Subversion, you can create your own repository and use a Subversion client to connect to it.

But an increasingly popular tool is Git, which takes a decentralized approach to version control and also offers numerous tools and hosting options for users who want to get started with a repository but don't necessarily want/need/understand all the extra installation and maintenance overhead that goes with it. One such hosting option for Git repositories is GitHub (https://github.com/), which allows users to create accounts and store and maintain as many open-source code repositories for free as they would like. GitHub also provides paid solutions for users who would like to maintain private code repositories.

Git and GitHub are highly recommended for users new to version control because of their relative ease of use and free, cross-platform tools. The GitHub Help site would be a great place to start: https://help.github.com. An added benefit of an already-free GitHub account is the ability to use Gist (https://gist.github.com), which enables you to share code snippets (or whole pages) with others; these snippets themselves are Git repositories and thus versioned and forkable in their own right. GitHub and Gist are both excellent ways to get started with version control of your work.

Summary

This hour's lesson provides a high-level overview of the process that developers go through to bundle and distribute applications to end users. It also introduces the nuances of mobile application distribution, as well as considerations for distributing your source code under an open-source license.

Q&A

Q. **Using version control seems like a lot of overhead for a simple set of scripts I want to distribute for free. Do I have to use it?**

A. No one requires developers to use version control or other backup systems, but it's a rare person who hasn't experienced some data loss or computer crash. In a corporate environment, the loss of any work such that it would need to be re-created from scratch is equivalent to spending money twice; hence, it is wise to work in a version control system.

Workshop

The quiz questions are provided for your further understanding.

Quiz

1. What is freeware?

2. What is the difference between freeware and shareware?

3. Why is distributing compiled programs more secure than distributing the source code?

4. What is an installation script?

5. What are the four primary services of the cloud computing stack?

6. Where do users of mobile devices primarily look for software applications to install?

7. What is one of the most important decisions to make when distributing open-source software?

8. What are two popular version control systems?

9. True or false: If you create an installation package for Windows users, Linux users can also double-click that `.exe` file and install the program.

10. True or false: You can bypass all stores, avoid manufacturing CD-ROMs and printed manuals, and simply put an executable installation file on your website for people to download for free.

Answers

1. Freeware is closed-source software that is distributed without a cost to the consumer.

2. Shareware is typically available only on a limited basis (for example, 30 days), whereas freeware is always available for free.

3. If you distribute source code, anyone with skills in the language can modify your work. This is the goal with an open-source project, but it could have terrible financial consequences if your product is supposed to be closed source.

4. An installation script is a script that controls the full installation process for the user.

5. Software as a Service (SaaS), Platform as a Service (PaaS), Function as a Service (FaaS), and Infrastructure as a Service (IaaS)

6. In the operating system–specific store for their device, such as the App Store for iOS or Google Play for Android

7. An important consideration is which of the many open-source licenses to choose for your work.

8. Subversion and Git

9. False

10. True. There's nothing stopping you from doing this, but would a user trust you? For all users know, your file contains a horrible virus. You would have to overcome marketing barriers before you began to earn revenue.

The Future of Programming

What's in store for you as a programmer? One thing is certain, and that's *change*. Change occurs rapidly in computing. The face of programming has dramatically changed since computers were first invented, and the rate of change is increasing. Today's programming tools were not even dreamed of 10 years ago, and now it seems that every day a new programming language, framework, database system, or utility pops up to help us innovate even more.

This final hour in Part V, "The Business of Programming," introduces you to some tools that are available to help you become a better programmer. More important than the tools, however, is understanding and maintaining proper code that is easily maintained by you and your future colleagues.

The highlights of this hour include the following:

- ▶ Improving your programs with the proper tools

- ▶ Using profilers to improve your program's efficiency

- ▶ Keeping efficiency and retaining maintainability

- ▶ Finding other resources available to improve your programming skills

Some Helpful Tools

As you develop more programming skills and work with more programming language environments, you will run across tools that you will want to add to your bag of coding tricks. The following sections briefly describe tools that you might run across as a programmer that you'll want to look into.

Profilers

Profilers, which are available for many different programming languages, analyze parts of a program and determine exactly which parts are sluggish. It is thought that 90% of a program's execution time is spent in less than 10% of the code. Of course, this rule of thumb is probably not scientifically provable, but the concept is understandable.

Perhaps a sorting algorithm is inefficient, and you want to look into how to speed it up. Perhaps you are performing a sequential search when a binary search might be faster. Perhaps a calculation is inefficient, and you can combine operations to make the program compute results more quickly. A profiler can analyze the execution of your program and tell you where the time is being spent during the execution.

CAUTION

Speed and efficiency are great factors, but don't forsake proper programming techniques just to eke out a microsecond or two of machine time. Clear code should be paramount in your coding. Computers are getting faster, not slower, so you know that your program will never run *more slowly* than it runs today. Some scientific and financial calculations, for example, get extremely complex. To clarify your code, you could break such calculations into several statements and store intermediate calculation results along the way. If you combined all the calculations into one long expression, although it might be more efficient and execute a few microseconds faster, it would later be difficult to debug or change if a problem arose. Therefore, unless a system's speed is critical (as might be the case in some medical or space exploration programs), don't make your code too tricky to be maintained later.

Many of the major programming languages used both in large corporations and by smaller programming shops and web application development agencies have profilers available for them. Java, .NET, Python, and Ruby programs can all be profiled and improved through computerized review. With these tools, you can find a balance between efficient code and clear, maintainable code.

Resource Editors

A Windows programming language brings its own requirements to the table. Many of the tools available to a Windows programmer were not needed in the DOS environment and make no sense in the mainframe world.

One such tool is called a *resource editor*. A Windows resource is just about anything used in Windows—such as an icon, a text string, a bitmap image, a menu, or a dialog box. As you work with programming languages, you will manipulate such resources.

Several ways exist for you to use resources in your Windows applications. You can, for example, designate an icon to use for the end user's installation of your application. The user can click that icon to start the application. You might want to create your own icon. A resource editor can help you create and edit icons and other Windows resources. Microsoft Visual Studio contains a resource editor, and there are several free and commercial programs that help you achieve the same goals (such as ResEdit, at www.resedit.net).

Integrated Development Environments

One of the ways coding has vastly improved in recent years is through the use of *integrated development environments* (*IDEs*). You have already seen IDEs used in the early parts of this book, particularly in the hours featuring Python and Visual Studio. As a reminder, you can think of IDEs as souped-up text editors that try to automate many common programming tasks. Within a unified graphical user interface (GUI), an IDE may offer a programmer a source code editor plus connections to a version control system, plus build automation tools, plus debugging and code inspection tools. While a programmer might operate all these types of tools independently, having installed several different applications to do so, one benefit of an IDE is that it simply allows the programmer to stay "in the flow" and not switch between applications to complete their tasks. In addition, many IDEs have secondary features that are specific to the programmer's development language of choice. For example, if you are a PHP developer using an IDE that has been finely tuned for use with PHP, you may be able to take advantage of autocomplete functionality such that the IDE reduces your need to memorize specific built-in function names or even complete syntax.

IDEs are not new technology but have been refined over many years of use. A common design paradigm for IDEs is to have a strong base feature set and allow developers to add custom functionality through the use of add-ons or plugins. Eclipse (www.eclipse.org) is an example of a popular IDE that provides the programmer with hundreds of plugins that enhance functionality, from changing the GUI theme to integrating automated diagramming functionality and a lot in between. Eclipse is a free and open-source IDE, as are many others. Microsoft Visual Studio is an example of a feature-rich commercial IDE. You can find a good list of IDEs and their feature sets at https://www.g2.com/categories/integrated-development-environment-ide. (As an added bonus, the programming languages you can use with each IDE is covered at that site. We've covered quite a few options in this book, but there's much more out there!)

Automated Testing

While software quality assurance (QA) testing is not a new concept, the handling of many types of tests through automated means has been on the rise in the past several years. This shift is due in part to the availability of better tools for programmers, and it is also due to a shift in attitude toward a development process known as *test-driven development*. In test-driven development, the developer examines the use cases and requirements for a feature and then writes the tests before actually writing any code. The developer then writes code until the automated tests pass, and the tests and the code both go through continual refinement throughout the development process.

Even if your programming group does not practice test-driven development, automated testing has a place in your work. There are automated testing frameworks and tools for many programming languages, such as Cucumber (https://cucumber.io) for Ruby and Selenium (http://seleniumhq.org) for front-end testing of web applications, among many others. When you begin to automate tests, you will likely find that your programs become more reliable and your process more efficient overall; after all, it is easier to fix something that is constantly being monitored than to have to continually (and manually) search through incrementally larger applications to find needle-in-a-haystack bugs.

Automated testing is *not* a replacement for a manual QA process or user acceptance testing. It is always important to have actual human eyes on programs and interfaces, especially when the target user of these programs and interfaces is a human and not a machine. I have personally experienced web applications in which code has significant test coverage and all of the automated tests pass, but the application itself is completely unusable. Don't create that kind of code!

Continuous Integration and Deployment

Automated testing often goes hand in hand with the continuous integration and deployment of applications. *Continuous integration* (*CI*) is a process in which work by multiple developers is merged together as it is completed—or checked in to the code repository—and the automated tests are run at that time to detect any errors in the merged code. The idea here is that if multiple developers are working on different parts of an application at the same time, these different parts have dependencies on each other or are in some way affected by each other such that if changes in one part break functionality in another part, it's much more efficient to detect these issues and fix them sooner rather than later. When using CI, a little up-front effort in writing tests and checking code into the repository saves development teams a lot of effort later in the process as there is less code to weed through to look for errors.

There are many CI systems available to developers, ranging from free and open source to proprietary and commercial. Popular free and open-source CI options include Jenkins (http://jenkins-ci.org) and Travis (https://travis-ci.org); Microsoft Team Foundation Server (https://docs.microsoft.com/en-us/visualstudio/releasenotes/tfs2018-update3) is an example of a proprietary solution.

A natural extension of CI is continuous deployment (or continuous delivery). With continuous deployment, tools assist developers in performing the next logical steps after a codebase has been verified and all tests pass: packaging and releasing the software into a staging environment for manual testing or into a final production environment for all to use.

Will Programming Go Away?

In the mid-1970s, *management information systems* (*MIS*) were going to be the answer to all computing needs. Each company would have MIS in place, and all data needed by the company would be at each computer user's fingertips. That kind of data filtering was to be so vast and efficient that ordinary and more specific programs would not be needed. Obviously, the promise of MIS was not only overpredicted but also never materialized.

For some time in the past few decades, people have predicted the demise of programmers. However, the demand for programmers has grown tremendously. The need for programming is increasing at a rapid pace, and at last count in North America, there were four job openings for every developer; the need is still there, and programmers haven't yet developed the tools that will replace their own jobs.

CASE Tools

In the late 1980s, *CASE (computer-aided software engineering)* was going to replace programmers. Instead of having coders who knew one or more programming languages, programming teams would master CASE tools. CASE is like a program generator, only instead of helping programmers write programs, CASE tools help the staff create programs starting at the initial design level. A systems analyst can use CASE from the inception of a program request to the program's movement into production.

CASE is a massive program on a computer that a systems analyst can use for the initial output design, data definitions, logic definition, and program generation. (Some CASE programs even draw flowcharts from a flowchart description entered by the systems analyst.) CASE often produces code based on the analyst's logic definition, but heavy programmer intervention is needed to implement any but the most general of programs and to ensure the overall success of a project.

CASE's proponents promised that it would revolutionize the programming environment and decrease the time and resources needed to produce a finished program. (Most of the newer programming advances promote quicker development time and easier maintenance as their primary goals.) The promise of CASE, however, never materialized. Although CASE has achieved some success, it has yet to produce the advances in software development that were originally envisioned.

NOTE

The CASE products of the 1980s were not bad tools. The problems that resulted from them were due to the fact that CASE helped systems analysts and programmers do more quickly what the systems analysts and programmers already did incorrectly. Pre–object-oriented programming (OOP) methods suffer from difficult maintenance and documentation problems that OOP does not introduce. CASE could not eliminate the inherent problems of non-OOP programming. (OOP has its own set of problems, but it is viewed as an improvement over other traditional methods.)

TIP

Think of CASE as a program that helps you and others design and write programs. CASE is good for handling minute details throughout a system's development, so you and other programmers and systems analysts can work on implementing all the users' requests.

In recent years, programmers' tools have certainly become sophisticated, as you've seen throughout this 24-hour tutorial. Programmers are needed more now than ever before because computer technology keeps changing, along with the programming tools. Early PCs brought new challenges to programs because of their lack of speed and high demand. As PCs got faster, people networked them together and connected them to mainframes, so distributed client/ server programs were needed. Windows required much more effort to program than the simpler, text-based DOS mode. The Internet brought a new set of requirements for programmers that had not been imagined before. With people relying on their mobile devices for much of their day-to-day computing needs, programmers have a whole new platform on which to apply their trade.

As you can see, programming demand keeps increasing because the nature of computing keeps changing and becoming more complex. This trend will probably continue for years to come. Programming language developers are recognizing that new tools are needed not to replace programmers but to help them perform their ever-more-complex jobs.

UML: Data Modeling

UML, or *Unified Modeling Language*, provides a uniform definition of modeling a program. A company that models one program can share that model with companies that are writing similar programs. The models are not code but are definitions of the applications.

UML is extremely useful, initially, for database designers and database application writers to share the components of each database and to transfer those components between computers. The concepts in UML, however, are also being applied to program design.

UML benefits the following five areas of computing:

- ▶ **Reuse:** After a company completes a design, that design can be reused.

- ▶ **Tool interoperability:** The UML design uses different programming and database systems. Therefore, a UNIX-based Java programmer will be able to use the same UML model as a Microsoft Visual Basic programmer.

- ▶ **Team development:** The UML tools work well in a team-programming environment.

- ▶ **Data resource management:** Resources that appear along with the required data in the UML design are tracked with UML's objects.

- ▶ **Dependency tracking:** If files are required by other files in the design, UML keeps track of those dependents.

Like other design tools, UML will not replace programming, but it should enhance programming and enable the design of a system to be used with other systems to improve programmer productivity.

Your Ongoing Training Needs

Only if you keep up with industry changes can you ensure that computer problems do not occur in the future. Programmers continually hone their skills to keep up with the changing technology in languages, operating systems, software, and hardware. As you learn more about programming, you should consider sharing your knowledge with others through training, consulting, writing, mentoring, or contributing to open-source projects. You will likely find that your own programming skills improve the more you practice and collaborate.

The need for training is never as apparent as it is in virtually every programming department in the world. Programmers are often called to offer a training class for others who do not possess some needed skills. In-house training enables a company to keep a cap on its training costs and control the material being covered.

Your own computer training does not stop. The computer industry changes rapidly. The skills you have today may be obsolete in five years, so part of your job is to continue your own training. It is incumbent upon you to stay up with current trends if you want to secure your computer position in the future.

Industry Standards

Not every new breakthrough in computer hardware and software becomes an industry standard. You do not have to be on the *bleeding edge* of technology (a pun describing very new and unproved technology), learning everything there is to learn. You do not even have to be on the *leading edge* of computer programming innovations. For instance, OOP is considered by most to be the best way to program, yet many computer programmers haven't learned how to program with objects. They might or might not have to master OOP, depending on where their jobs take them and the language they must master in their companies. While it is a good idea to stay on top of the latest trends, it isn't necessary to learn them all because today's breakthrough might be tomorrow's flop (though OOP is not a flop).

You will find your own niche in the computer field, and specialization is often the way to go, since it is very difficult to master everything. However, there are plenty of developers who are quite successful as generalists—people who know quite a bit, if not at an expert level, about many different aspects of development. As you learn more about programming, you will find the area that best fits your own interests, and you will master that area.

Try to read one good computer book or online tutorial every month or two. Every few months, research a new computer programming topic to improve your skill levels. Most computer people do not balk at self-study; the field of programming is exciting and never gets old. The new innovations everywhere you look are always exciting and hold the promise of powerful computing power in the future.

Now that you have a more solid foundation than almost any other beginning programmer has ever had, you are ready to direct your education toward more specific goals. You should now begin tackling a programming language in depth. Mastering a programming language takes a while, and people learn at different rates. Nevertheless, the biggest problem budding programmers face is that they jump in too fast. After reading *Sams Teach Yourself Beginning Programming in 24 Hours*, you will not have that problem. You might be surprised at how well this book's concepts prepare you for your programming future, whether that future is just for fun or for a career.

NOTE
___
Computer books are known for their series approach. As you already know, the *Sams Teach Yourself in 24 Hours* series is designed to teach you the basics of a subject in as little time as possible. In addition to the highly successful *Sams Teach Yourself* series, you'll want to use the *Unleashed* books to master the advanced aspects of a programming language.
___

The following Sams Publishing titles are a sampling of some books that you might want to look at to improve your skills as a programmer. These books were specifically chosen to get you up to speed in specific areas of programming:

▶ *Sams Teach Yourself HTML and CSS in 24 Hours; Sams Teach Yourself Visual Basic .NET in 24 Hours; Sams Teach Yourself Java in 24 Hours; Sams Teach Yourself JavaScript in 24 Hours; and Sams Teach Yourself C++ in 24 Hours*: These books are the perfect next step from this book to take you more deeply into the language of your choice.

▶ *Sams Teach Yourself Java in 21 Days; Sams Teach Yourself Web Publishing with HTML and CSS in One Hour a Day; and Sams Teach Yourself C++ in One Hour a Day*: These books take you far into the languages to prepare you for your career or hobby.

TIP
___
To keep up with the latest in programming titles, regularly check out Sams Publishing's website, at www.informit.com/sams.
___

Summary

Programming tools go far beyond just the languages themselves. Throughout this 24-hour tutorial, you've seen examples of languages and programming tools that help you be a better programmer. This hour showed you additional tools that programmers can use to become more efficient and productive programmers. The most important part of programming is writing clear and concise code so that others can maintain your programs when needed.

After you've mastered programming, what's next? Keep mastering! Continuing education is almost as vital in the field of computers as it is in the medical profession. Rapidly changing computer technologies require that programmers stay on top of current trends by reading books and magazines and taking courses when possible. Share your knowledge with others to help improve the programming community and reduce the backlog that the computer industry faces. Knowledge shared is knowledge improved.

Q&A

Q. Is it important to know multiple programming languages?

A. Depending on your job or the company you work for (or want to work for), knowledge of several different programming languages might be overkill. If you work for a large corporation that develops software products, everyone in the company might use the same programming language all the time. But in case you want to move to a different company, you don't want to pigeonhole yourself as a developer in only one language. If that language falls out of popularity, you will find yourself competing for only a handful of available jobs. Therefore, it's important to stay familiar with the concepts in different programming languages; many of these concepts are the same, even if the languages differ in their specific syntax, so you can ramp up your knowledge as needed.

Workshop

The quiz questions are provided for your further understanding.

Quiz

1. How can a profiler improve program efficiency?

2. What is an IDE?

3. True or false: Automated testing goes hand in hand with CI and delivery processes.

4. Should programmers and other computer professionals continually update their skillsets to keep up with changes in the industry?

5. True or false: Automated tools are a good replacement for manual testing and review.

6. What does a resource editor do?

7. Are you a bad computer professional if you don't learn about every single bleeding-edge technology that comes along?

8. True or false: The computer industry changes often, so you must continually hone your skills to maintain your competence and stay in demand.

9. What is CASE?

10. What is UML?

Answers

1. A profiler locates inefficiencies in code.

2. An IDE is an integrated development environment, which brings together tools for completing common programming tasks into a unified GUI.

3. True

4. Absolutely

5. False

6. A resource editor is a program that helps you create and keep track of Windows resources.

7. No. Many technologies have come and gone; focus on knowing concepts and general information and be selective about what you learn (unless you have infinite time and brainpower).

8. True

9. CASE is a complex design technology to help organizations design, build, test, and implement complete computer systems.

10. Unified Modeling Language provides a uniform definition of modeling a program.

APPENDIX A
Installing Python

To follow along with the program examples in the first nine hours of this tutorial, you need to have Python on your computer. There are several options for using Python, regardless of whether you use Windows, macOS, or Linux. You can either enter your code in a text editor and run the programs at the command line or you can install an integrated development environment (IDE) for the editing and running of your code. Ultimately, it is your preference, but there are advantages to using an IDE in terms of better debugging support: If you make an error in your code, you will often get better clues as to what went wrong with an IDE.

If you choose an IDE, you can either select a Python-specific IDE, like Jupyter Notebook or PyCharm, or an IDE that you can use for multiple languages, like Visual Studio or Eclipse. (I do not recommend the latter for beginners as you need a plugin named PyDev for Eclipse to be an effective Python development environment. It might be your environment of choice in the long run, but for a beginner, it probably makes more sense to start simple.)

Downloading Python from the Python Software Foundation

NOTE

Follow the directions in this section if you don't want to install an IDE. If you'd like to use an IDE like the one in the examples in the first section of the book, jump to the "Installing Anaconda" section that follows.

To get started with Python, navigate to www.python.org. Clicking on the Download option on the menu below the Python logo will take you to a page with options for downloading Python for Windows, macOS, or Linux (see Figure A.1). The default is the latest version of Python 3 (3.7.3 for this installation, but 3.7.4 as of this writing), but you can also scroll down to download a version of Python 2 (most likely 2.7.16).

FIGURE A.1
Downloading Python from python.org. *(©2001-2019 Python Software Foundation)*

Clicking the Windows button to install Python brings up the dialog box shown in Figure A.2; I'm sure you've seen similar ones when you've installed other software. Click Run.

FIGURE A.2
Your computer prompts you to ensure that you want to make the requested changes to your computer.

When the setup file has completed downloading, you see the installation dialog box shown in Figure A.3. You can choose to customize your installation, but you're better off with the default installation.

FIGURE A.3
The default installation of Python should give you everything you need.

When the download is complete, you can then start running Python programs that you create at the command prompt. Again, the recommendation is to use an IDE, such as the one covered in the next section.

Installing Anaconda

Anaconda not only gives you access to an IDE but also simplifies the installation and use of Python libraries. To install Anaconda, go to the website https://www.anaconda.com/distribution/ (see Figure A.4).

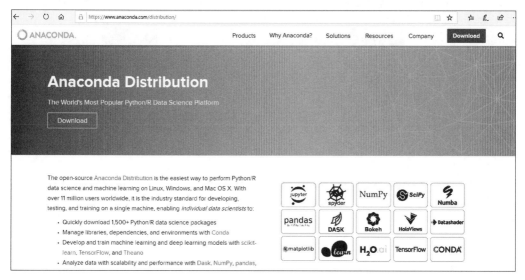

FIGURE A.4
The Anaconda distribution home page. *(www.anaconda.com/distribution/ © 2019 Anaconda, Inc.)*

Click the Download button in the upper section of the page. You can then click whether you want to proceed with a Windows, macOS, or Linux installer (see Figure A.5). For each operating system, you can choose whether to install Python 2 or 3.

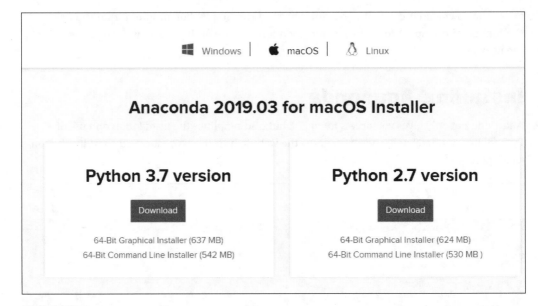

FIGURE A.5
With each operating system, you have numerous choices.

Once you've made your operating system and Python version choices, you can proceed with the installation (see Figure A.6). After you click Next to proceed, you have the opportunity to make advanced changes to your installation. At this point, I recommend going with the default options (see Figure A.7).

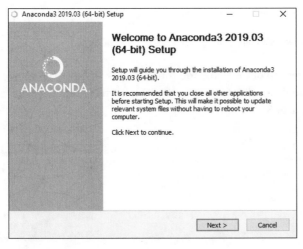

FIGURE A.6
Beginning the setup process.

FIGURE A.7
Keep the first option unclicked and the second one clicked.

Click Install to complete the installation. Then you can launch the Anaconda Navigator (see Figure A.8). There are several options for you here, and I recommend doing some exploring on your own if you are so inclined. For this book, the second option on the first line, Jupyter Notebook, is where you will be doing the bulk of you coding. Launch it.

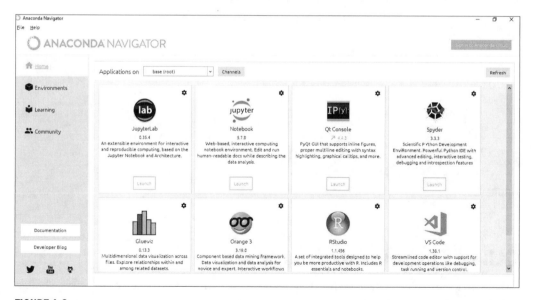

FIGURE A.8
The Anaconda dashboard.

Jupyter Notebook launches within your web browser (see Figure A.9).

FIGURE A.9
Once Jupyter Notebook launches, you can either create a new notebook or open an existing one
(if you have one). *(Credit: © 2019 Project Jupyter)*

On the right side, click the New button to launch a new notebook. In the pop-up menu that
appears, highlight Python 3. A new tab opens in your browser with your new notebook, ready for
your coding adventures (see Figure A.10). Start following along with the book's examples!

FIGURE A.10
Who's ready to code?

Other Python Environments

If you want to use a different Python IDE, you can go to PyCharm's home page (https://www.jetbrains
.com/pycharm/) or the Visual Studio installation page (https://visualstudio.microsoft.com/) and follow
the download directions. Ultimately the code will run the same, regardless of the environment; it's up
to you to pick the IDE you like the best.

Index

I

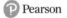